Collins

AF513306

Cascade 8

A SKILL-BASED COURSE IN SOCIAL STUDIES

Archna Golcha
Urmi Chakraborty
Swati Shukla

PREFACE

Cascade is a skill-based course on Environmental Studies and Social Studies for the foundational, preparatory and middle stages. This series for classes 1 to 8 is aligned to the National Education Policy, 2020. Taking into account the multidisciplinary nature of Environmental Studies and Social Studies, the series follows an interactive approach through a variety of tasks and stimulating content. This series deals with the study of human behaviour, relationships, resources and institutions in local as well as global contexts, all of which are fundamental to our conception of society.

Cascade and the NEP

Based on an interactive pedagogy, the books focus on:

- Conceptual development encouraging students to learn how to learn through Constructivist learning tasks
- Thinking critically, solving problems and learning essential life skills to imbibe 21st century learning
- Creative skills aimed at developing all capabilities of learners and to increase individual happiness from childhood
- Multidisciplinary teaching which aligns to the NIPUN initiative for young learners
- Inquiring, analyzing and absorbing new information in a world of increasing interconnections through inferential and experiential tasks
- Sustainable Development Goals that hold the key to the future of mankind sensitizing young learners through a gradual study that builds environmental and social awareness
- The promotion of Indian arts and culture to inculcate a sense of identity as well as an appreciation of other cultures and identities
- Competency-based Structured Assessments For Analyzing Learning (SAFAL)

About the authors

Archna Golcha is a resource person for CBSE and a master trainer. She has conducted several training programmes for educators and students. She also has been an observer CBSE for NEET and JEE exams on several occasions. She is presently working with Manikgarh Cement English School as the principal.

Urmi Chakraborty has over three decades of teaching experience. She has taught in Sardar Patel Vidyalaya, New Delhi, Welham Girls' School, Dehradun and The Shriram Millennium, Noida. She has been selected as a mentor by The Council for Secondary Education.

Swati Shukla has over two decades of teaching experience. She is currently teaching in Sanskriti School, New Delhi.

Key Features

Cascade offers features that focus on essential skills to assist learners achieve holistic learning through a multidisciplinary approach. In so doing, the series is aligned with the guidelines given in the National Education Policy, 2020.

Learning

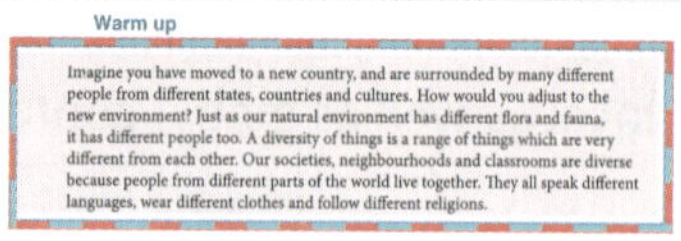

Warm up has pre-reading tasks for discovery-based learning

Conceptual Development

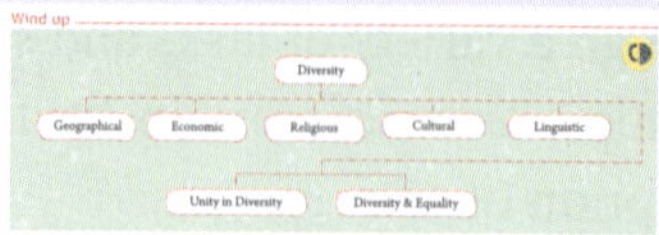

Wind Up has concept maps to assist in learning

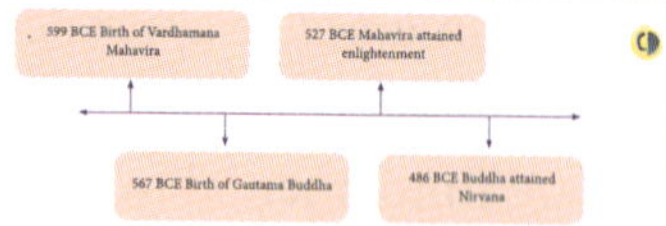

Timeline helps learners understand the chronology of events

Extended learning

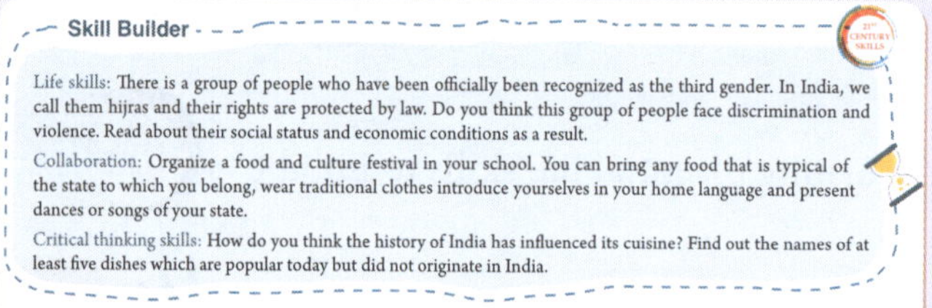

Skill builder has 21st century skills necessary in the age of information

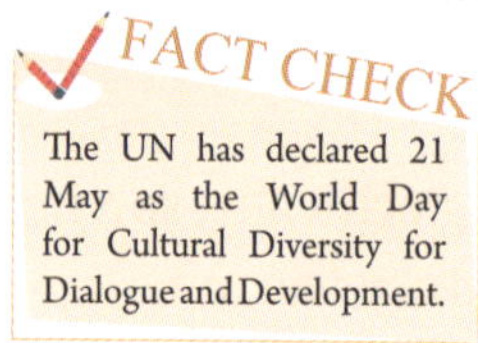

Fact check provides interesting titbits of information

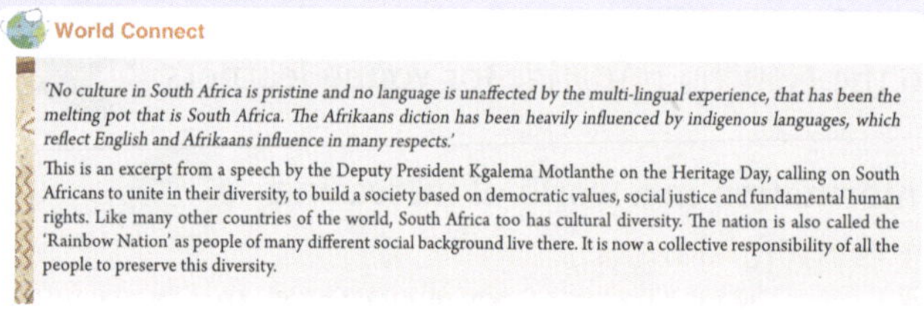

World Connect highlights stories and events from around the world related to the chapter.

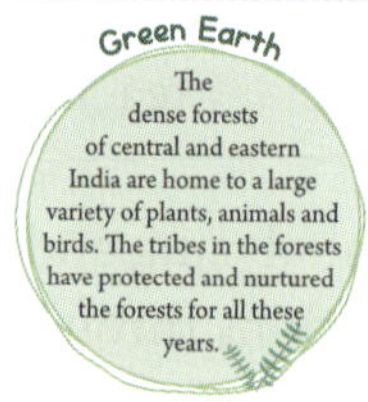

Green Earth sensitizes learners towards conservation of the environment.

Constructivist learning

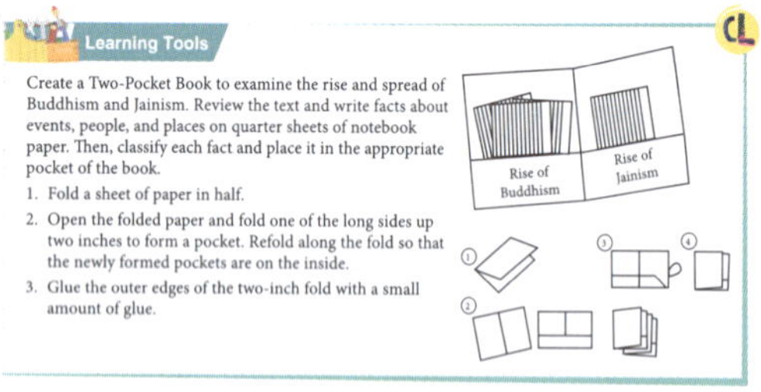

Learning Tools are student-made study guides to organize and arrange data encouraging self learning

Creativity and happiness

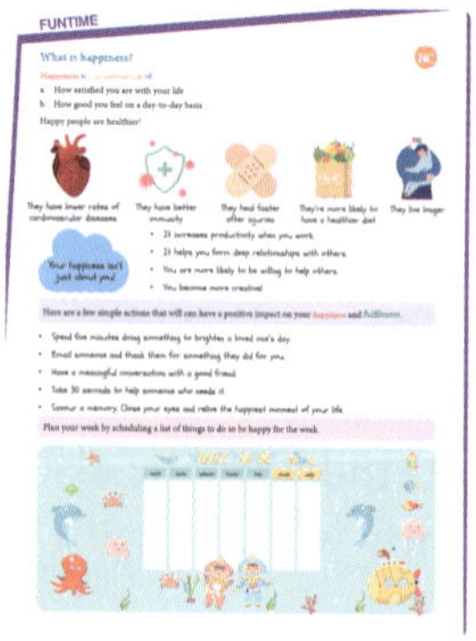

Fun Time addresses wellbeing and happiness of the students through creative and fun tasks

SDG Posters encourage sustainable living

Cross-curricular learning

What's in the picture?

How does this advertisement influence people? Find out ways in which you can recycle water at home.

SAFAL

What's in the picture? provides exercises for inferential learning

Geography skills

On a political map of India highlight all the different states to which your classmates belong. Also highlight the states of India that you have visited. Then, hold a discussion on the special dishes and places of interest in these states.

SAFAL

Geography skills build map skills and improve world overview of learners

Think Big — Integrate with Science

A. Listed below are some of the many ways that we can try to save the endangered animals. Make a chart with the given points and display it in class.

1. Learn more about wildlife by reading books, watching television programmes about nature, visiting zoos and nature preserves.
2. Try to volunteer for a wildlife organisation.
3. Do not pet wild animals.
4. Do not buy products that have been tested on animals.
5. Try to create awareness about endangered species by writing articles and drawing posters.
6. Do not disturb the habitats of wild animals.

B. Discuss the ways in which you can help prevent animal extinction in your country.

Think Big provides varied activities for multidisciplinary learning

Observation and application

Apply it!

'Efforts must be made by all the people, to uphold the dignity of labour in our country. All professions must be treated with respect, because all jobs are important for the smooth functioning of society.'

Write a comprehension on what you understand from these lines.

Apply it! provides application-based activities for experiential learning

Case Study

Discrimination on the Basis of Physical Disability

Nine year old Gabi Shull was just like any other girl of her age very active, and had hobbies, like dancing, singing, reading and playing. She was a talented ballet dancer but her hopes of becoming a dancer came crashing down when she was diagnosed with bone cancer at the age of nine. Her condition required the lower part of her leg, knee down to be amputated. She now had to get an artificial leg. Her road to recovery was very tough but she never gave up hope. She is now back to dancing on her toes as is the requirement of ballet and she is a competition level dancer.

Gabi Shull

Read about some other famous personalities who have overcome similar challenges.

Case Study re-counts in-depth investigations of a single person, group, event or community.

SAFAL

Assessment and practice

Exercises

A. Fill in the blanks.

1. .... is a vast country with diverse geography and cultures.
2. Each period of .... had a distinct influence on the lives of people.
3. The UN has declared 21 May as ....
4. Religion, languages, food, festivals and rituals form ....
5. The Constitution of India promotes and supports .... and national integration in which all people from different races, religions, cultures, castes and backgrounds are treated equally

ASSESSMENT 1

D. Read the following passage and answer the questions. 3

The Indus Valley Civilization also known as the Indus Civilization, was a Bronze Age civilization in the northwestern regions of South Asia, lasting from 3300 BCE to 1300 BCE. It flourished in the basins of the Indus River, which flows through the length of Pakistan. The civilization's cities were noted for their urban planning, baked brick houses, elaborate drainage systems, water supply systems etc. The large cities of Mohenjo-daro and Harappa very likely grew to contain between 30,000 and 60,000 individuals. The Harappan language is not directly attested, and its affiliation is uncertain as the Indus script has remained undeciphered.

The Indus civilization is also known as the Harappan Civilization, after its type site, Harappa, the first of its sites to be excavated early in the 20th century. The discovery of Harappa and soon afterwards Mohenjo-daro was the culmination of work beginning in 1861 with the finding of the Archaeological Survey of India during the British Raj. By 2002, over 1,000 Mature Harappan cities and settlements had been reported, of which just under a hundred had been excavated. However, there are only five major urban sites: Harappa, Mohenjo-daro (UNESCO World Heritage Site. Dholavira, Ganeriwala, and Rakhigarhi. The early Harappan cultures were preceded by local Neolithic agricultural villages, from which the river plains were populated.

1. The Indus Valley Civilization flourished near the .... river.
2. Name any two Harappan sites.
3. "The Harappan towns were well-planned". Explain the statement.

E. On the outline map of India locate and name the following. 3 × 1 = 3

1. The strongest Mahajanapada.
2. The capital of Vajji.
3. Avanti in present-day Madhya Pradesh.

SAFAL

Exercises, **Assessments** and **Outline Maps** for assessment

CONTENTS

HISTORY

GEOGRAPHY

SOCIAL AND POLITICAL LIFE

1. Where, When and How

Warm up

For centuries, explorers have travelled around the world for adventure. In 1492, Christopher Columbus, an Italian explorer, decided to sail westward from Spain hoping to reach Asia. He landed on an island which blocked the westward movement to the East. This new island came to be called the West Indies. He later explored parts of the Atlantic coast, not realizing that he had discovered the Americas. In 1519, Ferdinand Magellan sailed westward and went around the world. Magellan's voyage became the first successful attempt to circumnavigate the Earth.

When the European ships first arrived on the shores of the Indian subcontinent, the Mughal Empire ruled over this vast region. The heart of the Mughal Empire was in the densely populated Ganges river basin. Initially, the Mughal rulers did not feel threatened by the Europeans dominating the seas. They were pleased with the money coming in from trade. The European traders needed to maintain a cordial relationship with the rulers in order to establish profitable trade in the region. However, the Mughal Empire began to decline in the early years of the 18th century, just as the East India Company began to increase its presence.

Periodization of Indian History

James Mill, a Scottish historian in his book *A History of British India* (1817), divided the history of India into Hindu, Muslim and British periods—in that order. However, this would prove to be incorrect as different cultures and religions have coexisted in India.

Therefore, later historians have divided Indian history into ancient, medieval and modern periods. However, this classification was taken from the West where the modern period was associated with modernity. It cannot be applied to India as, in the 18th century, India did not have freedom, liberty, economic growth and progress—all ideas associated with modernity. Historians, therefore, call it the colonial period, which is a period when India was **colonized** by the British.

FACT CHECK

The British Raj is a historical term. 'Raj' is a word in the Hindi language which means 'rule', so 'British Raj' means rule by the British in India. This rule was before 1947 and was over parts of four countries, the Republic of India, Pakistan, Bangladesh, and Myanmar. At that time, these four countries were all parts of the British Indian Empire, known at the time as the Indian Empire and sometimes now spoken of as the 'British Raj'.

colonize: if people colonize a foreign country, they go to live there and take control of it

Case Study

India and the Industrial Revolution

The published accounts of European travellers show that India had flourishing industrial centres in the 17th and the early part of the 18th century. Traders from various parts of the world exchanged their gold, silver and precious stones with cotton textile, saltpetre, tobacco, indigo and silk brocade. Indian spices, such as peppercorns, cloves and nutmeg were extremely valuable as wealthy Europeans used them to cook elaborately flavoured dishes as well as to preserve food. Spices were also used in medicines and perfumes. In the early seventeenth century, pepper was the most important part of the East India Company's trade. Much of the pepper made its way from London to other countries.

During the eighteenth century, the main industries in India were involved in weaving cotton and silk textiles, ship building, handicrafts, tannery, perfumery, paper-making and other things. With the Industrial Revolution in progress, the British needed both raw materials for their factories and markets to sell their finished products.

India had many skilled weavers and dyers, who produced beautiful designs. The demand for Indian textiles increased at a fast pace, and a number of unique patterns and designs made their way to England from India. Unfortunately, the imperial policy of the British industries to provide cheaper machine-made goods slowly led to a decline in the popularity of Indian handicrafts.

Q1. Why were spices so important to European traders?

Q2. How do you think a trading company extended their influence over an entire country?

Sources to Study the Colonial Period

There is no shortage of sources through which we learn about the colonial period. The British were particular, not just about keeping records, but also in maintaining them. Numerous **archives** and museums were built as a result. Let us learn about them.

Archaeological Sources

These comprise monuments, artefacts, inscriptions, coins and pots. Some examples of the monuments in Delhi built during the British period are India Gate, the Secretariat Complex, the Parliament House (originally known as the House of Parliament) and the Teen Murti Bhavan.

Official Records

These cover all levels of administration, from the district to the central government. The British Crown also kept a variety of official records. By reading these, one can trace every development and follow the processes of decision-making.

Inside the National Archives of India (NAI)

Records of European Companies

The records of the Portuguese, the Dutch and the French are important, as they give us an insight into the histories of the 17th and 18th centuries. They are important from the point of view of economic history, but one gets information of the political set-up too.

archives: a collection of historical documents or records providing information about a place, institution or a group of people

Indigenous Literary Sources

The *Siyar-ul-Mutakherin* (*A Review of Modern Times*) by Mir Gholam Hussein Khan is an important Indian literary source. It covers a period of 70 years, chronicling the decline of the Mughals, the rise of the Marathas and the steps that led to the occupation of the country by the British. Another important source is the diary of Ananda Ranga Pillai, Chief Interpreter to Governor Joseph François Dupleix of Pondicherry. Writing in Tamil, he recorded the reversals seen in politics and everyday life in the southern kingdoms of India during the governor generalship of Dupleix.

Some institutions are a treasure trove of historical artefacts and documents. Such an institution, the Bharat Itihas Samshodhak Mandal, was founded in 1910 by the **doyen** of historians, Vishwanath Kashinath Rajwade and Sardar K C Mehendale. It is a premier research institute. The original manuscript of the famous travelogue *Maaza Prawas* (*My Travels*) by Godse Bhatji gives a first-hand account of the revolt of 1857, including the last moments of the Rani of Jhansi.

Surveys and Census

Different kinds of surveys were conducted to provide the government with information regarding certain matters like population, topography, archaeology and forests. The British began conducting surveys so that territories could be **earmarked** for fixing land revenue. This data provides valuable information.

Apply it! E

If a historian cannot find written primary sources, what other sources can he or she look for? What about buildings, archaeological finds, artwork or craft tools? What do these types of objects tell us about the past? What do they leave out?

Newspapers, Pamphlets and Letters

Through these, one gets to understand people's opinions. The first newspaper published in India was the *Bengal Gazette*, started by James Augustus Hickey, in January 1780. It was a weekly newspaper consisting of two pages, with three columns of printed material on each side. It did not have a circulation of more than two hundred and was discontinued in less than two years.

What's in the picture?

Photographs also serve as sources of history. They provide rare glimpses of a second in time. Although not all photographs can be taken as accurate historical records, what can you infer about position and hierarchy in British India by looking at this photograph?

This was followed by the *Bombay Herald*, established in 1789. A few years later, the paper's name was changed to *Bombay Gazette*. It became a leading paper of the city. The first session of the Indian National Congress (1885) was covered by this paper.

Difficulties of using Original Records

One cannot take primary sources at their face value. Historians evaluate these sources based on when and where they were created, who created them and why. This is called interpretation. Historians then compare this interpretation with secondary sources of information. Examples of secondary sources are bibliographies, reference books commentaries and treatises.

doyen: respected or prominent people in a particular field; earmarked: funds or resources designated for a particular purpose

Skill Builder

Referencing skills: Even though India has been invaded by the Arabs, Turks, Afghanis and has been colonized by the British, India never invaded any country in her last 10,000 years of history. What qualities do we learn about this Indian policy?

Critical thinking skills: The Behriyar-Gareriya nomads is a community of sheep wool weavers which has almost given up weaving blanket due to a lack of funds. One weaver says, 'we cannot compete with the blankets being sold in the markets'. Another says, 'we are forced to sell our products in villages because of limited access to urban markets'. Compare the situation of the weavers in British India and in the present times. Is it the same or different? What steps would you suggest to improve their conditions?

Information literacy: Observe images of pre-Independence newspapers and list at least three differences that you can find between the newspapers of the past and present-day newspapers.

World Connect

European Influence in Trade

In the 16th and 17th centuries, China witnessed a flourishing economy and a high standard of living. China was a prosperous region with a large population and abundant natural resources. China's population doubled from 150 million in 1650 to 300 million by 1800. Meanwhile, European powers, such as the British and the French, attempted to entice China into the new world economy. But China refused to open its ports for trade with these states. As a result, a series of wars took place between the European powers and China. The western military force was far superior, and China was forced to sign treaties that opened the Chinese ports, first to the European and then to American and Japanese traders. The Chinese had to give up their rights of legal control over certain sections of these ports, where the foreigners resided. Between the first major **confrontation**, the Opium War of 1839–42, and the early 19th century, the British, French, German, Americans and the Japanese competed for spheres of influence within China.

Wind up

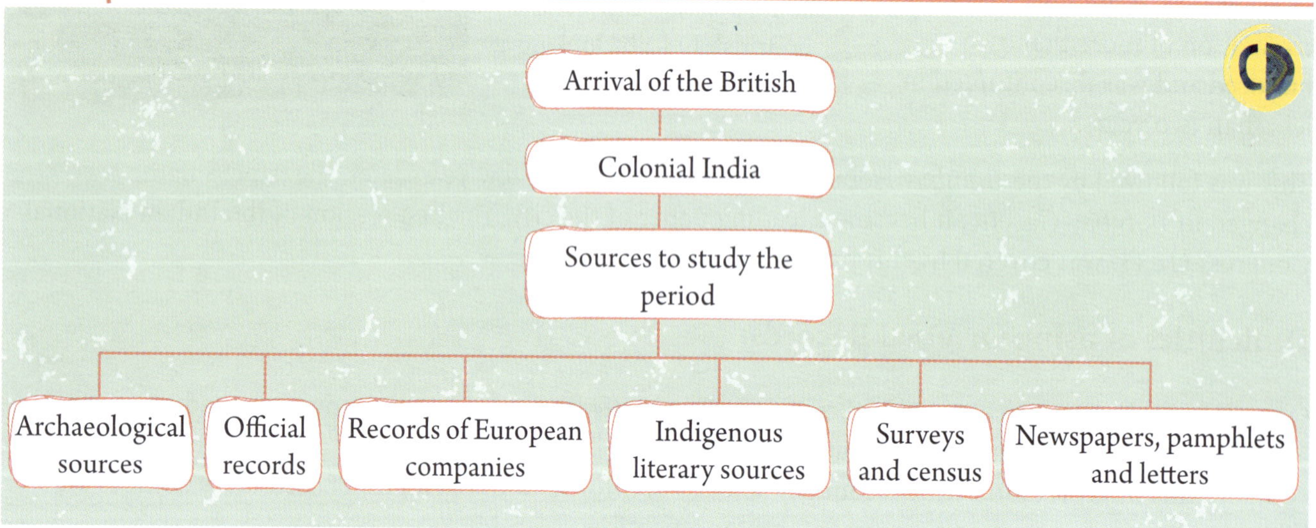

confrontation: a hostile or argumentative situation or meeting, between opposing parties

Exercises

A. Choose the correct answers.

1. These sources comprise of monuments, artefacts, inscriptions, coins and pots.
   a. Literary sources b. Archaeological sources
   c. Newspapers d. Surveys
2. The Bharat Itihas Samshodhak Mandal was founded in 1910 by Vishwanath Kashinath Rajwade and
   a. Godse Bhatji b. Sardar K C Mehendale
   c. Governor Joseph François Dupleix d. Mir Gholam Hussein Khan
3. The first newspaper published in India was the
   a. *Bengal Herald* b. *Bengal Gazette* c. *Bombay Herald* d. none of these
4. Bibliographies, reference books, commentaries and treatises are examples of
   a. primary sources b. secondary sources c. both a and b d. none of these
5. Historians call the period when India was colonized by the British the
   a. imperial period b. modern period c. colonial period d. medieval period

B. Write T for true and F for false.

1. Archaeological sources are primary sources of studying the past. ☐
2. The British did not build any buildings or monuments in India. ☐
3. The records of the Portuguese, the Dutch and the French are important, as they give us an insight into the history of the 16th century. ☐
4. The modern period refers to the period when the British ruled India. ☐
5. The Gateway to India is in Mumbai. ☐

C. Fill in the blanks.

1. *A History of British India* was written by ....
2. The original manuscript of the famous travelogue *Maaza Prawas* (My Travels) was written by ....
3. The *Bombay Gazette* was first called ....
4. The *Bengal Gazette* was started by ....
5. .... is an example of an archaeological source during British rule.

D. Answer these questions in brief.

1. Name two archaeological sources to study the colonial period in India.
2. Name two newspapers from the colonial period.
3. What are archives?
4. What do you understand by the term colonial period?
5. List the items of trade that India exported to other countries.

E. Answer these questions in detail.

1. Describe the periodisation of Indian history.
2. List the difficulties in using primary resources.
3. How did the British policy of imperialism affect industrialization in India?
4. Explain how British official records, surveys and census helped historians learn about history.
5. What are the difficulties historians face while using original records?

Think Big

Integrate with Geography

How did the geography of India affect its history? Read the points below and look at a map to locate the features through which foreign invaders entered.

i. A mountain pass in the Himalayas through which foreigners could enter India. ....

ii. India's coastline is approximately 7516 kms. How did European travellers enter India? ....

Learning Tools

Dates are significant in the study of history. But it can get quite difficult to remember all the dates of important events. Here are a few steps that will help you remember historical dates:

- If you have to remember a year, for example, 1857, try leaving out the first two digits as you would probably already know the time period or century that you are studying and recall only the number 57.
- Now, let's try a mathematical approach to this.

  Take the year 1615, when the company acquires its first territory in Bombay. Here, you will notice that you are working with only three numbers—1, 6 and 5 making it easier to remember.

  If you explore further, you will find that some numbers can be put into equations. For example, 6 - 1 = 5
- Connect the date to something you know, such as birthdays, festivals or other significant dates.
- Use rhymes. Take the last two digits of a year and try attaching it to a rhyme. For example,

  India attains independence in 1947: *47 seventh heaven*

  Jallianwala Bagh massacre in 1919: *19 unforeseen*

  Now, pick up a few dates from this book and try these techniques.

Web links:

https://www.history.com/this-day-in-history/vasco-da-gama-reaches-india

Last accessed on 31 August 2021

2. Establishment of British Rule in India

Warm up

Rupesh read that India was once called '*Sone ki Chidiya*', which means golden bird. He was unfamiliar with the term and asked his elder sister to explain what this means. Rinku, his sister explained, 'In the 17th century, India could boast of many things—the Kohinoor diamond, the priceless peacock throne, agricultural land, towering mountains ... India had it all. India was once a wealthy land and did not have problems like population explosion or poverty that we have now.' Rupesh understood the concept of 'golden bird', but he felt sad realising that India no longer fits that title.

The discovery of the sea route to India by Vasco Da Gama, a Portuguese explorer, opened up new possibilities and opportunities for trade in India. Spices, sugar, indigo and textiles were major items of export. As trade in India proved to be a profitable venture, many European countries started establishing trade links with India. The aims of such **mercantile** companies, which emerged from Portugal, the Netherlands, Great Britain and France, were to exclude competition, as well as buy cheap goods and sell them in their country as well as others, at the highest possible price. This led to rivalries amongst these trading countries, eventually leading to bitter trade wars.

European Trading Companies in India

The 18th century was an era when two notable European powers, France and Britain, struggled to achieve superiority in India. The English East India Company was established to engage in trade with east and southeast Asia and India. By a royal charter on December 31, 1600, the Company was given exclusive rights to trade in the region. As the company tasted success, more settlements were established in Chennai (Madras), Mumbai (Bombay) and Kolkata (Calcutta).

The French East India Company, founded in 1664, made the first expedition to India and reached Surat in 1667 and established the first trading post in Surat. France also tried to exert influence on the Indian subcontinent. Joseph François Dupleix, who was appointed the Governor General of all French establishments in India in 1742, endeavoured to acquire for France vast territories in India and, for this purpose, entered into relations with the native princes in the Indian subcontinent. French factories were established at Chandannagar (Chandernagore) and Puducherry (Pondicherry) in India. Two other companies that were set up in India during this period were the Dutch East India Company and the Portuguese East India Company.

The Dutch East India Company was formed in 1602. Their important factories were in Masulipattanam, Pulicat, Surat, Chinsura and Pipli. In the year 1628, the Portuguese East India

mercantile: relating to trade or commerce; commercial

Chennai. Since the Portuguese, the English, the French and the Dutch all wanted to buy the same goods, rivalry was inevitable. They would sink each other's ships and block routes that led to the trading ports. The English and the French companies were very powerful, hence, the Dutch could not establish themselves and finally sold their trading centres to the British.

Geography skills

On an outline map of India, mark the trading centres established by the Portuguese, Dutch, British and the French. Use different colours for different countries. Remember to give a key indicating the colour, representing the country.

India in the 18th Century

Anglo-French Rivalry: The Carnatic Wars

Both the French and the British took advantage of the rivalry among the Indian rulers. They allied themselves with rival Indian rulers and fought three wars. The British began by attacking the French trade settlements in Pondicherry, while the French attacked the **fortified** British settlement in Madras. Altogether, they fought three wars, known as the Carnatic Wars, between 1746 and 1763. The Treaty of Paris ended the Third Carnatic War, with the defeat of the French in the hands of the British. The French were allowed to retain Pondicherry and Chandernagore. Madras was restored to the British, and thus, they emerged as the main European power in south India.

British Control of Bengal

The Battle of Plassey (1757)

The Bengal province was known for its silk and textiles. It included modern-day Bihar, Jharkhand and Odisha. After the death of the Mughal emperor, Aurangzeb, the Nawabs asserted their power over Bengal. The British had to now deal directly with the Nawabs to get trade-related grants and permissions. However, the Nawabs of Bengal—Murshid Quli Khan, Alivardi Khan and then Siraj-ud-Daulah—were irked by the English and French fortifications and were also suspicious of their growing power. Moreover, they did not like the fact that the Company had not only gained **concessions** from Mughal rulers, but were also misusing them to amass more wealth. In 1756, the British began reinforcing their fort, anticipating an attack by the French. This was the last straw for the newly crowned, twenty-year-old Nawab Siraj-ud-Daulah. He attacked and seized the British factory at Kasim Bazar, acquired all the goods and then captured Fort William.

fortified: (a place) with defensive works as protection against attack; concessions: something that is granted, especially in response to demands

The British commander-in-chief, Robert Clive, was fully aware that the British could not win with their army alone. They had to win by way of **conspiracy.** They found a willing supporter in Mir Jafar, the commander-in-chief of the Nawab's army. Nawab Siraj-ud-Daulah commanded a well-equipped army of 50,000 foot soldiers and horsemen and Robert Clive led the British forces to Plassey. The Battle of Plassey broke out on June 23, 1757. Keeping his end of the bargain with the British, Mir Jafar remained inactive during the course of the war and the British were victorious. Clive returned to Murshidabad and made Mir Jafar the Nawab of Bengal. Mir Jafar was exactly what the British wanted—a puppet ruler who granted **24 parganas** to the East India Company, along with personal presents to Clive. This was the first major success of the English East India Company in Bengal.

What's in the picture?

Study the painting and identify two features that show that the British were successful.

However, Mir Jafar was unable to keep his promise of making regular payments to the company, and when his son died in July 1760, he retired broken-hearted. Supported by the British, his son-in-law Mir Qasim succeeded him to the throne.

The Battle of Buxar (1764)

Mir Qasim handed over Burdwan, Midnapur and Chittagong to the East India Company to maintain their troops. He moved his capital from Murshidabad to Monghyr to lessen the Company's interference in political matters. Next, he tried to stop the Company workers from conducting private trade, as it affected the native traders of Bengal. As a result, a war broke out between the English and the Nawab. Mir Qasim lost four battles with the British in the summer of 1763 and was forced to flee Bengal. He joined forces with the Mughal Emperor Shah Alam II and Shuja-ud-Daulah, the Nawab of Awadh. The combined forces engaged in a battle with the British troops at Buxar, led by the British commander-in-chief, Hector Munro, and lost the battle on October 22, 1764. The victory at Buxar proved to be of great advantage to the British, as it marked the beginning of a strong British power in India. From this, the British got the *diwani* rights (right to collect revenue) for Bengal, Bihar and Orissa.

Dual System of Administration in Bengal

Clive was instrumental in introducing the dual system of administration in Bengal. It was based on a traditional Mughal system of administration, according to which the powers of the government were divided into *diwani*, the power of collecting revenue and administering civil justice, and *nizamat*, or the power of commanding troops and dispensing criminal justice. Based on this system, the British took up *diwani*, and *nizamat* was to be done by the Nawab. Therefore, power was separated from responsibility. The responsibility of looking after the affairs of the people was with the Nawab, but the actual power was with the English. The Company used a portion of the revenue to fund administrative costs, the rest was sent to England. This resulted in quick depletion of the wealth of Bengal.

conspiracy: a secret plan by a group to do something unlawful or harmful; 24 parganas: a former district of the Indian state of West Bengal

Case Study

The Subsidiary Alliance

The East India Company preferred to use political, economic and diplomatic means to achieve their goals rather than engage in wars. One such strategy, called the 'subsidiary alliance', was introduced by Governor General Richard Wellesley, after he arrived in 1798. He tried to reduce French influence while the Nizam of Hyderabad and Tipu Sultan of Mysore allied with the French and employed French officers to train the army. Therefore, he made the Nizam sign a subsidiary alliance with the Company, according to which the Indian rulers could not have their own army. The British would provide 'subsidiary forces' to the Indians on condition of a payment. Failure to make the payment would lead them to lose a part of their territory. The British also installed a resident who was a British official and all the Indian rulers were expected to act in **subservience** to the resident.

Q. Which Indian state had to cede its territories immediately after the subsidiary alliance came into force?

The Expansion of the British Empire

The Anglo-Mysore Wars (1767–1799)

After establishing their position in Bengal, the English wanted to expand their control and conquer more territories. Mysore was a powerful state with profitable trade in pepper and cardamom. Hyder Ali, the ruler of Mysore, had the support of the French. Not only was his infantry trained by the French, but most of his artillery was also manned by them. The British saw this as a threat, and eventually, four Anglo-Mysore Wars were fought between the years 1767 and 1799. Hyder Ali died in 1782, and his son, Tipu Sultan, succeeded him.

The storming of Seringapatam

In 1789, Tipu Sultan attacked Travancore, which was a British ally. This gave the British an excuse to wage war on Mysore. Tipu's tactical skills and well-trained army was leading him to a win. It was then that the British Governor General, Charles Cornwallis, managed to convince the Marathas and the Nizam of Hyderabad to ally with the British. This was a humiliating defeat for Tipu. The Treaty of Seringapatam was signed in 1792, with Tipu having to surrender half of his kingdom to the British.

Tipu was hungry for revenge and tried to ally with the French and Zaman Shah of Kabul, against the British. He also refused to get into a subsidiary alliance with the British. This led the British to attack. The forces of Mysore were surrounded by the British and the Marathas. The heavily outnumbered Mysore troops were taken by surprise, and faced a final defeat, with the death of Tipu Sultan. Thus, large chunks of territories went into the hands of the British and Tipu's family was exiled to Vellore.

subservience: the quality of being too willing to obey other people

Anglo-Maratha Wars (1775—1818)

The way in which the Marathas allied with the British to defeat the rulers of Mysore, one would think that their alliance had some permanence. However, the British wanted to curb the power of the Marathas, as they were gradually strengthening after the Mughal rule began to weaken. The Marathas and the British fought three wars between 1775 and 1818, before the British managed to defeat the Marathas completely. The British exploited the disunity and rivalry that existed in the Maratha clans, particularly in the house of the **peshwa**. Under the British Governor General, Warren Hastings, the Peshwa was completely defeated and pensioned off and the Maratha territories were annexed by the British.

FACT CHECK

The first rulers to accept the subsidiary alliance were the Nizam of Hyderabad, and the Nawab of Awadh. Tipu Sultan refused to do so.

The Anglo-Sikh Wars (1845—1849)

The Sikhs became very powerful under Maharaja Ranjit Singh. Maharaja Ranjit Singh not only had a cordial and diplomatic relationship with the English, but he had an efficient army too. The death of Ranjit Singh in 1839 led to a civil war. By 1843, Ranjit Singh's youngest son was placed on the throne. The relationship between the Sikhs and the British were strained, as the Sikhs had refused passage to the British during the Anglo-Afghan war. The British made use of this situation and fought two wars with the Sikhs between 1845 and 1849. Ultimately, the Sikhs were defeated, and Punjab too became a part of the British Empire.

Ranjit Singh

- 1600, East India Company acquired exclusive trade rights
- 1602, Dutch East India Company was formed
- 1628, Portuguese East India Company was formed
- 1664, French East India Company was established
- 1746, Carnatic Wars started
- 1757, Battle of Plassey
- 1763, Carnatic wars end
- 1764, Battle of Buxar
- 1767, Anglo-Mysore war begins
- 1775, Anglo-Maratha wars begin
- 1799, Anglo-Mysore wars end
- 1818, Anglo Maratha wars end
- 1845, Anglo Sikh wars start
- 1849, Anglo Sikh wars end

Doctrine of Lapse

Lord Dalhousie, the Governor General from 1848 to 1856, devised a policy of annexation known as the doctrine of lapse. According to this policy, if the ruler of a kingdom which was either protected or dependent upon the British died without a natural heir, his state would either lapse, or pass on to the company. Examples of the kingdoms annexed using this policy were Satara (1848), Jaitpur and Sambalpur (1850), Udaipur (1852), Nagpur (1853) and Jhansi (1854).

Another clause in the policy for annexation of a kingdom was alleged mismanagement in administration. On this basis, the kingdom of Awadh was annexed in 1856. All this led to a lot of discontent among

peshwas: prime minister of the Maratha ruler

Indian rulers. They became highly suspicious of the objectives of the British and this feeling of insecurity became one of the factors that led to revolt.

The other factor that generated intense discontent was the abolition of titles and pensions. The titles of many ex-rulers, like the Nawabs of the Carnatic, Surat, and the Raja of Tanjore, were not recognized by Dalhousie and many others were refused pensions. Dalhousie's policies intensified the displeasure of the affected rulers to the extent that a revolt broke out soon after Dalhousie left in 1856.

Administration of the British Empire

The army played a very important role in the British administration, as it was with the help of the army that the British were able to expand their empire. A uniform military culture came to be adopted. Soldiers were given European-style training, drill and discipline that regulated their life far more than before. One of the first responsibilities taken on by Warren Hastings, when he was appointed the Governor General of Bengal, was to recruit sepoys from Bengal, Awadh and Benaras. Therefore, the sepoys from this area formed a majority of the Bengal army. However, they did not rise above the position of a subedar but remained loyal to the British.

Charles Cornwallis developed a regular and permanent police force in India to maintain law and order. Each district was brought under a *thana*, headed by a *daroga*. Towns and villages had *kotwals* and *chowkidars* to maintain law and order. The post of the District Superintendent of Police was created with the entire district being brought under him. There were a lot of disparities in the police department too. Higher posts were filled only by the British.

Indians used to follow their own varied customs and traditions regarding the imposition of justice. There was no common law in the entire subcontinent and the English law only applied to the English. Steps were taken by Warren Hastings and Charles Cornwallis to introduce a systematic judicial administration in India. The Cornwallis Code was introduced in 1793, according to which justice continued to be handed out in accordance with local Hindu and Muslim laws.

The Supreme Court was at the top of the judicial structure, followed by the high courts of Bombay, Calcutta and Madras. The district courts were under these three.

Policy of Paramountcy

Warren Hastings, the first Governor General of India from 1813 to 1823, introduced a new policy of **paramountcy**, according to which the company proclaimed that its power was superior to that of the Indian states, and therefore, they were justified in annexing any of the Indian states to protect their interests.

Apply it! E

History is full of examples of brave Indian queens who resisted the British occupation of their country. Can you name two such Indian queens?

However, there was a resistance to this policy. Rani Chennamma, the queen of Kittur, a princely state in Karnataka, rebelled against this and led an anti-British movement. She was the first female Indian ruler to do so, but was subsequently arrested and put in prison in 1823 and died in 1829.

paramountcy: the state or fact of being of greater importance than anything else

Skill Builder

21ST CENTURY SKILLS

Critical thinking skills: Imagine you are 15 years old and the nephew/niece of a ruler of a princely state in 19th century India. Your uncle has no child of his own, so you are made the heir to the throne. What steps would you take if the British imposed the doctrine of lapse in your kingdom and didn't allow you to succeed after your uncle?

Life skills: Prepare a speech on the 'Divide and Rule policy', as applied by the British.

Communication skills: Write a speech that Hyder Ali could have given to inspire his soldiers to fight against the British. In your speech, mention the enemies that Hyder Ali had to face, and stress on the importance of unity against an external force, such as the British.

World Connect

Colonial Rule in America

After Christopher Columbus's historic discovery of America, many European nations reached there to increase their wealth. The Spanish people were among the first to explore the United States of America. In 1606, King James I of England granted a charter to a new venture, the Virginia Company, to form a settlement in North America. This Company would explore the entire eastern coast of North America, and search for gold and silver deposits in the 'New World', as America was called. The Virginia Company also planned to find a river route to the Pacific Ocean that would allow them to establish trade with the Far East. Thus, the first colony in America was founded in 1607, at Jamestown, Virginia. Tobacco was a popular item of export by the Virginia Company, from America. By 1770, more than two million people lived and worked in Great Britain's thirteen North American Colonies.

Wind up

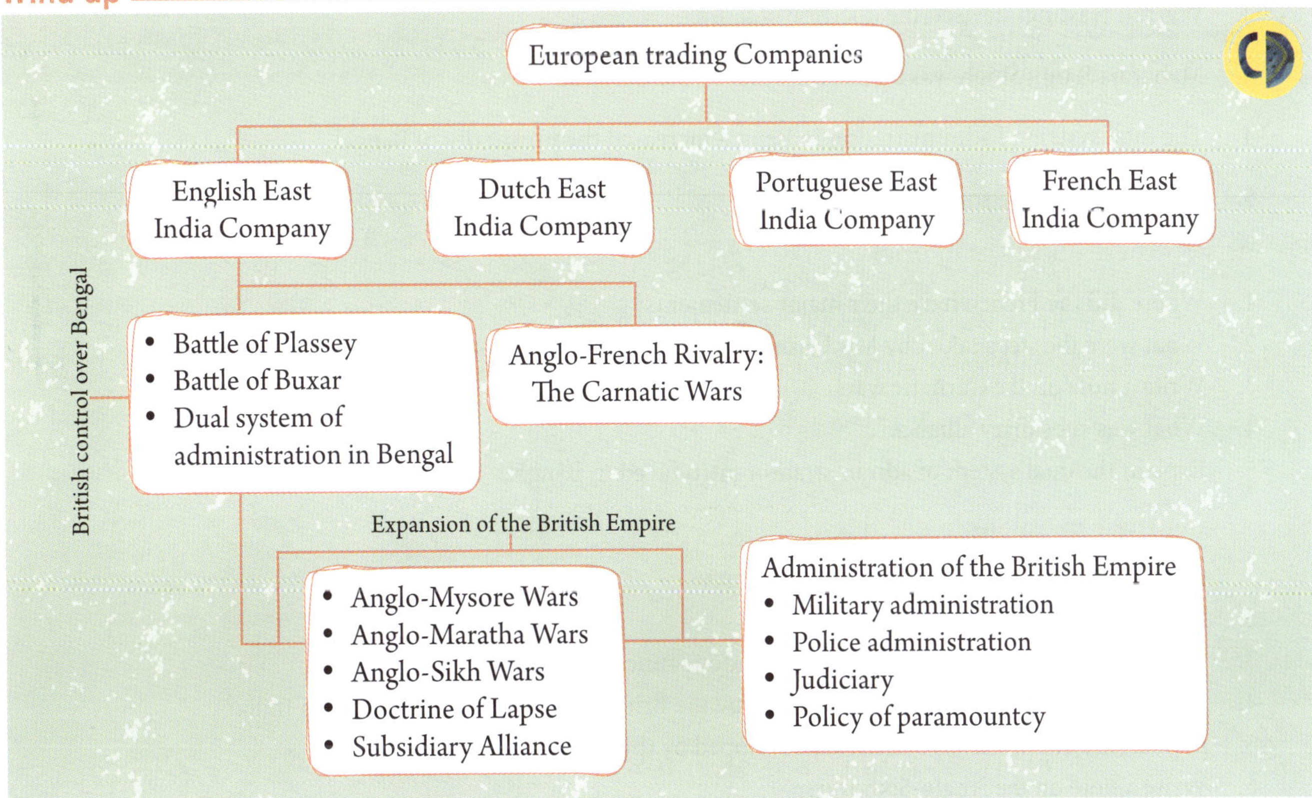

Exercises

A. Choose the correct answers.

1. The Battle of Plassey took place in the year
   a. 1707 b. 1757 c. 1764 d. 1773
2. The Subsidiary Alliance was started by
   a. Lord Dalhousie b. Lord Cornwallis c. Lord Wellesley d. Lord Hastings
3. The permanent police force in India was established by
   a. Robert Clive b. Thomas Roe
   c. Warren Hastings d. Lord Mountbatten
4. The Supreme Court was at the top of the judicial structure, followed by the high courts of
   a. Delhi, Bombay and Calcutta b. Madras, Bombay and Delhi
   c. Bombay, Calcutta and Madras d. Calcutta, Delhi and Madras
5. She was the ruler of Kittur.
   a. Madhav Rao b. Baji Rao II c. Rani Chennamma d. Ranjit Singh

B. Fill in the blanks.

1. .... introduced the dual system of administration in Bengal.
2. The British and the French fought the .... wars in India to establish their monopoly in trade.
3. Tipu Sultan's family was exiled to .... after the Siege of Seringapatam.
4. .... was associated with the policy of doctrine of lapse.
5. The new policy of paramountcy was introduced by ....

C. Write T for true and F for false.

1. Lord Dalhousie was a French general. ☐
2. Warren Hastings devised the doctrine of lapse. ☐
3. Maharaja Ranjit Singh was a powerful ruler of the Carnatic. ☐
4. The dual system of administration in Bengal increased the prosperity of Bengal. ☐
5. Mir Qasim was the son-in-law of Mir Jafar. ☐

D. Answer these questions in brief.

1. Where did the French have their major settlements?
2. What were the steps taken by Mir Qasim to check the ambitions of the English?
3. Write a note on the Carnatic wars.
4. What was subsidiary alliance?
5. Explain the dual system of administration introduced in Bengal.

E. Answer these questions in detail.

1. Give a detailed account of the Battle of Plassey.
2. What was the impact of the Carnatic wars?
3. What is the doctrine of lapse? Name a kingdom annexed by this means.
4. What were the different methods adopted by the British for annexing territories in India?
5. Explain the administrative structure developed by the British.
6. Write a note on the Anglo-Sikh wars.

Think Big

Integrate with language

Imagine that a small island on the other side of the world took over your country, changed its laws and insisted that you follow its commands. Prepare a speech imagining that you are the prime minister of India and want to motivate your countrymen to stay brave and learn from the sacrifice of Indian revolutionaries during the British rule.

Learning Tools

Create an accordion book to record a timeline of the key events in the history of India when the British established their rule. You can do this by pasting several folded papers together. Conduct research and make short annotations for the events on their timelines.

When folded, this project is used like a book, and it can be stored in student portfolios. When open, it makes a nice project display. Accordion books can be stored in file cabinets for future use, too.

Web links:

https://www.britannica.com/event/British-raj

Last accessed on 31 August 2021

3. Rural Life and Society

Warm up

One day a young child went out for a walk with his father one evening. His father was accompanied by a friend. They were chatting as they walked on and went beyond the village. The elders were walking along the edge of a field. Not hearing the footsteps of the boy, the father stopped and looked back. He saw that the boy was sitting on the ground and seemed to be planting something.

The father became curious. He approached the child and asked, 'What are you doing son?' The boy replied innocently, 'Father, I am planting guns all over the field.' His eyes shone with the strong faith that guns would grow in the field. Both the elders were struck with wonder upon hearing these words.

This little boy was none other than the great revolutionary Bhagat Singh. Once, when he was in school, Bhagat Singh asked his classmates, 'What do you wish to become when you grow up?' Each boy gave a different answer. One of them said, 'I want to become a doctor.' Another wished to become a government officer; and some other wished to become a merchant'. At this, Bhagat Singh remarked, 'I will drive the British out of India.' This shows how patriotism flowed in his veins right since childhood.

In the previous chapter, we learnt how the East India Company took up the *Diwani* of Bengal in 1765. For seven years, the company let their Deputy Diwan in the Mughal court, Muhammad Reza Khan, collect revenue on their behalf. In 1772, the then Governor of Bengal, Warren Hastings, abolished the post of the Deputy Diwan and the company 'stood forth as Diwan'. This meant that the company had to devise new ways of calculating the area under cultivation and of collecting revenue. Having become rulers, but retaining the 'trader' mentality, the company wanted to make the maximum profits from this new role.

System of Land Revenue Collection

Till the 18th century, agriculture and cottage industries in India were interconnected. India held a prominent place in both the fields of agriculture and handicraft production in the world. The coming of the British, however, destroyed the handicraft industry and caused extensive modification in the country's agrarian structure by introducing new systems of land tenure and policies of revenue administration.

Permanent Settlement

This was a land revenue system introduced by Charles Cornwallis in 1793. This system was introduced in Bengal, Bihar, Orissa and some parts of the Madras Presidency.

Charles Cornwallis

- The land was auctioned off to the highest bidder, who became the owner of the land.
- They were expected to pay a fixed amount as tax and the date of payment was also fixed.

- The zamindars were free to fix the rent, paying only the percentage agreed upon by the British and keeping the rest to themselves.
- If the zamindars were not able to pay the fixed amount, they would be turned out from the land and the land would be sold to someone else.
- Administrative and judicial functions lay on the hands of the British and not on the zamindars.

On the one hand, the permanent settlement created a group of loyalists called *zamindars* in Bengal and Bihar, on the other hand, it ensured a regular fixed amount for the Company. The British had thought that the *zamindars* would invest in new technologies to increase the produce or fertility of land. Greater produce would translate into greater profits for *zamindars*, as the revenue they had to pay the company was fixed under the new policy. However, *zamindars* made no efforts to improve it. They had the right to remove tenants from their land or seize the land belonging to a cultivator on non-payment of dues. All these factors left the cultivators in pitiable conditions.

Green Earth

Smart farming that uses modern digital technologies, such as sensors, location data derived from GPS and satellites, robotics and analytics, is changing the face of agriculture in India. Big Data helps improve the yield, reduces risk and increases efficiency.

The Ryotwari System

The permanent settlement did bring in a fixed revenue for the company. However, the company realised that the *zamindars* were exploiting the peasants and making huge sums of money for themselves, while remitting a fixed amount to the company. So, while the Permanent Settlement continued in Bengal and Bihar, the Ryotwari system was introduced by Sir Thomas Munro in 1799–1801 in Bombay and Madras Presidencies. According to this system,

- There was no mediator, and the revenue was collected directly from the cultivator or the *ryot*.
- The land revenue was fixed for a period of thirty years, after which it could be reassessed.
- Peasants were expected to pay half the estimated net value of the total produce.
- The method of collection was strict and at times, the cultivators were compelled to borrow money from moneylenders to pay their dues to the company.

While the cultivator was acknowledged to be the legal owner of the land, this new system hardly benefited the farmers. He was nothing more than a tenant of the land, with the government as the owner. The rigid system of revenue collection only pushed farmers to borrowing money. The government too had the right to increase revenue at will.

The Mahalwari System

This system was formulated by Holt Mackenzie in 1822. The Mahalwari System was based on the common ownership of land. This system was introduced in north western India, Punjab, parts of central India and parts of Bengal.

- Settlements of tax collection were made with village elders, who distributed the land settlements among cultivators, as the importance of the village as a social unit was recognized.
- The person responsible for collecting revenue was the village headman.

Impact of the Land Revenue Systems

The land revenue systems had many drawbacks:

- These land settlements damaged the economy of the country and the self-sustaining character of the villages. Revenue was paid in cash, and this increased money-lending amongst farmers.
- As the British were very strict in their revenue collection, many peasants had to borrow money by mortgaging their belongings, and many were forced to become bonded. Money lenders loaned money at high interest rates, thereby leading to growing debt and impoverishment of farmers.
- These land settlements led to stark differences in the society. The rich could turn to the courts to defend their properties, however, the poor had no access to them and were often left to themselves.
- The cash payment of tax forced cultivators to produce cash crops, like cotton and sugarcane, rather than food crops, as cash crops brought in more money than food crops. This led to a dearth in the country's food production.
- No effort was made to improve or modernize agriculture. The majority of the people in villages depended on agriculture and related activities. They became miserable if crops failed in any given year.

Cultivation of Indigo

Indigo, a crop cultivated in India, yielded a blue dye. It was in great demand among European cloth manufacturers. This was due to its brightness as compared to the other dyes, like violet and blue dyes from a plant called woad. Indigo was in short supply in the European markets, and therefore, its price was very high. The British decided to increase the production of indigo in India and rake in profits by supplying it in Europe. Business agents began investing in indigo farming. They rented land and hired labourers. This was known as nij cultivation. But this type of cultivation had many problems. The planters found it difficult to expand indigo cultivation, as indigo needed large pieces of compact land for cultivation and most of the fertile land was already densely populated. Therefore, only 25 per cent of indigo-producing land was under this system. The rest was under another mode of cultivation, known as the ryoti system, under which, the planter forced the ryots to sign a **contract**. Those who signed the contract could avail of cash loans at low rates of interest. Seeds were provided by the planters and once the crop was delivered, the ryots were sanctioned fresh loans. So, the cultivators remained caught in a vicious cycle.

Peasant Uprising

Peasants were burdened with high taxation, low profits and the gradual loss of a self-sustained lifestyle. This led to peasant rebellions. The failure of the *zamindars* to pay the land revenues was also a factor contributing to these rebellions. Kisan Sabhas were set up, which tried to represent the peasants and create awareness about their problems.

Apply it!

The Bengal famine of 1770 killed over 1 million people over a period of 6-7 months. It was due to the stringent East India Company policies and negligence towards grain shortages caused by drought.

Today, there are over 8 million people around the world who are undernourished and cannot afford to have three square meals a day. List some of the causes of hunger and malnutrition in today's world. Suggest measures on how they can be eradicated.

2 ZERO HUNGER

contract: a written or spoken agreement, especially one concerning employment, sales, or tenancy, that is intended to be enforceable by law

Indigo Revolt in Bengal

The loans sanctioned to the peasants for indigo cultivation initially seemed reasonable, but the cultivators soon realized the strictness and rigidity of the terms of the loan. The labour put in by the indigo farmers did not match the price they got from the indigo planters, as it was too low. Moreover, they were unable to free themselves from the loans. Also, the deep roots of the indigo plant made it impossible for the farmers to grow rice or any other crop, as indigo plantation exhausted the soil.

What's in the picture?

This photo shows an indigo factory in Allahabad, India. Study the picture and describe the condition of farmers during that time.

Green Earth

Launched to aid farmers, Skymet's weather website offers services such as weather forecast, crop insurance and agri-risk management. Prediction of weather conditions can help prepare a farmers for a drought or heavy unseasonal rainfall and help them take appropriate preventive measures. They, claim to accurately measure and predict yield at the village level for any crop.

The outcome of all this was that many peasants in Bengal refused to grow indigo in the early months of 1859. The situation became so oppressive that those who worked for indigo planters were **ostracized**. The planters were not paid rent, and the *gomasthas*, that is, the record-keepers, were beaten up.

The indigo farmers gained tremendous support from the intellectuals within the city as well as the local zamindars, who were angry because they were forced to lease out their land for a long period. Dinabandhu Mitra wrote *Neel Darpan*, a forceful play that depicted the real situation of the indigo farmers and the highly exploitative nature of the planters. The British, too, got unnerved by such an agitation and realized the consequence it could have on their own government.

Indigo production in Bengal came to a standstill and the planters shifted their attention towards Bihar. Mahatma Gandhi visited Champaran to observe the condition of the indigo farmers during this time. This visit was the beginning of the Champaran Movement against indigo cultivation and would eventually grow into a nationwide movement against British dominion.

Case Study

Comparative study of Punjab, Bengal, and Bihar

Punjab: Punjab was annexed by Lord Dalhousie. It was a very fertile region irrigated by five rivers. The British took advantage of this and encouraged the cultivation of cotton, as it was required for their industries in England. The British laid down an extensive network of canals in Punjab. This step increased productivity and the peasants prospered.

Bihar and Bengal: The land revenue policies adopted by the British in the region of Bengal and Bihar were not peasant friendly. Non-payment of land revenue allowed the zamindars to throw out peasants from

ostracized: excluded from a society or group

their land. Due to these factors, peasants became debtors. Cultivation of cash crops led to the commercialization of agriculture and impacted the rural economy in an adverse manner. As the soil became unsuitable after the cultivation of cash crops, like indigo, farmers could no longer raise food crops. The result of this was that the farmers were no longer self-contained and were left in an impoverished condition.

Q. What commonalities were there in the agrarian policies adopted by the British in these three regions?

Skill Builder

Critical thinking skills: Why did the British introduce different land revenue systems for different states under their control? As a British official, if you were to select a particular land revenue system, which one would you have chosen?

Creativity skills: Imagine you are a rice cultivator and you have been told to cultivate indigo in your farm land. Write a note expressing your concern on growing indigo instead of rice. Read it in the class.

Life skills: The British had all rights for revenue collection and no responsibility towards the peasants. Is this attitude appropriate for a ruler?

World Connect

Indigo Cultivation in South Carolina

The Pinckney family reached a British plantation in South Carolina, America, in 1738. Eliza Lucas Pinckney, the daughter of the family, was determined to successfully grow some cash crops to pull the plantation out of debt. She asked for indigo seeds from her father and hoped that it would be the answer to their financial problems. In a few years, she became the first to successfully grow and process indigo in South Carolina. She then distributed the seeds to her neighbours in 1744, making it a new trade commodity for the colony. Not only that, she effectively put South Carolina on the map of British colonies that grew indigo. She became involved in slave trade, as she required slaves in the entire process of sowing, reaping and processing indigo.

Wind up

Land revenue systems
- 1793 CE — Permanent Settlement, Bengal
- 1799-1801 — Ryotwari System, Bombay and Madras
- 1822 CE — Mahalwari System in North West Provinces

Exercises

A. Choose the correct answers.

1. Cultivation of this crop was also called nij cultivation.
   a. Cotton b. Jute c. Indigo d. Wheat
2. Kisan Sabhas were set up to represent the
   a. peasants b. zamindars c. collectors d. planters

3. The Mahalwari System was conceived by
   a. Charles Cornwallis b. Warren Hastings c. Holt Mackenzie d. none of them
4. The indigo planters shifted to this region after the production stopped in Bengal.
   a. Orissa b. Rajasthan c. Gujarat d. Bihar
5. The term 'ryot' refers to
   a. zamindars b. peasants c. moneylenders d. options a and b

B. Fill in the blanks.

1. The British Governor who introduced the Ryotwari System was ....
2. The peasants had to borrow money from the ....
3. The Champaran Movement was started by ....
4. Punjab was annexed by Lord ....
5. The Champaran Movement was against ....

C. Write T for true and F for false.

1. Lord Cornwallis introduced the Permanent Settlement system. ☐
2. Indigo farmers benefited from British rule. ☐
3. Land revenue was fixed for a period of thirty years in the Ryotwari System. ☐
4. Indigo is a plant which yields blue dye. ☐
5. India was the biggest supplier of indigo in the world in the 19th-century. ☐

D. Answer these questions in brief.

1. Name the benefits of the Permanent Settlement.
2. Name two features of the Ryotwari System.
3. Give reasons as to why the British planters grew cash crops.
4. Who wrote *Neel Darpan*? What was the subject of the play?
5. Name any two demerits of the Permanent Settlement.

E. Answer these questions in detail.

1. Discuss the different land revenue systems as introduced by the British.
2. Explain the main reasons that led to the crumbling of indigo production in Bengal.
3. Draw a comparison between the Mahalwari and the Ryotwari System.
4. Give reasons for peasant rebellions.
5. What led to the Champaran Movement?
6. Explain the harmful effects of British agrarian policies on Indian agriculture.

Think Big

Integrate with science and maths

Visit a farm and ask the farmer to show you around the crops he is growing and provide you with information related to it.

Observe the field and see if it is approximately rectangular in shape. By pacing the field, estimate the length (metres) and width (metres). What could you use to make the measurements more accurate?

Prepare a chart like the one given below to assess the farmland.

Theme	Examples
Micro-organisms	Helpful and harmful microbes in food production, health of plants and animals, biosecurity
Chemical analysis	Assessment of nutrient deficiencies Environmental risk management of pollutants
Products from living things	Food, wool, silk, cotton, leather, pharmaceuticals, dyes Intensive and organic farming Controlled environments for plants and animals

Learning Tools

CL

Make a three-tab book to list the points you have studied about under the Permanent Settlement, Ryotwari System and Mahalwari System.

1. Fold a sheet of paper like a hot dog.
2. With the paper horizontal, and the fold of the hot dog up, fold the right side toward the centre, trying to cover one half of the paper.
3. Fold the left side over the right side to make a book with three folds.
4. Open the folded book. Place your hands between the two thicknesses of paper and cut up the two valleys on one side only. This will form three tabs.

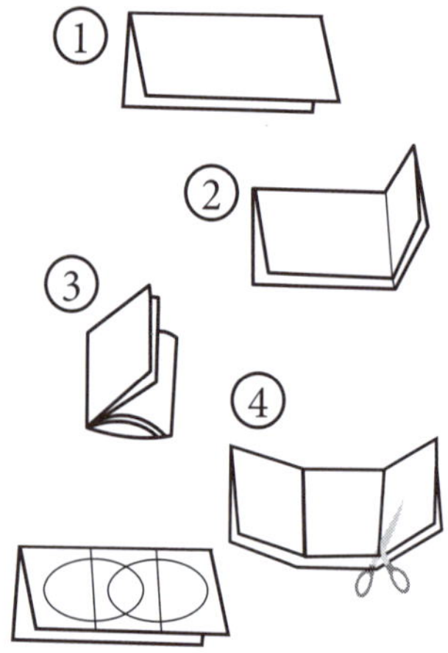

Web links:

https://niu.edu.in/sla/online-classes/BHS-401_Land-Revenue-System-in-British-India.pdf

Last accessed on 31 August 2021

4. Tribal Societies

Warm up

The *adivasis* or the aboriginal people of India inhabited different forested and hilly regions of the country. The word *adivasi* is a combination of *adi* which means 'the beginning of time' and *vasi* which means 'inhabitant'. So, *adivasi* literally translates to 'inhabitants since the beginning of time'. The Gonds, Bhils, Santhals, Mundas and the Kols are names of some tribal groups in India.

During the British era, tribal people lived in various parts of India. They used to practise shifting cultivation (*jhum*), hunting, gathering and fishing for their livelihood. They had a distinct socio-economic and political structure and formed an important part of the Indian society.

Social Life

In tribal societies, women enjoyed great respect and dignity. They believed a lot in the institution of family and marriages could not be performed within the same clan. Tribal people were religious people and believed in **animistic** spirits. Sacrifices were performed to please these spirits. Ancestors were worshipped and they believed in the death rituals which were performed by priests.

Economic Life

Adivasis were self-sufficient and were minimally dependent on the market. They would clear small areas of land in forests or hilly regions for shifting cultivation. The cut vegetation was dried and burnt, and the ashes scattered on the cleared land. Once the crops ripened and were reaped, the land was left fallow for about 20–30 years to allow the forest to regenerate. Meanwhile, another part of the forest was cleared for another crop. This is why it was called shifting cultivation. The food items grown by them included rice, millet, maize, potatoes and cotton.

What's in the picture?

This is a photo of the Santhali folk dance. Observe the picture and list three points that show the uniqueness of this tribes' traditional dress.

Forest produce was used for the purpose of building houses, making mats, etc. Besides this occupation, they engaged in cattle rearing, fishing and weaving. Soon, they started getting

animistic: the belief in a supernatural power that organizes and animates the material universe influenced by the lifestyle and culture of the people from the plains. They adopted the barter system and exchanged forest produce for what they needed from the market.

Policies of the British Towards the Tribals

During the British period, tribals were not only exploited by *zamindars*, but they also came under the control of the British.

The British encroached upon the lands of the tribals and disturbed their peaceful existence with the objective of expanding their political power. They curtailed the functions and powers of tribal chiefs and asserted their dominance over tribal land. This became the primary cause of discontent among the tribals. Other factors that led to their rebellions were:

- The British seized large areas of land cultivated by *adivasis* to grow cash crops such as indigo, jute and cotton.
- Their land was sold to the *zamindars* who were made owners of that land. Zamindars adopted oppressive methods to evict cultivators and extracted as much money as possible. This was profitable for the British.
- The tribal policy of the British did away with many of the rights that the tribals had enjoyed and forced them to work as landless labourers with minimum wages, especially in the tea plantations of Assam.
- As a result of the land settlement policy introduced by the British, the British claimed their right to the forested areas and made use of the forest resources for their benefit.
- Taxes were levied on tribal products, thus hampering the traditional economy.
- The tribals retaliated and were in conflict with the local police and company officials, as they refused to work for the British without being given any wages.
- The new developments, such as the postal and railway services, were a constant threat to the survival of the tribal people.
- The tribals of Jharkhand were forced to cultivate silk cocoons, which were sold at exorbitant prices.

Other factors were the introduction of forest laws, exploitation by the moneylenders and traders and unavailability of work. All these led to their exploitation and contributed to the revolt. At times these revolts were against the British, and at times, against the *zamindars*.

Apply it! E

The British intruded into the traditions of the tribals and tried to introduce them to a modern way of life. Do you agree with their actions?

The well-known revolts by the tribals were those of the Bhils in Madhya Pradesh, the Santhals in Bihar and the Khasis and Garos in Meghalaya. The British had all kinds of arms and the latest weapons, whereas the tribals had very primitive weapons. However, when we study the tribal movement, it can be broadly classified into three stages. The first one was before the revolt of 1857 and the second one during 1860–1920. This was due to the political and economic development of the British. The third one was during 1921–47, which was to show their support and solidarity towards the national movement.

Tribal Revolts in the Chhota Nagpur Region

The Santhal Rebellions

Adivasis had become highly suspicious of the British, who had gained control of their land. Suddenly, their forests and its produce belonged to these 'outsiders'. These outsiders or *dikus*, as they referred to anyone who were not *adivasis*, had also proved to be treacherous. For example, Santhals used to rear cocoons for their silk, in the jungles of Hazaribagh. Traders dealing in silk sent in their agents, who bought the cocoons for one-fifth of the price that they were sold for. The Santhals, who had been used to the barter system, not trade, were exploited.

In 1784–85, Baba Tilka Manjhi organized the Santhals to form the Mukti Dal, to fight against the British. This was the beginning of the liberation movement of the Santhals, known as the Santhal Hul. Many Santhals joined this movement. On June 30, 1855, a large group of Santhals declared their independence, and decided to fight *zamindars*, moneylenders and the British. On June 7, 1855, the British sent police officials to arrest Sidhu and Kanhu, who were the leaders of the Hul movement. A huge confrontation followed, where some British officials and *zamindars* were killed.

The British suppressed the uprising by January 1856. However, the movement caused the British to rethink their policies. Finally, the government passed a law to protect the interests and rights of the Santhals, which was known as the Bengal Tenancy Act.

The Munda Rebellion

The Ho, Oraon, and Munda tribes joined the Kols and Santhals in their revolt. The reasons were the same. *Zamindars* and their agents, the *thikadars*, would not only force them to pay high rents, but also evict them from their land when they failed to do so. Birsa Munda was a famous leader of the Munda tribe who inspired the people to stand against the British and fight for their rights to their lands.

The people of Ho tribe had fought with the rulers of Mayurbhanj and Chhota Nagpur, to maintain their independence. So, when the other tribes joined the revolt, they did so too. There are many milestones in the *adivasi* rebellion, such as the Tamarh revolt (1795), the Bhumij revolt (1798–99), the Munda revolt in Palamau (1819–20), the Kharia and Kairwar movements, in the two decades from 1860 to 1880.

FACT CHECK

The people of the hills showed their solidarity in fighting against the oppressive ways of the British. They even used guerilla tactics and burnt police stations, but U Kiang Nangbah was captured and hanged to death in 1862.

Case Study

Alluri Seetha Ram Raju, popularly known as *Manyam Veerudu* or 'hero of the jungle', was a revolutionary from Andhra Pradesh. He inspired local tribals to stand against the British by teaching them guerrilla warfare. In 1922, he led the Rampa Rebellion which was a tribal uprising in the Godavari district of the Madras Presidency. The sole purpose of the rebellion was to protect their land from the British who wanted to commercially exploit it. The revolt ended in 1924 with the death of this revolutionary leader.

Q. Why did Alluri Seetha Ram Raju lead his people into revolt?

Tribal Uprisings in the North East

The British imposed heavy land tax in the North East. In Kamrup and Darrang, it was increased from 50 per cent to 70 per cent. This led to an agitation in 1893–94. The peasants had been unable to pay the imposed taxes, so the British seized their land and ruthlessly suppressed their agitation.

In 1872, armed forces were sent to the Garo hills. The Garo tribals rose in revolt under the leadership of Pa Togan Sangma. This too was suppressed. U Kiang Nangbah, a young man in his thirties, rebelled against British injustice in Jaintia hills.

In Manipur, there was a war of succession between Surchandra, the eldest son of the King of Haripur, and his stepbrother Tikendrajit. Surchandra took the help of the British forces. Tikendrajit was defeated and hanged.

Tribal Uprisings in the South

The Hill Reddis of the Rampa region of Andhra Pradesh rose in a revolt against the British and the *Zamindars* in March 1879. This was because the Madras government had not only trebled the land revenue, but also restricted shifting cultivation (*podu*) in most areas. *Podu* had been the main source of livelihood for the Reddis. This rebellion, known as the Rampa rebellion, spread like wildfire among the local tribes. The Paderu rebellion by the Koya, Paraja and Kandha tribes, led by a non-tribal, Alluri Sitaram Raju, followed in 1922–23. Raju was an admirer of Mahatma Gandhi and his tactics. He led the tribal people in their first guerrilla warfare against the English. The rebellion gradually died down after Raju's capture and killing in May 1924.

Skill Builder

21ST CENTURY SKILLS

Critical thinking skills: 'Ancient tribes and modern civilizations do not mix'. Do you agree with this statement? Give reasons for your answer.

Life skills: There are five tribal languages that are moving towards extinction in India. Linguist experts say that the most threatened language is Majhi in Sikkim. According to a research conducted by People's Linguistic Survey of India, there are just four people who currently speak Majhi and all of them belong to the same family.

Collaboration: Divide the class into five groups. Each group has to make a presentation about any one tribe from the list given below. The presentation may include the location of the tribe, their social and economic lives, their art and any other interesting facts about them.

- Santhal
- Khasi
- Mizo
- Naga
- Bhil

World Connect

Native American Tribes: The Inuit and the Aleut

The Inuit and the Aleut were indigenous people who lived in the cold, flat and treeless region of present-day Alaska, Canada and Greenland. Both these groups spoke the Eskimo-Aleut language. The Inuit were nomads and hunted seals and polar bears as they moved across the tundra region. The Aleut lived a more settled life in small fishing villages along the shore. Both the Inuit and the Aleut lived in dome-shaped houses. They used seal and otter skins to make warm and weatherproof clothes. The open fishing boats of the Inuit were called kayaks.

By the time the United States took over Alaska in 1867, decades of oppression and exposure to European diseases had taken their toll. The native population had dropped to just 2,500. The descendants of these survivors still make their home in the area today. According to the U.S. Census Bureau, there are about 4.5 million Native Americans and Alaskan Natives in the United States today. That is about 1.5 per cent of the total population of the United States.

Wind up

British policies

- Zamindari oppression, exploitation by moneylenders and traders
- Forced to work as landless labourers without wages, land settlement policy, taxes, forest laws
- New developments proved to be a threat to them
- Unavailability of work

Tribal revolts

- Santhal rebellion
- Munda rebellion
- Uprisings in north east
- Uprisings in the south

Exercises

A. Choose the correct answers.

1. The term 'jhum' refers to
   a. step farming b. shifting cultivation c. contour ploughing d. both options a and b
2. The agitation by the Santhals was known as
   a. Hul b. Satyagraha c. Dharna d. none of these
3. The Bhils were tribes from
   a. Meghalaya b. Madhya Pradesh c. Bihar d. Andhra Pradesh
4. A tribal group from Meghalaya
   a. Santhal b. Khasi c. Pampa d. Kayathas
5. Pa Togan Sangma was the leader of the revolt in
   a. Khasi Hills b. Assam c. Garo Hills d. central India

B. Fill in the blanks.

1. The Santhal rebellion was led by ....
2. The British seized large areas of land cultivated by the adivasis to grow .... crops.
3. Adivasis were the... inhabitants of India.
4. There was a war of succession between .... and .... when the king of Manipur died.
5. The Hill Reddis of the Rampa region of .... revolted against the British.

C. Write T for true and F for false.

1. The Santhals belonged to the Chhota Nagpur area. ☐
2. The zamindars supported the tribals in their revolt. ☐
3. The Bengal Tenancy Act was passed to protect the rights of the Mundas. ☐

4. Tikendrajit sought the help of the British.

5. Alluri Seetha Ram Raju was known as the 'hero of the jungle'.

D. Answer these questions in brief.

1. Who were the adivasis?
2. State the religious beliefs of the tribals.
3. Who was Birsa Munda?
4. Give some examples of tribal occupations.
5. Mention the areas in India that were occupied by the tribal people.

E. Answer these questions in detail.

1. Discuss the reasons for tribal revolts in India.
2. Do you agree that the Santhal rebellion was a massive uprising? Support your answer with reasons.
3. Give reasons for the tribal uprising in the south.
4. Discuss the role of Alluri Sitaram Raju in the Rampa Rebellion.
5. Describe the economic life of the tribals.

Think Big

Integrate with geography

The Jarawa people are one of the last surviving tribes in the Andaman and Nicobar Islands. Four years ago, the last speaker of the Bo tribe passed away. A learned linguist, Professor Anvita Abbi, has stated that the rapid extinction of these tribes is due to the abrupt contact the tribes have had with other people over the last decades. She states that the loss of language is the catalyst for the extinction of one of the oldest civilizations in the world.

Can you look for more tribal communities who have been in the process of extinction due to certain reasons?

Learning Tools

Create a two-tab book to describe the cause-and-effect relationships related to tribal uprisings against the British. Select events from the period and identify two or more causes for each event.

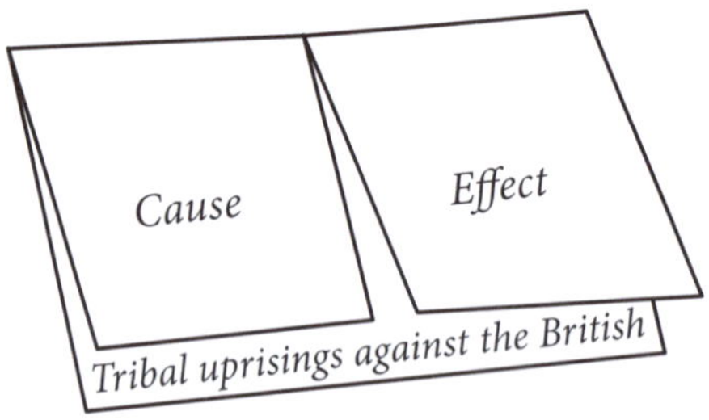

Web links:

https://www.jagranjosh.com/general-knowledge/summary-of-the-tribal-rebellions-during-british-rule-in-india-1521541943-1

Last accessed on 31 August 2021

5. Crafts and Industries

Warm up

A little girl sits on the couch, eyes twinkling with excitement. Her parents have brought her a gift from their trip. It was a beautiful doll, the most colourful one she's seen! She claps and clutches the doll to her chest. It is different—softer and vibrant. Her father tells her, 'This puppet doll is called Kathputli and the art of making such dolls started thousands of years ago in Rajasthan. Beautiful dolls are made from wood and cloth by hand and are strung by strings. They are used for entertainment, when the puppeteers hold these wooden dolls and make them dance and enact a play'. The little girl was thrilled!

Green Earth

India's landforms, climate, and terrain were ideal for the growth of cotton tea, sugarcane and other crops. This was the reason for India's wealth.

India has always valued its age-old customs and age-old crafts that have been passed from one generation to another. Before the British arrived in India, there were different industries in both the urban and rural areas. Weaving, pottery, sculpturing and metals were the main industries in the rural areas. Family-run businesses were common in the villages.

The arts and crafts industry thrived in towns and cities. These people not only made utility-based objects, but also luxury items that were exported to South East Asia, West and central Asia. Towns like Surat, Ahmedabad and Madurai were the centres of these industries. Surat was the centre for the cotton textile industry. Ship building was also one of the major industries of India.

Romesh Chunder Dutt, an economic historian, said that 'India in the 18th century was a great manufacturing as well as a agricultural country, and the products of the Indian loom supplied the markets of Asia and Europe.'

Decline of Industries

The English East India Company was a trading company till 1757. Their main objective was to purchase goods, such as cotton, silk, spices, indigo and sugar, which they then sold in the European markets at a huge profit. The Indian rulers of that time were in favour of establishing factories in different parts of the country. Eventually, the Indian handicrafts industry suffered a great setback because of the policies of the British.

As per the laws of the British Parliament, the use of Indian cotton and silk was not permitted in England. The English East India Company was ruthless with the Indian craftsmen and artisans. The weavers were paid poorly. They ultimately left their jobs and started working as farmers. The Indian handicraft industry suffered a huge misfortune because of this.

Impact of the Industrial Revolution

The significant inventions of the Industrial Revolution, such as the spinning jenny and the steam engine brought a novelty in textile weaving in England. From being the largest supplier and exporter, India now became a consumer of British finished products. The British imported their manufactured products to India on a massive scale.

Thus, there was a shift from handmade products made by specialized artisans to mass production by industrialists, caused by the invention of machines in England. The taking over of the princely states by the British resulted in artisans losing the patronage of the rulers.

Deindustrialization

The native industries collapsed and disintegrated due to the policies of the British. Merchants and bankers ceased to be involved in the textile trade.

The situation of the weavers changed when the East India Company became a political power. The Company dealt with the weavers directly. They prohibited them from selling their goods to any Indian merchants. The Company adopted many legislative measures to make its relationship legal and formal. The rules and regulations pertaining to the allowance that the weavers got were subject to many strict conditions. Each weaver during British rule was registered under an **aurang**. Records of every producer's residence, name and annual account were maintained. Later, these rules became strict and a code of behaviour was specified. The Company gradually became more of an employer than a buyer. Eventually, discontentment rose amongst the weavers. They were no longer independent workers. The increasing rising yarn prices were also detrimental for the weavers, as they brought about a decline in the imports of textiles.

FACT CHECK

Monopsony is a form of market with many sellers but only one buyer, who dictates the terms to the sellers.

The one-way free trade imposed by the English East India Company in 1813 made the situation worse. Under this policy, Indian cloth materials were made highly taxable in England, whereas British goods were sold at extremely cheap prices in the Indian market.

Growth of Industries

The end of the 19th century saw the development of two types of industries in India—the plantation industry and the machine industry.

Plantation Industry

The demand for indigo, tea and coffee attracted many European nations to explore the rich plantations of India. Indigo, a natural dye obtained from plants, was mainly grown in Bengal and Bihar. Indigo was in a huge demand overseas. However, this demand reduced when cheaper synthetic dye was introduced into the market. The tea industry

What's in the picture?

Study the photograph and write a few lines about it.

aurang: warehouse for storing finished goods or a place where goods are stored before being sold became the biggest plantation industry. The location, climate and the slopes of the mountains facilitated tea growth and made it the most flourishing business. Many tea companies emerged in south India and British India became the largest exporter of tea, with England as its largest buyer.

Machine Industry

In the second half of the 19th century, the machine industry emerged in India. Jute was already a popular material in India. It was woven by hand into a coarse cloth. In 1855, mass production of jute started. The first jute mill was set up in Rishra in Bengal. By the end of the 19th century, there were more than 5000 looms functioning in the mills.

Bales of cotton at the Mumbai (Bombay) railhead for export to Britain

Cotton Textile Mills

The first cotton textile mill was opened in Bombay because of the favourable climatic factors and availability of a port to import machines and export cotton. Later, more mills came up in Ahmedabad, Kanpur, Sholapur and Madras. A demand for steel, cement, chemicals and coal started soon after.

Coal

Coal was **indispensable** for the development of industries. With the expansion of railways, the demand for coal increased. Coal industries were set up in Bengal, Bihar and Orissa.

Apply it! E

Why was coal important for the development of industries? Is it still important today? Write a report on the uses and effects of coal.

Attitude towards Indian Industrialists

The Indian industrialists were not provided enough banking facilities. The rate of interest on the loans was very high and they were not exposed to the technical knowledge needed for the job.

Impact on the Indian Economy

Although foreign trade expanded and India established trade relationships with the USA, Japan and Germany, there was a decline in the export of manufactured goods as the new India became an importer of manufactured goods. Heavy taxes were levied on Indian goods, while British goods entering India were exempted of heavy taxes.

Economic Condition of the People

People were very poor as they were paid poor wages. They worked long hours in unhygienic conditions.

The main factors which led to the poor economic condition of the people were:

- The British did not take steps to protect and develop industries in India.
- They made no efforts to improve rural life and agricultural practices.
- The high land revenue turned small peasants into debtors and ultimately turned them into landless labourers.
- The British government's policies drained India's wealth.

indispensable: very essential

Emergence of a New Social Class

With the development of modern industries, two social groups came up—the capitalists and the working class. They had new ideas and a fresh outlook and were interested in the development of the country. This factor also helped to bring people closer.

Case Study

Carpet-weaving is one of the oldest industries in the country. Emperor Akbar brought in the finest carpet makers from Persia and established carpet weaving in India. In north India, it is an elaborate art. Uttar Pradesh, Rajasthan, Haryana and Kashmir are known for producing some of the best tapestries. Uttar Pradesh has the biggest carpet-weaving industry, and its carpets are known the world over for their unique colours and designs.

In Kashmir, carpets are handwoven entirely with intricate designs. Carpets of Rajasthan are traditionally well known for fine-quality hand-knotted woollen fibres.

Q. Name three states known for their carpet-weaving industries.

Skill Builder

21ST CENTURY SKILLS

Critical thinking skills: How does agriculture promote industrial development?

Creativity: Imagine you are a batik printer in British India. Write a diary entry describing your work and the impact of British rule on your art.

Information literacy: Prepare a short report on the handloom-weaving industry of India, with a special focus on the promotional policies of the Government of India.

World Connect

The Industrial Revolution in Britain

The Industrial Revolution began in Britain in the 18th century, as machines and industries revolutionized the manufacture of goods and improved the economy of the country. In the 18th century, Britain was a land of opportunity. With the acquisition of numerous colonies, Britain had access to ample supply of coal, cotton and other resources required for setting up industries. Political stability and freedom of thought allowed British scientists to develop new technologies. These new inventions stimulated Industrial Revolution in Britain, which soon spread over other parts of the world. By the early 19th century, Britain was producing more than half of the cotton and iron goods and the majority of steam engines of Europe.

Wind up

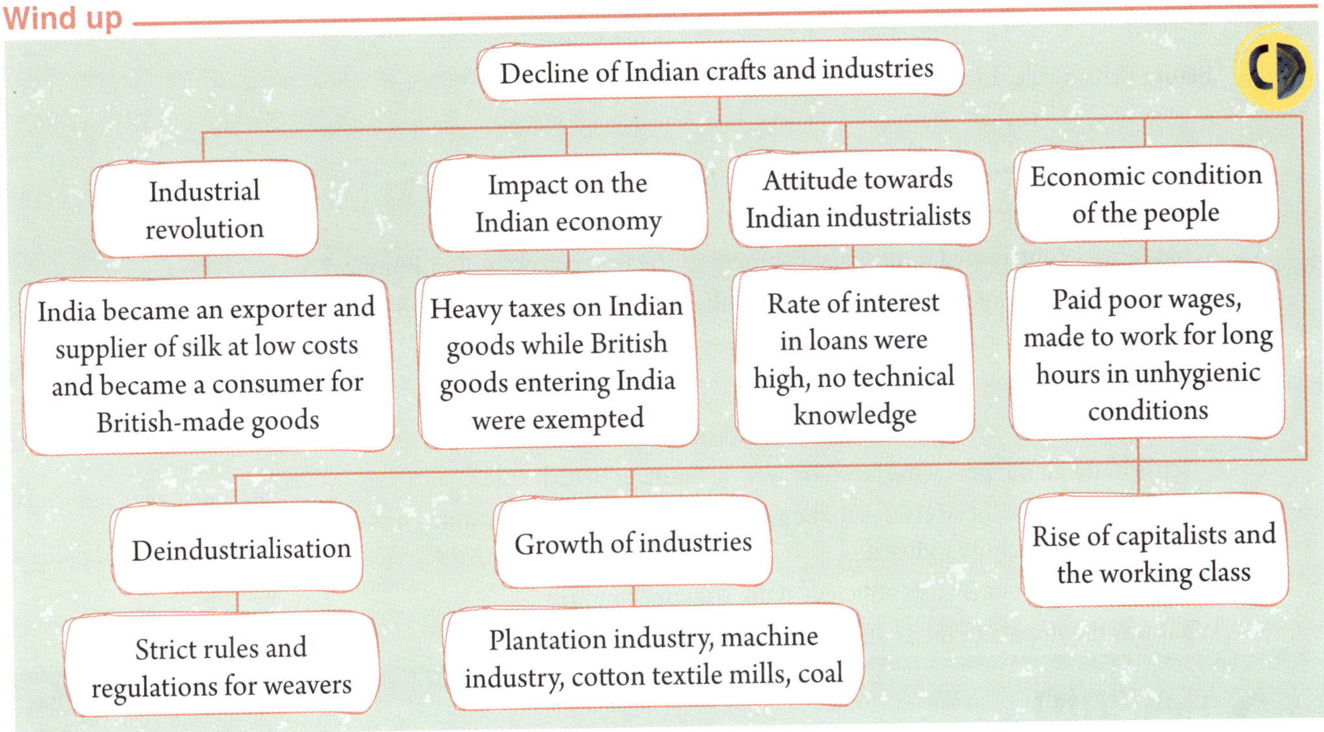

Exercises

A. Choose the correct answers.

1. The first cotton textile mill was opened in
   a. Surat   b. Ahmedabad   c. Banaras   d. Bombay
2. The plantation industry in India comprised of tea, coffee and
   a. cotton   b. jute   c. rice   d. indigo
3. The first jute mill was started at
   a. Kanpur   b. Jamshedpur   c. Surat   d. Rishra
4. The Industrial Revolution in England flourished at the cost of Indian
   a. landlords   b. merchants   c. traders   d. handicrafts
5. England did not import this item from India.
   a. tea   b. cotton   c. indigo   d. modern machinery

B. Fill in the blanks.

1. India supplied .... to the European countries.
2. The spinning jenny was invented during the ....
3. Coal industries were set up in Bengal, Bihar and ....
4. Mass production of jute started in India in the year ....
5. The British imported their .... products to India on a massive scale.

C. Write T for true and F for false.

1. In pre-colonial times, India was renowned for its handicrafts. ☐
2. Surat was the centre for cotton textiles in the medieval period. ☐
3. The one-way free trade made Indian goods extremely cheap in the British markets. ☐
4. The British carried machine-made goods from India to England. ☐

5. Indigo, a natural dye obtained from plants, was mainly grown in Bengal and Bihar. ☐
6. Before British rule, India excelled in the craft industry. ☐

D. Answer these questions in brief.

1. Describe the industrial sector in India before the advent of the British.
2. Explain the term 'deindustrialization'.
3. What factors contributed to the establishment of the first cotton mill in Bombay?
4. Describe the one-way free trade imposed by the East India Company in 1813?
5. Why did the tea plantations become the biggest industry in India?

E. Answer these questions in detail.

1. What were the reasons for the decline of traditional Indian industries?
2. Discuss in detail the problems faced by weavers during British rule.
3. What were the new social classes that emerged due to industrialization? Draw a comparison between plantation and machine industries.
4. Explain the impact of British policies on the Indian economy.
5. What was the impact of the Industrial Revolution on India?

Think Big

Integrate with art

Painting pots

You will need poster paints, glitter, beads and a paint brush.

1. Pick up a pot and remove any dust from it using a soft cloth or a brush.
2. If you have earthen pots, give them a coating of paint in any colour that you like.
3. When the base colour is dry, you can paint a variety of patterns on top to decorate your pots. Designs can range from geometrical, floral or even modern art. Just give it lot of colour, sprinkle glitter and paste some beads on the dry, painted pot.

Learning Tools

Create your own study guides by compiling the necessary information for swift recap.

Main ideas	Why it matters	Important terms and names
....	....	....
....	....	....
....	....	....
....	....	....

Web links:

https://www.historydiscussion.net/british-india/decline-of-industries-and-changing-conditions-of-artisans-in-india-during-british-rule/644

Last accessed on 31 August 2021

6. The Revolt of 1857

Warm up

Mangal Pandey, one of main heroes of the revolt of 1857, was was a sepoy (infantryman) in the 34th Bengal Native Infantry (BNI) regiment of the British East India Company. He was born in a village in Uttar Pradesh and joined the Bengal Army in 1849. In 1984, the Indian government commemorated Mangal Pandey by issuing a postage stamp in his honour. His life and actions have also been portrayed in several films and TV serials.

British domination over India was so powerful that the changes were felt not only in administration, but also on the economy of India. The setting up of railways and roadways was with the objective of facilitating the supply of raw materials from one British outpost to the other. It was only a matter of time before the people of India started a rebellion to protest against the oppressive administrative and economic policies of the British.

Causes of the Revolt of 1857

Political Causes

Lord Dalhousie was the Governor-General of India from 1848 to 1856. He introduced an oppressive annexation policy, called the doctrine of lapse, whereby any princely state would automatically come under the control of the British if the ruler was considered incompetent or died without a male heir.

The annexation of Satara (1848), Jhansi (1853) and Nagpur (1854) also angered the affected people. Nana Saheb, the adopted son of Baji Rao II, was not recognized as an heir by the British. He too became an enemy of the British, along with Rani Lakshmi Bai of Jhansi and Bahadur Shah, the last Mughal emperor. Dalhousie's policy of annexation unnerved the rulers of the princely states, as one kingdom after the other passed into the hands of the Company. Awadh was annexed on the pretext that the state was misgoverned. The Nawab of Awadh submitted without any resistance, but this caused a lot of ill-will against the British.

Social Causes

Many changes took place in the traditions and customs of the Indians. Lord William Bentinck made the practice of *sati* punishable. Widow remarriage was made legal. Female infanticide, child marriage and polygamy were banned. The common people did not like this transformation of their society, as they considered these reformers to be a threat to their social system. Developments, such as the introduction of the railways and telegram, were not received well. Developments in science were a challenge to the social order and brought about social unrest.

Economic Causes

As more and more territories were annexed under the doctrine of lapse, the company officers received huge salaries and a lot of wealth was sent to England. Many people lost their jobs because of industrialization. Huge taxes were collected from the zamindars and the peasants. Cultivators were like mere tenants and zamindars were mere revenue-collectors and not the real owners of the land. Pathetic agricultural conditions led to famines.

Religious Causes

The introduction of western education was thought of as an attempt to convert people to Christianity. Some missionaries criticized the practice of *sati* and child marriage as unreasonable and pressurized people to convert to Christianity. **Levying** taxes in the lands on which temples and mosques were built lent further support to the idea that people's religions were under threat.

FACT CHECK

Field allowance was also known as *batta*. It was an extra allowance made to the officers, soldiers, or other public servants, when in the field, or on other special grounds. The question of the right to batta created great agitation among the officers of the Indian Army.

Military Causes

The plight of the Indian soldiers in the army was also one of the causes of the Revolt of 1857. The British officers were given all the important posts in the army, while the Indians were given the lower ranks. The high-ranking British officers treated their Indian subordinates with total disregard. Indian soldiers were paid less than the British soldiers. They were not promoted beyond the rank of a subedar and the claims they made for field allowances were turned down by the British.

Indian sepoys preparing rifles during a training

The General Enlistment Act 1856 was formulated by Lord Canning, the Governor-General of India. It stated that the Bengal Army shall serve overseas if needed. Initially, only the armies of Bombay and Madras presidencies were under this obligation. The soldiers of the Bengal Army faced immense strain of being deployed at the Burma and China borders. This caused great **resentment** towards the British.

What's in the picture?

This scene shows the beginning of the revolt of 1857. Who are the people fighting the British in this picture?

Immediate Cause

The introduction of the Enfield Rifles is considered to be the immediate cause of the Revolt of 1857. It was believed that the cartridges used in the rifles were greased with the fat of animals like cows and pigs. Before the cartridges could be used, their greased paper covers had to be bitten off, and the Indian soldiers refused to do this. The unrest first started at Barrackpore and then in Berhampore. Mangal Pandey belonged to the

levying: imposing a tax, fee, or fine; resentment: a feeling of anger or unhappiness

34th Infantry, stationed at Barrackpore. Along with other soldiers, he revolted against the use of the greased cartridges. He was arrested on March 29, 1857 and hanged to death on April 8.

Following this incident, a rebellion sparked off in the Meerut cantonment. The Meerut Mutiny that started on May 9, 1857, was the beginning of the Revolt of 1857.

Many who participated in the rebellion were imprisoned. The rebels killed the European soldiers and took control of the garrison area of the British. Many soldiers joined the rebels. On 11 May, Bahadur Shah Zafar was proclaimed to be the leader of the revolt and the Emperor of Hindustan. Delhi also became the centre of the revolt, which aggravated the British. Many Indian chiefs expressed their loyalty to Bahadur Shah Zafar.

Centres of the Revolt

The six main centres of the revolt were Kanpur, Lucknow, Bareilly, Jhansi, Gwalior and Arrah.

Great Revolt of 1857

Kanpur: The revolt was led by Nana Saheb, the adopted son of Peshwa Baji Rao II. Nana Saheb had brave commanders, like Tatya Tope and Azimulla, but they were defeated and Kanpur was ultimately re-annexed by the British in December 1857. While Nana Saheb escaped to Nepal, both Tatya Tope and Azimulla were arrested.

Lucknow: Begum Hazrat Mahal took an active part in the uprising. She had declared Birjis Qadr, the son of Wajid Ali Shah, as the new Nawab. The new Nawab too recognized Bahadur Shah Zafar as the emperor. The uprising gathered strength because of the cooperation Begum Hazrat Mahal received from the peasants and soldiers, who were highly motivated by Maulvi Ahmadullah. They were successful in blocking the Lucknow Residency, where the British had taken refuge to escape the revolutionaries. The siege lasted for six months. Sir Henry Lawrence, the British Chief Commissioner, died during the siege.

Jhansi: The revolt in Jhansi was led by Rani Lakshmi Bai, as the British were not accepting her adopted son Damodar Rao as the heir to the throne. Due to their superior military arms and ammunitions, the British captured both the fort and the city. Rani Lakshmi Bai fled to Kalpi, where she was joined by Tatya Tope, and they took over Gwalior. However, they were defeated by the forces of Hugh Gough, a British Army officer.

Bareilly: The uprising was led by Khan Bahadur Khan Rohilla. When the revolt failed, he escaped to Nepal. But the Nepalese handed him over to the British and he was hanged in 1860.

Bihar: In Arrah, Bihar, an elderly zamindar, Kunwar Singh, led the revolt. He also extended help to the rebels in Kanpur and Lucknow. They destroyed the indigo factories.

Delhi: It was very important and a matter of prestige for the British to recapture Delhi. The Indian troops did everything to protect the city from the British siege. Ultimately, under General Nicholas and his strong troops, the city was recaptured.

The Revolt of 1857 was not a success because the British authorities in Lahore were warned about the revolt. The British contingent was successful in recapturing Delhi in September 1857. Bahadur Shah was made captive and exiled to Rangoon (present-day Myanmar), where he spent the rest of his life. He died in 1862. His sons were killed, putting an end to the Mughal Dynasty.

Bahadur Shah Zafar being captured by the British

1848	1853	1854	1856	1857	1862
Lord Dalhousie became governor general of India; annexation of Satara	Annexation of Jhansi	Annexation of Nagpur	General Enlistment Act	Revolt of 1857	Death of Bahadur Shah

Reasons for the Failure of the Revolt

The main reasons for the failure of the revolt were:

- The leadership of the movement was weak. Most of its leaders were motivated by narrow and personal gains. They fought to liberate their own territories.
- The revolt did not spread to all parts of India. The regions in the south and north did not participate in the revolt. Many groups and large sections of the Indian society did not support the revolt.
- There was a lack of common purpose amongst the rebels. The revolt was largely unorganized and the rebels lacked any **ideology**.
- The rebels lacked resources. They were short of finances and weapons. The British had more sophisticated weapons as well as an organized army. The Indian rebels lacked planning and had no clear direction.

Consequences of the Revolt of 1857

Although a failure, the Revolt of 1857 brought far-reaching changes in both the political and social aspects of the Indian society. The British East India Company's rule ended in India and the country was placed under the direct rule of Queen Victoria of England. The designation of the Governor-General of India was changed to viceroy. Lord Canning became the first viceroy of India.

The Government of India Act, 1858 was issued by Queen Victoria. According to the act:

- The social customs and traditions of the people of India would be respected and no discrimination would be made on the basis of caste or religion.
- The people of India would be given jobs in public offices based on their qualification.
- The policy of annexation and expansion, along with the doctrine of lapse, was discontinued.
- Promises were also made regarding industrial and public welfare development.

However, these promises were short-lived. The Indians expressed their resentment by raising the demand for self-government.

ideology: a set of beliefs that influences the way people behave

Case Study

Divide and Rule

The Revolt of 1857 was devoid of any communal barriers. It seemed that the two communities had one objective, to challenge the oppression of the British. The combined strength of the people frightened the British rulers. This changed the British policy in India. Sir John Strachey, a British Indian civil servant said, 'the existence side by side of the hostile creeds is one of the strongest points in our political position in India'.

This policy of divide and rule can be observed after 1858, when efforts were made to turn the princes against their people, province against province, caste against caste, and above all, Hindus against Muslims, as the unity displayed by them during the Revolt of 1857 made the British feel insecure.

Later, they also made an attempt to turn the upper- and middle-class Muslims against the national movement.

After 1857, it was observed that there were many Sikhs and Gurkhas in the modern Indian Army. Rajputs, Brahmins, and upper-class Muslims were removed. This was a deliberate move, so that the majority did not influence the Army.

Finally, the system of separate electorates also defeated the idea that India was one nation.

Q. In your own words, explain the policy of divide and rule.

Skill Builder

21ST CENTURY SKILLS

Critical thinking skills: Why did many sections of the society, particularly educated Indians, not join the revolt?

Life skills: Make a list of three leadership skills that you think are required to lead a mass movement.

Collaboration: In groups of five, prepare a timeline of the events of the Revolt of 1857. Draw the timeline on a chart paper and present it in the classroom.

World Connect

In China, a political and religious rebellion had started in 1850. It lasted for about fourteen years, and spread over seventeen provinces. The Taiping Rebellion, as it was known, began under the leadership of Hong Xiuquan, who was influenced by Christianity. He was against the traditional religions practised in China, such as Confucianism and Buddhism. Hong propagated equality and universal brotherhood of mankind. He was popular among the impoverished peasants, workers, and miners, as he encouraged the sharing of property, and made no class distinction among people. The Taiping Rebellion was crushed by the ruling Qing dynasty, with the help of the British and French forces operating in China.

Wind up

Causes of the Revolt of 1857

- Economic causes: Decay in traditional industries, land revenue policies and indigo cultivation
- Military causes: Discrimination, low wages, General Service Enlistment Act
- Immediate cause: Introduction of greased cartridges for the Enfield Rifle
- Political causes: Doctrine of lapse
- Socio-religious causes: Abolition of sati, female infanticide, Widow Remarriage Act, women's education, railways, telegraph, missionaries

Exercises

A. Choose the correct answers.

1. The Mughal Emperor Bahadur Shah was exiled to
   a. Malaysia b. Ceylon c. Indonesia d. Rangoon
2. The greased cartridge first became a source of disturbance in
   a. Meerut b. Lucknow c. Jhansi d. Barrackpore
3. A popular name associated with the 1857 uprising was
   a. Bhagat Singh b. Chandrasekhar Azad c. Sukhdev d. Mangal Pandey
4. In Bareilly, the uprising was led by
   a. Kunwar Singh b. Khan Bahadur Khan Rohilla
   c. Bahadur Shah Zafar d. Mangal Pandey
5. The main centres of the revolt were
   a. Bihar b. Kanpur c. Bareilly d. All of these

B. Fill in the blanks.

1. .... policies of the British led to discontentment among people.
2. According to an Act in 1858, India came under the rule of the ....
3. Rani Lakshmi Bai's son was not recognized as the heir under the .... policy of annexation.
4. .... made the practice of sati punishable.
5. The Governor-General of India was proclaimed as the .... under the act of 1858.
6. In Arrah Bihar, an elderly zamindar, ..., led the revolt.

C. Write T for true and F for false.

1. The Revolt of 1857 was initiated by Mangal Pandey. ☐
2. The doctrine of lapse was started by Lord Bentinck. ☐
3. Bahadur Shah Zafar was the last Mughal ruler. ☐
4. Nana Saheb was the adopted son of the Rani Lakshmi Bai. ☐
5. The revolt ended Company rule in India. ☐

D. Answer these questions in brief.

1. What was the significance of the Revolt of 1857?
2. Which policy was adopted by Dalhousie to extend the British Empire in India?
3. What was the immediate cause of the Revolt of 1857?
4. Why did the General Enlistment Act 1856 cause resentment amongst the Bengal Army?
5. How was Jhansi annexed?

E. Answer these questions in detail.

1. Explain the social, political and military causes of the Revolt of 1857.
2. What methods were used by the British to suppress the Revolt of 1857?
3. Why was the revolt of 1857 not a success? Give two reasons.
4. Explain the consequences of the Revolt of 1857.
5. What were the main features of the Government of India Act 1858?

Think Big

Integrate with language

Imagine your great-grandparents had participated in the 1857 revolt. You have found a journal maintained by them in an old trunk in the house. Write a diary entry about the same. Mention the important events/incidences and atrocities faced by Indian sepoys during mutiny.

Learning Tools

Fill up the boxes below to create a study guide of the chapter for quick recap.

Causes of the Revolt of 1857

Political causes:	Social causes:	Economic causes:
....	....	....
....	....	....
....	....	....
....	....	....
....	....	....
....	....	....

Religious causes:	Military causes:	Immediate causes:
....	....	....
....	....	....
....	....	....
....	....	....
....	....	....
....	....	....

Centres:	Reason it failed:	Consequences:
....	....	....
....	....	....
....	....	....
....	....	....
....	....	....
....	....	....

Web links:

https://www.britannica.com/event/Indian-Mutiny
https://www.nam.ac.uk/explore/why-did-indian-mutiny-happen

Last accessed on 31 August 2021

7. Colonial Education

Warm up

Babita lives in a small village in Odisha. Her father is a potter, and he loves Babita and her younger sister, Manda. Babita is 12 years old. She often helps her father with small errands. She loves going to school, but she had to discontinue going, as money was hard to come by. Babita often sees her father hanging his head low and she knows that he worries about making ends meet. One day, he found out about the Kishori Shakti Yojana, which is a scheme for young girls that aims to provide nutritional, educational and financial support to adolescent girls in the state. Through this scheme, she was able to go to school again.

Traditionally, education in India was provided by *patshalas* and *madrasas*. Education was mainly related to religion, philosophy, logic and astronomy. Sanskrit, Persian and Arabic were the major languages that were taught. These languages were used in the teaching of the religious texts. Persian became an official language. Sanskrit was the language used in scriptures. However, the learning of Sanskrit was limited only to some people.

Most of the educational institutions in India provided religious education. *Patshalas* provided Hindu religious education, while *madrasas* propagated Islamic education. The education provided in the Gurmukhi schools was also purely based on religion.

Education During the Colonial Rule

The British wanted to educate the Indians for two main reasons:

- The introduction of the English language would expose educated Indians to western culture, literature and science.
- They wanted to employ educated Indians in administration as it would benefit them economically.

The British opened schools in Chennai and Kolkata for teaching English language and science. In 1781, Warren Hastings founded the Calcutta Madrassa. In 1784, the renowned linguist and law expert, Sir William Jones, started the Asiatic Society. The main aim of this society was to collect old manuscripts of India. Even today, the Asiatic Society has an enormous collection of books and journals published in the major languages of the world.

FACT CHECK

The Charter Act of 1813 sanctioned a sum of one lakh rupees to be spent annually, for the promotion of modern education in India.

There were two schools of thought—orientalists and anglicisits. There was a disagreement regarding the medium of instruction used in the educational institutions. H. H. William

There were two schools of thought—orientalists and anglicisits. There was a disagreement regarding the medium of instruction used in the educational institutions. H. H. William and Dayananda Saraswati were **orientalists** and supported the use of Indian languages. Others believed that exposure to English as a medium of instruction would make education more progressive and advanced. John Stuart Mill was against the orientalists. According to him, the purpose of education was to provide modern and scientific education.

Dayananda Saraswati

Thomas Babington Macaulay, supporter of **anglicists**, a famous British politician and historian, was instrumental in introducing the English language as a higher medium of instruction in India, as he believed that it would enhance the knowledge of Indians in western science and philosophy. The recommendation suggested by Macaulay was accepted and put an end to the controversy over education.

Raja Ram Mohan Roy

The English Education Act was passed in 1835 by Lord William Bentinck. According to this act, the East India Company, which supported the usage of native languages as a medium of instruction, would no longer do it. Only the institutions that taught western education with English as the medium of instruction would be supported financially by the Company. Those who supported the English medium of instruction were known as anglicists. Raja Ram Mohan Roy was an anglicist. William Bentinck received support and encouragement from Raja Ram Mohan Roy, and they established the Kolkata Medical College, the Elphinstone College in Bombay in 1834 and the Hindu College in Banaras in 1791.

What's in the picture?

This image shows the Elphinstone College in Mumbai. What type of architecture is this called?

Wood's Despatch, 1854

Charles Wood was the president of the Board of Control of the English East India Company. In 1854, he sent the Wood's Despatch to Lord Dalhousie. The recommendations made according to this were:

- To set up an educational institution in every province of India.
- Educational institutions based in the model of the London University should be established in Bombay, Calcutta and Madras.
- To give grants and aid to private institutions in India.
- To use vernacular languages as the medium of instruction besides English.
- Setting up an education department in all the provinces.

Apply it!

Conduct a group discussion in your classroom about the importance of teaching the native languages in the schools.

Based on the recommendations made by Charles Wood, universities were established in Kolkata, Mumbai and Chennai.

orientalist: someone from the West who studies the language, culture, history, or customs of countries in eastern Asia; anglicist: an expert in or the student of English literature or language

The Demerits of Wood's Despatch

- The small amount of money allotted for education was not enough to be spent appropriately.
- The company's main objective was to produce clerks for the English government. The company did not bother whether education was accessible to all sections of the society.
- English language was propagated and vernacular languages were ignored. People who could speak English considered themselves to be superior.
- No efforts were made to improve women's education.
- Scientific and technical subjects were mainly open to the Europeans. Thus, Indians were not exposed to any kind of development.

However, to say that English education did nothing towards the development of the Indian society would be baseless.

The British appointed several commissions and committees that were important for the Indian education system. Many nationalists also formed their own organizations to improve the education system of the country. One of these organizations was the National Council of Education (NCE) in Bengal. Satish Chandra Mukherjee formulated this idea and set up the Bengal National College and schools in Calcutta, with Sri Aurobindo Ghosh as the first principal.

FACT CHECK

Ishwar Chandra Vidyasagar set up 35 schools for girls and developed an innovative method of teaching Sanskrit.

The aims of the National Council of Education were:

- to impart education in regional Indian languages.
- to encourage the study of culture, arts and natural sciences.

Aurobindo Ghosh

The Non-Cooperation Movement of 1920 enhanced the idea of national education and led to the establishment of many renowned universities such as the Jamia Millia Islamia and Visva-Bharati.

Colonial Education after Wood's Despatch

The Indian University Commission (1902) and the Indian Universities Act (1904): The Commission suggested that the government should exercise control over universities and universities over colleges. They also recommended that hostels should be built for students. The Indian Universities Act was based on the recommendations of the Commission in 1902.

Gokhale's Resolution on Indian Education (1913): It recommended that elementary education should be made free and compulsory throughout the country for the age group from 6 to 10 years.

Apply it!

Conduct a group discussion in your classroom about the importance of teaching the native languages in the schools.

The Sadler Commission (1917–19): It recommended that the minimum qualification for getting admission in universities should be intermediate and not matriculation. It also urged that the medium of instruction in high schools should be the native language of that particular place.

The Hartog Committee (1929): It recommended that commercial and industrial courses be introduced in the middle school to make it interesting. Also, vernacular middle schools should be established in rural areas.

The Radhakrishnan Commission (1948): After Independence, the University Commission was set up under Dr S Radhakrishnan. It recommended the setting up of rural universities based on the models obtained from Santiniketan and Jamia Millia. It also urged that the grants for scholarships and stipends be considerably increased so that the poor would be able to receive education.

Rabindranath Tagore's Unique Concept of Education

Rabindranath Tagore wanted to establish an educational system where students would be happy, carefree, creative and free to explore. He believed that this would be possible only if a child was exposed to a natural environment. Therefore, he established a school and the Visva-Bharati University in rural Shantiniketan, which meant 'the abode of peace'. This was a place where children could harness and nourish their creativity and talent and could be taught art and culture.

Rabindranath Tagore

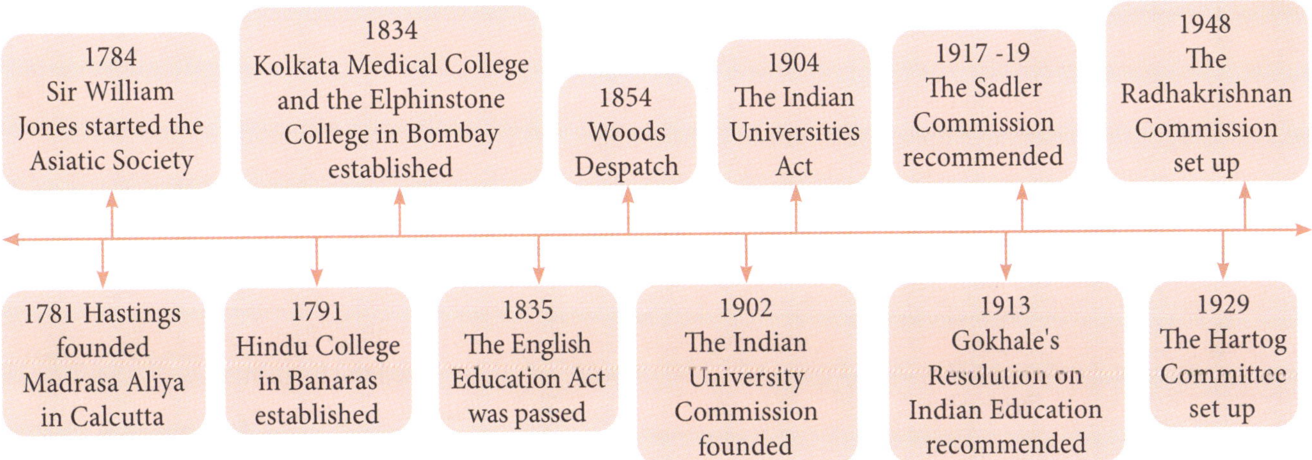

Case Study

Right to Education Act

The Right to Education Act 2009, also known as the RTE Act 2009, was enacted by the Parliament of India on 4 August 2009. It describes the modalities of the importance of free and compulsory education for children aged between 6-14 years in India under Article 21 (A) of the Constitution of India. This act came into effect on 1 April 2010 and made India one of the 135 countries to have made education a fundamental right for every child. It prescribes minimum norms for elementary schools, prohibits unrecognised schools from practice and advocates against donation fees and interviews of children at the time of admission. The Right to Education Act keeps a check on all neighbourhoods through regular surveys and identifies children who are eligible for receiving education but do not have the means to.

Educational challenges have been prevalent at both the centre and states for many years in India. The Right to Education Act 2009 maps out the roles and responsibilities for the centre, state and all local bodies, to rectify gaps in their education system, in order to enhance the quality of education in the country.

Q. What is the Right to Education Act?

Skill Builder

21ST CENTURY SKILLS

Information literacy: "Education is the most powerful weapon which you can use to change the world". Who pronounced these powerful words?

Life skills: In many parts of the world, boys go to school while girls stay home to take care of the house. Do girls need education and equal opportunities as boys even in the villages?

Critical thinking skills: Do you think western education has alienated us from our culture?

World Connect

During the early 19th century, England saw only the children of rich families going to schools. Most poor children worked to earn for their families. Children from the affluent families received education, with girls usually being taught at home by a governess. Children from poor families did not go to school. Till the 19th century, the Church of England carried out most of the formal education. The British Government established free and compulsory education for all children only by the end of the 19th century.

Wind up

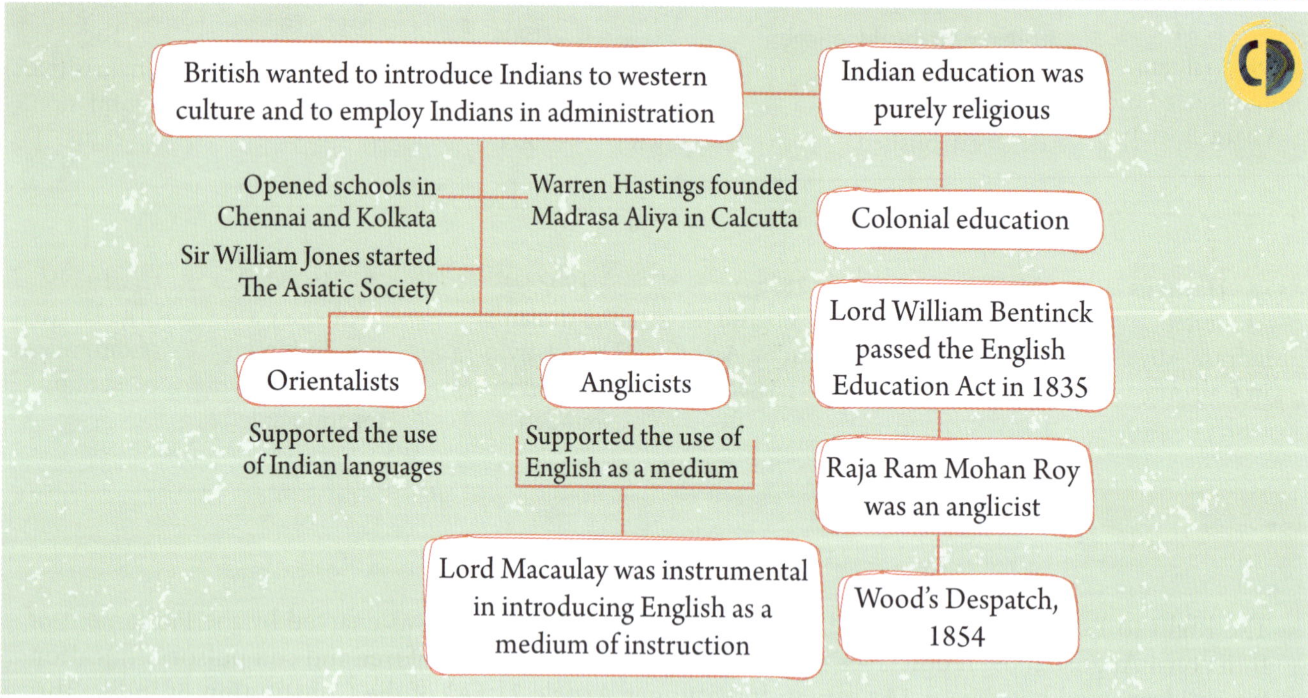

Exercises

A. Choose correct answers.

1. He set up the Asiatic Society in Bengal.
   a. Thomas Macaulay
   b. Mountstuart Elphinstone
   c. Nathaniel Halhed
   d. William Jones
2. Visva Bharati University was established by
   a. Mahatma Gandhi
   b. Raja Ram Mohan Roy
   c. Sri Aurobindo
   d. Rabindranath Tagore

3. Hindu College was established in Banaras in
   a. 1784 b. 1791 c. 1780 d. 1799

4. Elphinstone University was located in
   a. Calcutta b. Madras
   c. Bombay d. Banaras

5. The first principal of the Bengal National College was
   a. Raja Ram Mohan Roy b. Ishwar Chandra Vidyasagar
   c. Aurobindo Ghosh d. Satish Chandra Mukherjee

B. Fill in the blanks.

1. Before the advent of British, the .... and the .... imparted learning.
2. The English Education Act was passed in .... by Lord William Bentinck.
3. The .... Movement of 1920 enhanced the idea of national education.
4. In 1781, ... founded the Madrasa Aliya in Calcutta.
5. A person who was a severe critic of the Orientalists was ....

C. Write T for true and F for false.

1. A school for the teaching of Arabic and Persian languages was opened in Kolkata by Lord William Bentinck. ☐
2. Charles Wood is known for his educational despatch. ☐
3. Shantiniketan means 'the abode of peace'. ☐
4. Raja Ram Mohan Roy encouraged English education in India. ☐
5. Macaulay was in favour of the Persian language as the official language of India. ☐

D. Answer these questions in brief.

1. How did Ishwar Chandra Vidyasagar contribute to education?
2. What were the shortcomings of the traditional system of education, according to anglicists?
3. What were the main recommendations of the Hartog Committee?
4. What were the aims of the National Council of Education?
5. Name the two school of thoughts in the educational institutions.

E. Explain these questions in detail.

1. What were the main objectives of the British in propagating western education?
2. What were the main recommendations of the Wood's Despatch?
3. What was the impact of English education on Indian people?
4. Why do you think that Rabindranath Tagore's system of education was unique?

F. Read the passage and answer these questions.

The Non-Cooperation Movement of 1920 enhanced the idea of national education and led to the establishment of many renowned universities such as the Jamia Millia Islamia and Visva-Bharati.

1. Name two institutes that were established after the start of the Non-Cooperation Movement.
2. What do you understand by the phrase 'national education'?

Think Big

Integrate with language

Beti Bachao Beti Padhao (BBBP) was launched by the Prime Minister on 22 January, 2015 at Panipat, Haryana. BBBP addresses the declining Child Sex Ratio (CSR) and related issues of women empowerment over a life-cycle continuum. It is a tri-ministerial effort of Ministries of Women and Child Development, Health & Family Welfare and Human Resource Development. Despite these efforts, girls especially in rural areas are discouraged to attend school.

5 GENDER EQUALITY

Write a letter to the Prime Minister of India, suggesting ways for him to promote education for the girl child. List its benefits.

Learning Tools

Create your own study guide on the sheet below.

Notes	Cues
1 During Class	**2 After class**
(Main points and details from class)	(Main ideas prompts and question)

Summary

3 After Class

(summary of the leasson)

Web links:

https://science.jrank.org/pages/9087/Education-in-India-Colonial-India.html

Last accessed on 31 August 2021

8. Women and Reforms

Warm up

Helen Keller was a famous author and teacher who could not see or hear. Her teacher, Anne Sullivan, taught her to read Braille. She graduated in 1904 and went on to become an author, a lecturer, a political activist and an advocate for the differently-abled. During her lifetime, she received many honours in recognition of her accomplishments. Her book, *The Story of My Life*, is still in print in over fifty languages.

After the British gained a foothold in India, they made several changes. A significant change was the introduction of the western system of education. The intellectuals of India, who were exposed to western education, realized that the **obsolete** system of education of India needed an **overhaul**. They realized that a good education system was the need of the hour. This intellectual consciousness led to many reforms. Therefore, it is often referred to as a period of re-awakening or renaissance.

Status of Women Before the Reforms

It is said that a society that provides education and freedom to women is civilized and progressive. However, many social evils against women were prevalent in the Indian society. Women were subject to the following social evils:

Sati: Women were supposed to **immolate** themselves on the funeral pyre of their deceased husbands.

Female infanticide: The girl child was killed soon after the birth. Girls were considered a burden to their families and a drain on their financial resources.

Polygamy: The practice of having more than one wife was prevalent in many families.

Child marriage: Children were married at a very young age, which affected their health and education.

Dowry: The huge amount of money to be given by the girl's parents at the time of the wedding, failing which either the wedding would not take place, or the girl would be ill-treated, and killed in some cases, by the boy's family.

Widowhood: Girls were married off to very old men. When these men died, the girls' heads were shaved. They were not allowed to wear colourful clothes, eat good food or remarry. They were completely **outcast** by their families.

obsolete: something which is no longer used because a better replacement has been found; overhaul: to make necessary changes; immolate: to kill somebody by burning them; outcast: one that is cast out or refused acceptance (as by society)

Purdah system: Women were supposed to stay inside their houses—the kitchen and bedrooms. Many areas of the house were not accessible to women. Women would go out in **palanquins**, so that people who did not belong to the family could not see them. Women were expected to cover themselves completely, even if they were not comfortable in it.

No right to property: Women had no right to inherit their family's or husband's property.

The Role of Social Reformers

The social reformers of the 19th century were concerned about the issues of women and wanted to improve their position in the society. They felt that the political transformation of the society was not possible unless social atrocities against women were put to an end. Some of the social reformers who made significant contributions to the cause of upliftment of women were Raja Ram Mohan Roy, Ishwar Chandra Vidyasagar, Begum Rokeya Sakhawat Hossain, Swami Dayananda Saraswati, Syed Ahmed Khan and Dadabhai Naoroji, amongst many others.

Raja Ram Mohan Roy

Raja Ram Mohan Roy (1772–1833) was called the 'father of modern India'. He was a learned scholar, well-versed in Persian, Sanskrit and English. He was a pioneer of western education and championed the cause of women empowerment. He pioneered the Brahmo Samaj movement.

Raja Ram Mohan Roy

He was against the practice of sati and started a movement against it, despite facing stiff opposition from **orthodox** Hindus. His efforts received support from Lord William Bentinck, the then Governor-General of India. He passed a law on December 4, 1829, making the practice of sati illegal and punishable by law. Raja Ram Mohan Roy also demanded equal inheritance rights for women. He was against **polygamy**. He extended help to the people who opened schools and colleges and encouraged women to receive modern education.

Ishwar Chandra Vidyasagar

Ishwar Chandra Vidyasagar (1820–1891) was an educationist and a social reformer who supported the cause of widow remarriage. He published the book, *Hindu Widow Marriage*, in 1855. His efforts were **pivotal** in the passing of the Hindu Widow's Remarriage Act, 1856. He called it the 'single greatest good deed' of his lifetime.

Ishwar Chandra Vidyasagar

FACT CHECK

Ishwar Chandra Vidyasagar was the secretary of the Bethune School in Kolkata. It was the first women's school in India and was established by John Elliot Drinkwater Bethune in 1849. It was called the Hindu Female School back then.

Begum Rokeya Sakhawat Hossain

Begum Rokeya (1880–1932) opened a school for Muslim girls, known as the Sakhawat Memorial Girls' School, in Kolkata in 1911. She wrote many articles, short stories and novels about the condition of the women in India. In one of her lectures she said, 'I have been crying for the lowliest creature in India for the last twenty years. Do you know who that lowliest creature in India is? It is the Indian woman...'

palanquin: (in India and the East) a covered litter for one passenger, consisting of a large box carried on two horizontal poles by four or six bearers; orthodox: following or conforming to the traditional or generally accepted rules or beliefs of a religion, philosophy, or practice; polygamy: the practice or custom of having more than one wife or husband at the same time; pivotal: of great importance

Swami Dayanand Saraswati

Swami Dayanand (1824–1883), the founder of Arya Samaj, also fought for improvements in the position of women in Indian society. He opposed the tradition of *sati* and strongly promoted widow remarriage. He opened many schools which imparted modern education and Indian culture.

Syed Ahmed Khan

Sir Syed Ahmed (1817–1898) believed that women should be educated to **alleviate** the social evils of a society. He urged Muslims to adopt western education. He established the Muhammadan Anglo-Oriental College in Aligarh in 1875. It was one of the first universities in South Asia. He believed that scientific and logic-based education was important to curb the social evils in the society. The university was later renamed as the Aligarh Muslim University.

Syed Ahmed Khan

Dadabhai Naoroji

Dadabhai Naoroji (1825–1917) was a leading reformer of the Parsis. His efforts improved the position of women, especially in the matters relating to inheritance of property.

Other Reformers

Other reformers were Keshab Chandra Sen, Rabindranath Tagore and Swami Vivekananda from Bengal. In Maharashtra, Gopal Hari Deshpande helped in founding educational institutions for women, like Paramhansa Mandali in Mumbai, which worked for the emancipation of women. Jyotirao Govindarao Phule started schools in Pune for girls belonging to lower castes. Another prominent social reformer from Maharashtra was Pandita Ramabai. With the support of Justice Ranade and R.G. Bhandarkar, she founded the Arya Mahila Samaj and Sharda Sadan, a facility to house the widows and school girls of Mumbai. Pandita Ramabai made an effort to provide education and vocational training to women. She was given the title of Pandita as she was very learned. The Veda Samaj was established in Madras by Sridharalu Naidu and Keshab Chandra Sen in 1864. It supported widow remarriage. Kandukuri Veeresalingam, from Andhra Pradesh, established the Rajahmundry Association, which worked for the upliftment of women and believed in gender equality.

Dadabhai Naoroji

Pandita Ramabai

What's in the picture?

This photograph was taken in c. 1870, and shows a school for Parsi girls in Bombay (India). In not more than 100 words, write an essay on what India would be like had education for women not been introduced.

alleviate: to make something less severe

Case Study

Acharya Vinoba Bhave, often called the National Teacher of India, was an advocate of nonviolence and human rights. His doctrines of nonviolence and equality were influenced by Gandhi, and he dedicated his life to help the poor. He is best known for his active role in the Bhoodan Movement, which was a land reform movement where protesters attempted to persuade wealthy landowners to voluntarily donate a portion of their land to the poor. Vinoba was the first recipient of the international Ramon Magsaysay Award for Community Leadership in 1958. He was also conferred with the Bharat Ratna (India's highest civilian awards) posthumously, in 1983.

Q. Write a note on the achievements of Acharya Vinoba Bhave.

- 1772–1833 Raja Ram Mohan Roy
- 1829 Sati made illegal
- 1820 -1891 Ishwar Chandra Vidyasagar
- 1856 Hindu Widow's Remarriage Act passed
- 1880 -1932 Begum Rokeya
- 1824 -1883 Swami Dayanand
- 1817 -1898 Sir Syed Ahmed
- 1911 Sakhawat Memorial Girls' School in Kolkata opened
- 1825–1917 Dadabhai Naoroji

Apply it!

Imagine you are a social worker working for the cause of women. Which are the issues that you would like to take up for the cause of women? Design an action plan to achieve the necessary results.

5 GENDER EQUALITY

Impact of the Women's Movement

- Positive changes in the attitude of people towards women.
- Many women stepped out of the house and gave up the purdah to receive education.
- Women became aware of their rights and also started taking interest in political matters.
- Issues of women were represented through various organizations.
- Many organizations worked to create social consciousness, like the All India Women's Conference and the National Federation of Indian Women.

Skill Builder

21ST CENTURY SKILLS

Critical thinking skills: Why do you think women were excluded from inheriting property?

Information literacy: The government launched the Mahila Shakti Kendra in 2017 to empower rural women. What empowerment policies are part of this skill development programme?

Life skills: In what forms does discrimination against women exist even today? Make a list and suggest measures to prevent it.

World Connect

Catherine the Great (1729–96)

Catherine the Great was the ruler of Russia from 1729 to 1796. Her reign was the longest amongst the rulers of Russia. Catherine the Great, as she was called, came to power, after her husband Peter III was assassinated. The period of Catherine's rule is called the 'Golden Age' of the Russian Empire. Peter III had issued a manifesto on the freedom of nobility during his short reign. Catherine the Great confirmed this manifesto on the nobles, and freed them from compulsory military training or state service. She was a patron of arts. It was during her rule that Smolny Institute, the first state-financed higher education institution for women in Europe was established.

Wind up

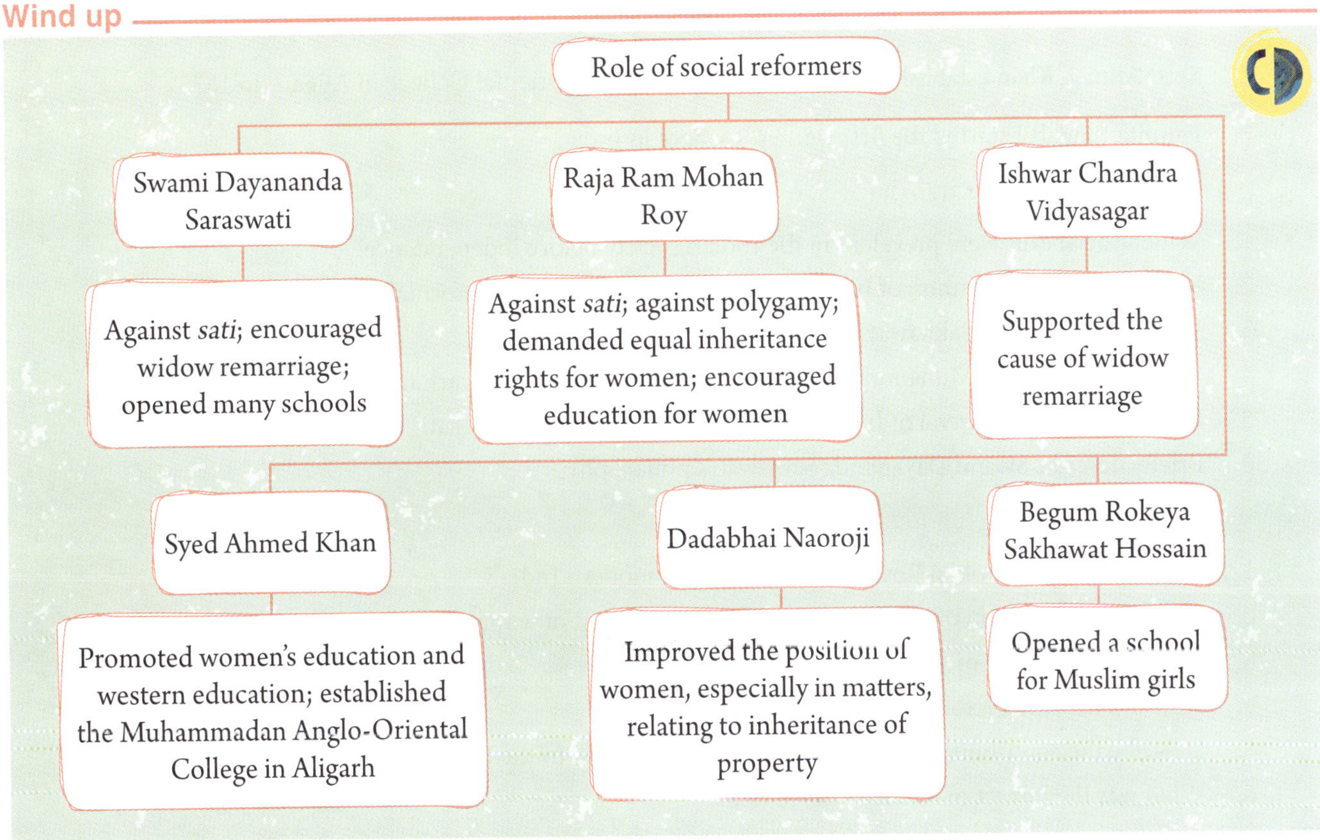

Exercises

A. Choose the correct answers.

1. Raja Ram Mohan Roy opposed the practice of
   a. western education
   b. working women
   c. sati
   d. widow remarriage

2. He was known as the father of the modern India.
   a. Ishwar Chandra Vidyasagar
   b. Jyotiba Phule
   c. Dadabhai Naoroji
   d. Raja Ram Mohan Roy

3. He founded the Arya Samaj.
   a. Dadabhai Naoroji
   b. Keshab Chandra Sen
   c. Swami Vivekananda
   d. Dayanand Saraswati

4. Sharda Sadan was established by
   a. Jyotiba Phule
   b. Begam Rokeya
   c. Kandukuri Veeresalingam
   d. None of these people
5. The Brahmo Samaj was founded by
   a. Swami Vivekananda
   b. Dayanand Saraswati
   c. Ishwarchandra Vidyasagar
   d. Raja Ram Mohan Roy

B. Write T for true and F for false.

1. Raja Ram Mohan Roy was not in favour of English education. ☐
2. Lord William Bentinck passed the law to abolish the practice of sati. ☐
3. Jyotirao Govindarao Phule established schools for girls in Pune. ☐
4. Syed Ahmed Khan established the Muhammadan Anglo-Oriental College in Aligarh in 1875. ☐
5. Pandita Ramabai started the first women's school in India. ☐

C. Answer these questions in brief.

1. Which social evils were prevalent in the Indian society before independence?
2. What was the contribution of Ishwar Chandra Vidyasagar to the reformation of women's condition?
3. Who established the Sakhawat Memorial Girls School in Kolkata?
4. Who established the Muhammadan Anglo-Oriental College in Aligarh in 1875?
5. Which Governor-General of India helped Raja Mohan Roy abolish sati?
6. Briefly describe Swami Dayananda Saraswati's philosophy.

D. Answer these questions in detail.

1. Why is Raja Ram Mohan Roy called the 'father of modern India'?
2. State the contribution of Ramabai towards the upliftment of women.
3. Discuss the position of women in the 19th century.
4. How did the social reformers change the Indian society?
5. Describe the contribution of Swami Dayananda Saraswati to the Indian society.
6. What was the impact of women's movement?

E. Read the passage and answer the questions.

Other reformers were Keshab Chandra Sen, Rabindranath Tagore and Swami Vivekananda from Bengal. In Maharashtra, Gopal Hari Deshpande helped in founding educational institutions for women, like Paramhansa Mandali in Mumbai, which worked for the emancipation of women.

1. Give the names of two other reformers who worked towards establishing educational institutions for women.
2. What was the purpose of the Paramhansa Mandali in Mumbai?

Think Big — Integrate with language

Speak out in a debate for and against these powerful words, '*One child, one teacher, one book, one pen, can change the world*' - Malala Yousafzai

5 GENDER EQUALITY

Learning Tools

Complete the table to summarise what you have learnt in the chapter.

Status of Women before the reforms	Social reformers	Contributions

Web links:

https://www.feministformations.org/sites/default/files/24.2.warner.pdf

Last accessed on 31 August 2021

9. Challenging the Caste System

Warm up

Babasaheb, once a struggling student, was caught eating food at a library in London. When the librarian threatened to terminate his membership, he apologized profusely and admitted that he could not afford the food sold in the cafeteria. After hearing this, the librarian said, 'From tomorrow, you will be joining me at the cafeteria and I will share my meal with you.' Today, we know this young student as Bhimrao Ramji Ambedkar. He grew up to become a jurist, economist, politician and social reformer. He spent his life campaigning against social discrimination against Dalits and supported the rights of women. He was the principal architect of the Constitution of India.

The caste system remains a major social evil in India. The oppressive conditions and menial occupations of the lower castes created great disunity among the people. The *Shudras* were banned from using public places such as temples, schools, wells and even rivers. They were treated as untouchables. People belonging to higher castes could not travel overseas, as they feared losing the purity of their caste. Thus, the caste system prevented people from developing a feeling of brotherhood.

The caste system was attacked by the Brahmo Samaj, the Prarthana Samaj, the Arya Samaj, the Ramakrishna Mission and the Theosophical Society.

Raja Ram Mohan Roy

Raja Ram Mohan Roy condemned the oppression of the lower castes by the upper castes. He wanted people to understand the meaning of the scriptures, so that they could free themselves from the meaningless rituals of religion. Therefore, he got the *Vedas* and *Upanishads* translated into Bengali. He established the Brahmo Samaj in 1828 as an expression of his concept of universal worship. After his death, the Samaj and the movement was taken forward by Debendranath Tagore. Over a decade or so later, Keshab Chandra Sen joined the Samaj. About two decades later, the Brahmo Samaj split into two, with Keshab leading the younger reformist group, the Brahmo Samaj of India. This group laid great emphasis on female **emancipation**, female education and a total abolition of caste distinctions.

Swami Vivekananda

Swami Vivekananda

Swami Vivekananada, a disciple of Sri Ramakrishna Paramhansa, was the founder of the Ramakrishna Mission. The mission was established to spread the message of Shri Ramakrishna Paramhansa. He explained that no religious text prescribed the caste system, and that it was a social, not

emancipation: the fact or process of being set free from legal, social or political restrictions; liberation

Dayananda Saraswati

religious system. He stressed on humanism and doing service to mankind. According to him, no religion spoke of untouchability.

Swami Dayananda Saraswati

Swami Dayananda tried to remove the evils of the caste system and untouchability through the Arya Samaj.

Justice Ranade

Justice Ranade and Dr Ramkrishna Gopal Bhandarkar

The Prarthana Samaj was founded by Justice Ranade and Dr Ramkrishna G Bhandarkar, who were greatly influenced by the Brahmo Samaj. They were opposed to the authoritative influence of Hindu priests. They emphasized that all gods were one, and stressed on the unity between Hindus and Muslims. Justice Ranade's wife, Pandita Ramabai, continued this work.

Jyotiba Phule

Jyotiba Phule

Sardar Gopal Hari Deshmukh, a social worker, opposed the caste system and protested against the pitiable state of the Hindu widows. He was a sessions judge and wrote many articles aimed at social reform. Jyotiba Phule stressed that the exploitation of lower castes, and the ill-treatment of women, were great social evils. He wrote both in Marathi and English. His book *Gulamgiri* (slavery) was published in 1872. He opened a school for non-Brahmin girls in 1848. He set up the Satyashodhak Samaj in 1873, which worked to liberate the oppressed classes.

Kandukuri Veeresalingam

Kandukuri Veeresalingam Pantulu

Kandukuri Veeresalingam Pantulu is known as the father of the Telugu Women's Movement. He was from Andhra Pradesh. He wrote *Satyavati Charitram* to highlight the importance of women's education in building a happy home. In another book, *Brahma Vivaham*, he made fun of the custom of old men marrying young girls. He led a movement for the marriage of child widows and campaigned for women's education.

Narayana Guru

Narayana Guru

Narayana Guru was born in Kerala in 1854 in the Ezhava community, who were considered untouchable by the upper castes. He believed in one caste, one religion, and one God for all human beings, and this concept was popularized through Sri Narayana Dharma Paripalana Yogam that was founded by him. He also established temples in which there were no images of gods and goddesses. He worked for the progress of the oppressed classes, especially the Ezhavas.

E.V. Ramasamy (Periyar)

E.V. Ramasamy (Periyar) was a champion of the cause of the downtrodden or low caste people. He fought against the domination by Brahmins. He also criticized Hindu scriptures openly. He encouraged lower castes to free themselves from the clutches of religion, in order to achieve social equality. He established a self-respect movement to fight for the rights of Dalits, especially securing government jobs through the reservation policy. This resulted in the very first amendment in the Indian Constitution to safeguard the rights of the lower castes.

E.V. Ramasamy

Mahatma Gandhi

After his return from South Africa, Mahatma Gandhi established the Sabarmati Ashram in Gujarat in 1916 and invited people of all castes and religions. He campaigned against untouchability as he felt it was an inhuman practice, and therefore, made all efforts to remove it. He also felt that the Indian society would become a free society once the caste system was removed entirely. The All India Untouchability League and a weekly magazine called *Harijan*, were initiated by him. He frequently undertook tours to interact with people of the lower castes and ate in their utensils, which was unheard of back then.

FACT CHECK

Mahatma Gandhi coined the word *Harijan* for the lower caste people which meant children of God.

Dr Bhim Rao Ambedkar

Dr Ambedkar belonged to a lower caste and experienced a lot of indignities because of this. He fought for the cause of removing untouchability. He organized the All India Deprived Class Federation. He organized many campaigns for lower castes to be allowed to enter temples, and draw water from the wells belonging to upper castes. Dr B. R. Ambedkar involved the deprived classes in the national movement. He published a paper known as 'Castes in India' and published a weekly called *Mooknayak*, which attacked the Hindu orthodox legacy. The Bahishkrit Hitkarini Sabha was formulated with the objective of promoting education and social upliftment for the backward and deprived classes.

B. R. Ambedkar

Results of the Efforts of Reformers

- The oppressed classes became aware of their rights.
- They played an important role in removing untouchability. Their criticism was diverted to the upper castes and they advocated progressive changes.
- People began to question the oppression by the upper castes.
- It was an effort to unite the people to participate in the freedom struggle, irrespective of caste or religion. Very soon laws were passed abolishing untouchability.

Apply it! E

Find pictures of five social reformers of India and write a few lines about each in your notebook.

However, the struggle to fight against the caste system still exists, especially in the rural areas.

World Connect

The African Slave Trade

In the seventeenth century, the new crops of sugarcane, tobacco and cotton required a large amount of workforce to assure timely production for the European market. Thus began slave trade from Africa. These slaves were brought in by European traders from Africa, and sold to the planters in America. The slave trade reached its peak in the mid-eighteenth century, when over 80,000 Africans crossed the Atlantic Ocean to work as slaves in the plantations owned by the white Americans.

Skill Builder

21ST CENTURY SKILLS

Critical thinking skills: Although Indian law prohibits discrimination and violence against Dalit people, in reality atrocities are a daily occurrence. Why do you think people in general have not been able to change their mindset?

Life skill: How did the knowledge of ancient texts help the reformers promote new laws?

Communication skill: Write slogans against any kind of discrimination in society and display in your class.

Wind up

Challenging the caste system

- Raja Ram Mohan Roy
- Swami Dayananda Saraswati
- Jyotiba Phule
- Narayana Guru
- Mahatma Gandhi
- Dr B. R. Ambedkar
- E. V. Ramasamy
- Kandukuri Veeresalingam Pantulu
- Justice Ranade and Dr Ramkrishna Gopal
- Swami Vivekananda

Exercises

A. Choose the correct answers.

1. He founded the Ramakrishna Mission.
   a. Rabindranath Tagore b. Keshab Chandra Sen
   c. Swami Vivekananda d. Raja Ram Mohan Roy
2. The Satyashodhak Samaj was set up in in 1873 by
   a. Gopal Hari Deshmukh b. Pandita Ramabai
   c. Jyotiba Phule d. B.R. Ambedkar

3. Founder of the self-respect movement.
   a. Sri Narayana Guru
   b. Mahatma Gandhi
   c. Kandukuri Veeresalingam
   d. E.V. Ramasamy

4. The organizer of the All India Deprived Classes Federation
   a. B.R. Ambedkar
   b. Mahatma Gandhi
   c. Gopal Hari Deshmukh
   d. Sri Narayana Guru

B. Fill in the blanks.

1. Kandukuri Veeresalingam .... is known as the father of the Telugu Women's Movement.
2. .... was born to the Ezhava caste.
3. The term *Harijan* was coined by ....
4. The attitude of the people regarding the caste system changed because of the efforts of ....
5. The caste system did not allow people to travel ....
6. Swami Vivekananda stressed on .... and service to mankind.

C. Write T for true and F for false.

1. Dr B.R. Ambedkar was a Brahmin by caste. ☐
2. Jyotiba Phule was also known as Mahatma. ☐
3. Raja Ram Mohan Roy founded the Ramakrishna Mission. ☐
4. *Satyavati Charitram* was written by Swami Vivekananda. ☐
5. Mahatma Gandhi campaigned against untouchability. ☐

D. Answer these questions in brief.

1. Name the reformer known as the father of the Telugu Women's Movement.
2. Describe one striking feature of the temples established by Narayana Guru.
3. Who founded the Prarthana Samaj?
4. Who believed in one caste, one religion and one god for all human beings?
5. Mention the name of the illustrious disciple of Sri Ramakrishna. What were his views on the caste system?

E. Answer these questions in detail.

1. Discuss the drawbacks of the caste system.
2. Examine the role of social reformers in removing the evils of the society.
3. What was the significance of the Brahmo Samaj?
4. State the efforts undertaken by B.R. Ambedkar to achieve equality in society.
5. Why do we say that E.V. Ramasamy was a campaigner of the right of the lower castes?
6. How did reformers bring change in the society?

Think Big — Integrate with language

Imagine you are an educated person from a lower caste, and you were rejected in a job interview because of your caste. Write a diary entry expressing your feelings.

Learning Tools

Fill up this organizational chart about each of the social reformers.

Reformer	Location	Contributions and Achievements
Raja Ram Mohan Roy		
Swami Vivekananda		
Dayananda Saraswati		
Justice Ranade		
Jyotirao Phule		
Veeresalingam		
Narayana Guru		
Periyar		
Gandhi		
Ambedkar		

Web links:

http://nammakpsc.com/wp/wp-content/uploads/2015/07/10.-Religion-reform-movement.pdf

Last accessed on 31 August 2021

10. Colonialism and Urban Change

Warm up

Gracy lives with her parents in a village near Gangtok. Her father sells locally-made handicrafts and incense sticks. Gracy loves gardening and plants seasonal ornamental flowers. One day, a massive landslide hits their village, and the family is struck with tragedy. She migrates to the beautiful Gangtok city and now lives with her uncle and aunt who run a bakery. Gracy brings a box full of seeds to her uncle's place and tries to stay optimistic after the disaster. She plants the seeds around her uncle's bakery and soon transforms the bakery with lush flowers and vegetables, bringing colour to the surrounding area and smiles to the faces of the customers. Her uncle and aunt are thrilled too. Even though Gracy migrates to the city, she keeps the memories of her garden fresh this way. Now her uncle earns more profit, as customers throng the bakery to view the exquisite flowers. Gracy gets a brilliant idea and becomes a florist, selling flowers and ferns. She slowly adjusts to living in an urban setup and enjoys it too.

Urbanization refers to the growth, progress and development of towns and cities, which is mainly due to two factors, namely, growing population and industrialization. Important amongst them were Delhi, Agra, Mathura, Varanasi, Fatehpur and Surat. As India entered the colonial rule, it underwent major changes due to the downfall of the Mughal Empire. With the disintegration of the Mughal Empire, many independent states, like Awadh, Bengal, Hyderabad and their capitals gained importance. Very soon, Delhi and Agra lost their importance, and regional capitals like Lucknow, Seringapatam, Tanjore and Nagpur became important. People moved to these new capitals in search of work. However, these places were gradually absorbed into the British Empire and lost their individuality. With time, many European powers established their colonies. For example, Goa and Daman and Diu were Portuguese settlements, while Chandernagore and Pondicherry were French settlements.

Green Earth

From 1990 to 2000, within ten years, there has been almost a three-fold increase in the number of motor vehicles in India. On an average, it is a ten per cent increase each year, which is a cause for serious concern, as it increases air pollution.

Deurbanization in India

The objective of the British was to formulate policies to boost their economy. This impacted the economy of India drastically by bringing about the complete destruction of the traditional economy of India. The decline of handicrafts led to the decline of handicraft centres like Surat, Murshidabad and Agra. The British adopted policies which were exploitative in nature. With the coming of the Industrial Revolution in the Great Britain, raw materials were in great demand. The British forced Indian farmers to grow cash crops in place of food crops. These raw materials were sold to Great Britain at extremely low rates. The finished products were imported to India and finally sold at exorbitant rates. Under British control, India was reduced to merely a source of cheap raw materials and a market for the finished goods. Craftsmen and artisans were rendered jobless. This ruined many industries in India, which were previously flourishing. Food crops were scarcely grown, leading to widespread famines throughout the country. At this point, under British rule, India witnessed a period of deurbanization wherein the country saw the total collapse of its economy.

Development of New Urban Centres

With the coming of European powers, India saw the development of new towns and cities. Many towns flourished as centres for British, French, Dutch and Portuguese settlements. Three port towns gained importance under the English—Bombay, Madras, and Calcutta. They were called presidencies, as those were the cities that the British ruled the subcontinent from.

Calcutta

The Battle of Plassey (1757) and the Battle of Buxar (1764) brought the whole of Bengal under the control of the British. In Bengal, the site of Govindpur was cleared for the construction of Fort William, around which Calcutta developed. This city was the capital of British India till 1911. Calcutta was one of the first cities which came up in India as a result of mass construction of houses, buildings, colonies and road networks. This urbanized the once-small town and made it a centre of political power. The position of the Governor-General of Bengal became very important and the governors of Bombay and Madras were brought under him.

FACT CHECK

Calcutta became a large city from a group of three villages, namely Sutanati, Kalikata and Govindpur.

Bombay

The control of Bombay was given by Charles II to the English East India Company. Charles II had received it as dowry from the king of Portugal for marrying a Portuguese princess. Bombay became a naval base soon after. The British would send their ships to Bombay for repairs. The city grew in importance. It became the head of the administrative circle of western India. Increase in trade led to many people settling in the city. The establishment of textile mills resulted in the immigration of more people.

Fort William

The first cotton mill came up in 1854 and many more followed. **Maritime** trade increased the prospects of the place. The laying of railway lines was another factor, due to which many people migrated to the city.

Madras

The search for textiles brought the English merchants to the east coast. A trading port was constructed at Madraspatnam, locally known as Chennapatnam. The British got the right to settle here from the Telugu lords who wanted to encourage trading activities. Madras was fortified due to English rivalry with the French. When the French were defeated in 1761, Madras developed into an important commercial centre.

maritime: used to describe things relating to the sea and to ships

Hill Stations

In addition to this, hill stations like Shimla, Nainital, Mussoorie, Darjeeling, Shillong, Ooty and Kodaikanal were established as summer resorts as the English were not used to the extreme summers. In the year 1864, Viceroy John Lawrence moved his council to Shimla, making Shimla the summer capital. It also became the official residence of the Commander-in-Chief of the Indian Army. Hill stations had a lot of economic importance because some of them were ideally suited for tea and coffee plantation. This resulted in the migration of labour from the plains to the hills.

Geography skills

On an outline map of India mark

- Three hill stations during the British rule
- Three presidency towns

Administrative and Infrastructural Development

During British rule, urban centres had civil lines and cantonment areas. While the civil lines had administrative offices and residential buildings of European officers cantonments were for the army. The development of mini cities and towns made it necessary to develop a system of transport to deliver manufactured goods from and transport raw materials to Great Britain. Therefore, an effort was made to connect major cities, ports, and markets by road. The postal system was introduced by the British and the first telegraph line was laid from Calcutta to Agra in 1853. Public works, like piped water supply, sewage, and streetlights, parks, and playgrounds, were set up in the civil lines and cantonment areas. Municipalities were set up to provide civic amenities like education, sanitation, and public works in major towns and cities. The District Magistrate was the ex-officio chairman of each municipality and he was assisted by commissioners. The oldest municipal corporation in India is the Madras Municipal Corporation. The British government was indifferent towards the well-being of Indians. A major part of the revenue was spent on administration and in wars.

What's in the picture?

This is a picture of Shimla in the month of May. Why do you think Shimla was made the summer capital?

The Indian railways were developed with the objective of quick movement of troops to different parts of the country. The first railway line introduced in India was from Bombay to Thane. This benefitted British capitalists through contracts given for construction. The profits earned by the railways were sent to England. Although these projects were undertaken with the motive of benefiting the English, eventually they were advantageous to Indians too. Indians increasingly came in contact with each other, thus inculcating a spirit of nationalism amongst them.

Police Administration

The police force was established by Lord Cornwallis. It was headed by the Inspector General of Police, who was assisted by the Deputy Inspector General, Senior Superintendent of Police, Deputy Superintendent of Police, Assistant Superintendent of Police, Head Constable and Constables. When Lord Curzon was appointed as the Governor General, he introduced many reforms to the administration of the police. The salaries of all police personnel were increased. Like in the army, high posts in the police force were reserved only for the English. The Indian Penal Code was drawn up in 1860 under Lord Macaulay. A jail code was also developed to administer jails.

Apply it! E

The costs outweighed the benefits of British rule in India, and thus led to the rise of an Indian nationalist movement. Do you agree? Give reasons for your answer.

Case Study

Delhi

Delhi is located on the banks of the river Yamuna. Remains of seven major cities have been unearthed in Delhi, from Indraprastha to Shahjahanabad. Edwin Lutyens designed New Delhi, that has landmarks like the Rashtrapati Bhavan, India Gate and the Parliament. The two secretariats in North Block and South Block were designed by Herbert Baker. The architecture of Delhi is unique. The famous Mughal Gardens is part of the Rashtrapati Bhavan. This was meant as the residence of the British Viceroy before Independence. The India Gate was built to commemorate the soldiers who laid down their lives for their country.

Soon after the revolt of 1857, the British realized how important the Mughal Emperor was to the people. Lord Lytton organized a lavish durbar in Delhi. This was to acknowledge Queen Victoria as the Empress of India. Following this, a durbar was held in Delhi to celebrate the occasion of the crowning of King George V. The decision to shift the capital from Calcutta to Delhi was made on this occasion. Thus, Delhi was made the capital of the British Empire in 1911.

New Delhi was built over a period of 20 years. This city was designed with the objective of representing law and order as compared to old Delhi. New Delhi had no crowded mohallas or by-lanes, as the British viewed overcrowded places as unhygienic. Today, Delhi is a city with magnificent buildings and a perfect amalgamation of new and old styles of architecture.

Q. Why was the India Gate built?

Skill Builder

21ST CENTURY SKILLS

Critical thinking skills: Which one of the following was the summer capital of the Government of India from the year 1865 to 1939?

a. Ooty b. Delhi c. Shimla

Life skills: What was the reason that all the important government buildings in New Delhi, constructed by the British, were constructed on a hill?

Communication skill: Imagine you are a tourist in Delhi during British rule. Write a diary entry describing your first day and the places you have visited.

Information literacy: Bombay originally was a group of seven islands. Can you name the islands?

World Connect

In eighteenth-century England, people still lived in the countryside and agriculture was the main occupation of the people. However, many towns developed during this time. Ports such as Bristol and Liverpool became prosperous because of extensive trading. Many seaside resorts also came into being at this time, which catered to the upper classes of society. The resort town of Bath became a vacation centre. Industrial towns, such as Birmingham, Sheffield and Manchester, attracted agricultural workers to migrate toward new industrial jobs.

Wind up

Colonialism and Urban Change

- **Deurbanization in India**
  - Decline of handicrafts: Destruction of the traditional economy; farmers forced to grow cash crops instead of food crops, leading to famine; craftsmen and artisans jobless
- **Development of new urban centres**
  - Calcutta, Bombay, Madras, Hill stations
- **Police administration**
  - Established by Lord Cornwallis: He introduced many reforms–salaries increased, high posts reserved for the British, Indian Penal Code and jail code were drawn up
- **Administrative and infrastructural development**
  - Developments: System of transport, postal system, telegraph lines, municipalities, Indian railways

Exercises

A. Choose the correct answers.

1. A prominent centre during the beginning of British rule in India.
   a. Delhi b. Calcutta c. Agra d. Bangalore
2. Before Delhi was made the capital of India, which major city was the capital of British India?
   a. Madras b. Bombay c. Kanpur d. Calcutta
3. The British capital was changed from Calcutta to Delhi in the year
   a. 1907 b. 1909 c. 1911 d. 1913
4. This was given to the Company by King Charles II of England.
   a. Bombay b. Calcutta c. Surat d. Madras

B. Fill in the blanks.

1. The first textile mill was established in 1854 in ....
2. The Indian Penal Code was drawn up under .... in 1860.
3. The first telegraph line was introduced from .... to .... in 1853.
4. Madraspatnam was locally-known as ....
5. A police force was established by .... to maintain law and order.
6. The first railway line was built between .... and .... in 1853.

C. Write T for true and F for false.

1. The British shifted their capital from Calcutta to Bombay. ☐
2. Shimla became the official residence of the Commander-in-Chief of the Indian Army. ☐
3. Varanasi was an important port town of the medieval period. ☐
4. Lord Curzon introduced many reforms to the administration of the police. ☐
5. Lord Cornwallis established the police force in India. ☐
6. The British set up the municipal corporation to take care of city administration. ☐

D. Answer these questions in brief.

1. Name the important cities of ancient India.
2. Give reasons for some places developing into cities.

3. Explain the term 'urbanization'.
4. State the purpose of the cantonment areas.
5. Name the hill stations that came up during British rule. What was the purpose of developing these hill stations?
6. Which cities rose up as Presidency cities during the late 18th century?

E. Answer these questions in detail.

1. How did Calcutta develop into an important town?
2. Explain how the British administered urban centres.
3. Give reasons as to why the British developed the Indian railways.
4. Write a note on the development of infrastructure and public works undertaken by the British.
5. Who designed New Delhi? Discuss the significance of some important buildings situated in Delhi.
6. Give a brief account of the origin and growth of Madras.

F. Read the passage and answer these questions.

The Indian railways were developed with the objective of quick movement of troops to different parts of the country. Although these projects were undertaken with the motive of benefiting the English, eventually they were advantageous to Indians too. Indians increasingly came in contact with each other, thus inculcating a spirit of nationalism amongst them.

1. Why were the Indian railways set up?
2. How did the introduction of railways benefit Indians?

Think Big Integrate with language

Kolkata's former name, Calcutta, is an anglicized version of the Bengali name *Kalikata*. According to some, Kalikata is derived from the Bengali word *Kalikshetra*, meaning 'ground of the goddess Kali'. Can you find out the reason for renaming of Calcutta as Kolkata?

Learning Tools

Make your own study guide by following these steps.

MAIN POINTS (*Note down the important headings and the main ideas*)

→ ....
→ ....
→ ....
→ ....
→ ....

Keywords

- ....
- ....
- ....
- ....
- ....

Assess yourself (Use the questions at the end of the chapter to assess how much you have learnt and understood)

Web links:

https://www.tcd.ie/Economics/staff/orourkek/Istanbul/JGWGEHNIndianDeind.pdf

Last accessed on 31 August 2021

11. Changes in the Arts: Painting, Literature and Architecture

Warm up

Ravi Varma is considered to be one of the greatest Indian painters. As a boy, his artistic talent did not go unnoticed and under the patronage of Ayilyam Thirunal, he received an education in arts and was exposed to western styles of painting. In 1904, he was awarded the Kaisar-i-Hind Gold Medal, whereby the title 'Raja' was mentioned for the first time against his name. He is best known for his paintings in the Amar Chitra Katha comics.

The exposure to English education and western culture greatly reformed the Indian society. The people were now exposed to scientific knowledge and they became aware of the new trends in literature, art and philosophy. Western ideas of reason, equality, liberty and humanity inspired them. The spread of liberal ideas in the west provided further **stimulus** for the emergence of reform movements. The weaknesses and decay of the Indian society became apparent to the educated Indians. They questioned the age-old practices, traditions and beliefs of the Hindu society, shifting the focus from religion to social and economic issues. This steered in a cultural awakening that completely swept the nation. Reform movements developed and brought about significant changes in the social and religious life of the people of India. Scholars like William Jones and Max Mueller, who recognized the rich heritage of India and considered it to be superior to the western culture, supported the emergence of these movements, further propagating them.

Green Earth

Before the printing press was invented, scribes, who lived and worked in monasteries, wrote and illustrated books by hand. This meant that fewer trees were cut for paper.

By this time, educated Indians had started to spread ideas of nationalism and patriotism in the nation. This was the beginning of a long and winding struggle towards reviving the glory of India. Raja Ram Mohan Roy was the pioneer of what has been called the Indian Renaissance.

Literature

Hindi

Inspired by European romanticism and nationalism, a wave of religious and cultural movements spread in the country. By the 19th century, India witnessed a shift in literature from topics related to tradition, mythology and religion to those related to the actual conditions that the people were living in.

FACT CHECK

Phanishwar Nath Renu's *Mare Gaye Gulfam* was adapted into a film *Teesri Kasam* directed by Basu Bhattacharya.

stimulus: something that causes a change or a reaction.

This came about as a means to signal an end to the degrading social practices like sati and female infanticide. Munshi Premchand was a renowned Hindi prose writer. His writings not only revolved around ordinary people, but also included social issues prevalent in the nineteenth century. He wrote a number of novels like *Nirmala, Seva Sadan* and *Godaan*. Historical novels also gained popularity, as they sought to rekindle the sensitivities of the people towards their rich historical past. Bhagwat Charan Verma has been attributed with notable historical works, which include novels like *Chitralekha*. Another notable writer is Phanishwar Nath Renu who is considered to be the most successful and influential writer of modern Hindi literature and his work *Maila Anchal* is considered to be almost as powerful as Premchand's *Godaan*.

Another notable writer of the 20th century was Jainendra Kumar. He was awarded one of India's highest civil honours—the Padma Bhushan in 1971 and the Sahitya Akademi award in 1966 for his work *Muktibodh*. Apart from these, we had many writers who revolutionized Hindi literature. One such example is Agyeya. His novel, *Sekhar: Ek Jeevani*, became very popular.

Short stories too had a special place in literature. They underwent tremendous changes in terms of quality and eminence. Short stories were preferred by the people as they did not take too much time to read. Munshi Premchand and Rajendra Singh Bedi wrote numerous short stories during this period.

Apart from these, there were some Indian writers who wrote in English. Famous writers belonging to this category were Raja Rao, Mulk Raj Anand and R.K. Narayan. Raja Rao's *Kanthapura* was the first Indian novel to be written in English. The story illustrates the birth of new ideas in a secluded village in south India as the freedom movement gains momentum. *Untouchable* is a novel written by Mulk Raj Anand. The novel tells the tale of a young sweeper who is 'untouchable' and is looked down upon by society. This novel criticizes the caste system and the injustices that come with it. R.K. Narayan highlights the social context of the everyday life of his characters through many of his novels like *Malgudi Days, Swami and Friends* and *The English Teacher*.

Urdu

During this period, the use of Urdu in literary pieces developed. Mirza Ghalib was one of the most prominent poets who wrote in Urdu. He was the last great poet of the Mughal era. His ghazals have since been sung in many ways, by different people. Muhammad Iqbal was one of the most renowned figures in Urdu literature. He composed the famous song *Saare Jahan se Accha*.

Regional Literature

Bengali literature and poetry during the time, was **articulate** and forceful. Some of the most well-known writers include Rabindranath Tagore, who was awarded the Nobel Prize in 1913 for *Gitanjali*. His song, *Jana Gana Mana*, became the national anthem of independent India. Apart from Rabindranath Tagore, Bankim Chandra Chattopadhyay too, has contributed a lot towards literature. His song, *Vande Mataram* is very famous. His novels, *Durgeshnandini* and *Ananda Math* have been translated into many different languages.

Bankim Chandra Chattopadhyay

The other famous writers who wrote in vernacular languages include Vishnu Shastri, who wrote Marathi prose, Hemchandra Barua, who wrote in Assamese, Mohan Senapati, who wrote in Oriya, Govardhan, who wrote in Gujarati, Rajagopalachari or Rajaji who wrote in Tamil and Vallathol Narayana Menon who wrote in Malayalam.

articulate: having or showing the ability to speak fluently and coherently

The 20th century literature saw the rise of women in the field of literature. Ashapurna Devi was a prominent Bengali novelist and poet. In her lifetime, she has received many awards including the Jnanpith Award, the Padma Shri, Deshikottam and the highest honour of fellowship, conferred by the Sahitya Akademi. Nayantara Sehgal wrote in English and Amrita Pritam wrote in Punjabi.

Amrita Pritam

Developments in Literature

Poetry was replaced by prose as it was easier to understand. It proved to be an effective medium of communication. As prose gained a larger readership, writers highlighted the different kinds of atrocities faced by the people. *Neel Darpan* by Dinabandhu Mitra chronicles the difficulties faced by the indigo workers that culminated in the Indigo revolt of Bengal. Writers gave a voice to the disadvantaged masses, by highlighting the exploitation that these people faced under British rule. They also wrote about nationalism and patriotism and ignited within the people, a burning love for their own country. The use of vernacular, colloquial words and local dialects added to the popularity of the literary works as they reached out to the masses including those who could not read in English. The printing press played a major role in this cultural awakening of the country. With this new tool, Indians could spread their ideas to a larger population, thereby spreading nationalism throughout the country.

Printing Press

By 19th century, the press emerged as an important tool and a medium through which people could voice their feelings. It made them aware of events that took place around the country. It acted as an effective instrument for underlining public opinion on social issues.

FACT CHECK

It is believed that the printing press was first introduced in India in the year 1556 CE by Portuguese missionaries to print Christian literature.

This kindled feelings of patriotism amongst the people, giving them a chance to reflect on the ruthless and repressive policies of the British. Most of the national leaders and reformers of the country themselves took the initiative of starting newspapers. Some of the newspapers by the national leaders were *The Hindu* and *Swadeshmitram* by Subramaniya Iyer, *Kesari Maratha* by Bal Gangadhar Tilak, *Sulubh Samachar* by Sharma Prakash and Keshab Chandra Sen, *Amrita Bazar Patrika* by S. K. Ghosh and Motilal Ghosh, *Indian Mirror* by N. N. Sen, *Voice of India* by Dadabhai Naoroji and *Young India* by Mahatma Gandhi.

The first printing press invented by Johannes Gutenberg

In India, English dailies such as the *Times of India* (1861), *The Pioneer* (1865), *The Statesman* (1875) and *The Hindu* (1878) still continue as leading newspapers. These papers were introduced in the second-half of the nineteenth century.

Unnerved by the growing sense of nationalism in the country induced by the press, the British took stringent measures to curb it. The Vernacular Press Act was passed in 1878 to control the circulation of what they termed '**seditious** material', to the masses. Some Indian newspapers were discontinued and

unnerved: not lacking in courage or confidence; seditious: of, relating to, or tending toward sedition publishers and editors were even sent to jail for inciting the public. However, despite all these restrictions, the Indian press persisted and continued to play a significant role in bringing people together during the freedom struggle.

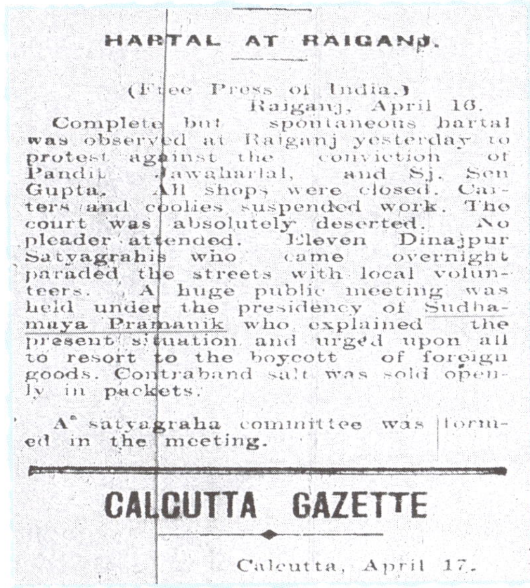

HARTAL AT RAIGANJ.

(Free Press of India.)

Raiganj, April 16.

Complete but spontaneous hartal was observed at Raiganj yesterday to protest against the conviction of Pandit Jawaharlal, and Sj. Sen Gupta. All shops were closed. Carters and coolies suspended work. The court was absolutely deserted. No pleader attended. Eleven Dinajpur Satyagrahis who came overnight paraded the streets with local volunteers. A huge public meeting was held under the presidency of Sudhamaya Pramanik who explained the present situation and urged upon all to resort to the boycott of foreign goods. Contraband salt was sold openly in packets.

A satyagraha committee was formed in the meeting.

CALCUTTA GAZETTE

Calcutta, April 17.

Calcutta Gazette

Europeans Who Contributed to Indian Literature

Many Europeans contributed significantly to India's journey towards independence. William Jones founded the Asiatic Society in 1784.

Its objective was to orient the English with the history, heritage, arts, science and literature of Asia. Many people were members of this society and they studied Indian literature and philosophy with passion. This resulted in the translation of Sanskrit texts to English. William Jones translated the *Abhijgyan Shakuntalam* into English. The Asiatic society also published a journal called the *Journal of the Asiatic Society of Bengal.*

James Prinsep deciphered the Brahmi script used in the Ashoka's edicts. Max Mueller was a German scholar who was passionate about the study of Indian history, philosophy and arts. He was successful in translating the *Rig Veda* into English. These scholars played an important role in creating a cultural awakening and the impact of this could be seen in the transformation of literature, painting, music and dance.

Music

India has always had a strong connection with music since the ancient period. One of the *Vedas*, the *Sama Veda*, is based on music as it is composed of primarily melodies and chants. Music was also considered to be divine. Therefore, musicians were always patronized by rulers. A popular musician belonging to the medieval period was Baijnath Mishra or Baiju Bawra.

FACT CHECK

The Mughals used two terms to refer to the Europeans. Name them.

Music, like other arts, declined after the Mughals. It was restricted to gatherings in the royal households, but did not get recognition as an art. However, two schools or *gharanas* of music came up under the British. In the south, Madras became the centre of Carnatic music between 1857 and 1947. Hindustani music was patronized by the people of the north.

Dance

Throughout the ages, dance has been a medium of entertainment. However, it had a very limited audience. Only rulers and nobles could enjoy it. Many people worked towards changing the negative attitude that the public had towards dance. Bharatanatyam and Carnatic music owe their elevation to the Thanjavur Quartet, which comprised of four brothers who excelled in this dance form. They were employed in the courts of the Maratha King Serfoji II at Thanjavur. Pandit Uday Shankar, an Indian dancer, was a pioneer of modern dance in India. Rukmini Devi Arundale was considered to have revived Bharatanatyam from its original style.

Bharatanatyam

Rabindranath Tagore was another great proponent of dance, as he merged various forms of dance and called it *Rabindra Nritya*. Pandit Uday Shankar also created a fusion style of dance, wherein he merged European dance forms, like the ballet, with the traditional Indian dance forms.

Painting

Raja Ravi Varma

Painting witnessed a number of styles during the British era. In fact, many paintings had European themes, but these paints became prominent only during the colonial period. With time, Indian artists were influenced by western styles.

Indian art was revived under the influence of the Government School of Art in Calcutta. The principal of this school was E. B. Howell. He emphasized on the finer nuances and the originality of Indian art. Under his influence, a new school of Indian painters, headed by Rabindranath Tagore, evolved. He drew a lot of inspiration from the paintings of Ajanta and Ellora.

Some of the renowned artists were Raja Ravi Verma, Dr Coomarasamy, Amrita Sher-Gil and George Keyte. Raja Ravi Verma, who was a painter from Kerala based most of his work on Indian epics. His paintings had the flavour of European nationalism. Dr Coomarasamy from the Bengal School of Art popularized Indian art internationally. Amrita Sher-Gil and George Keyte—well-known names, were both highly skilled and knowledgeable in European art and modern expression. The theme of Amrita Sher-Gil's paintings included the day-to-day life of the people, Indian women and many other diverse themes in oil painting. George Keyte was a Sri Lankan modern painter, and his style was influenced by cubism. Cubism was a style of painting created by Pablo Picasso.

During this phase of the freedom struggle, Indian artists were filled with the spirit of nationalism. This was expressed in their paintings as artists continually depicted scenes of everyday lives of the people.

Drama and Theatre

Prithviraj Kapoor

The Sanskrit theatre was the earliest form of theatre in India. Hundreds of plays have been written in India since long before British rule. It saw a sudden halt with the coming of the Turks and the Mughals, but was revived during colonial rule. The Indian People's Theatre Association was founded with an objective to bring about a cultural awakening. Prithviraj Kapoor, Bijon Bhattacharya, Ritwik Ghatak, Utpal Dutt, Khwaja Ahmad Abbas, Salil Choudhuri and Pandit Ravi Shankar constituted of this association at its inception. They heavily influenced the masses by conveying messages and critiques relevant to contemporary times. In south India in particular, dance drama became a popular mode of expression. Rabindranath Tagore wrote plays centred around the themes of nationalism, identity, spiritualism and material greed. His play, written in Bengali, include *Chitra, The King of the Dark Chamber, The Post Office* and *Red Oleander*. Vijay Tendulkar and Mahesh Dattani are two important playwrights who displayed some of the most relevant social issues of that period.

Photographs

The art of photography reached Indians in the 19th century. Many European photographers came to India and set up studios. One of the most famous European photographers was Samuel Bourne, who set up his studio in Calcutta. Rulers and people from royal families took an interest in this vocation, like Maharaja Bin Chandra Manikya of Tripura and Maharaja Ram Singh of Jaipur. Lala Deen Dayal was appointed as a court photographer, who recorded and documented architecture, geography, historical ruins, events and the people of the country, in his photographs.

Architecture

Like all other aspects, the Europeans made an impact on architecture too. The development of big cities, such as Bombay, Madras and Calcutta began during British rule. The Europeans started building houses that were palatial. Intermixing of European and Indian styles of architecture can be seen at the Victoria Memorial of Calcutta and the Parliament House in Delhi. There were other buildings, designed by Edwin Lutyens in New Delhi, such as the Rashtrapati Bhavan, earlier known as Viceroy's House, which depict both Buddhist and Islamic traditions. Chandigarh was designed by Le Corbusier and Louis Kahan designed the city of Islamabad. The British constructed institutional and civic structures, that is, buildings of utility such as post offices, railway stations and rest houses.

Construction of Victoria Memorial

The styles adopted in architecture were styles which were prevalent in England. Power was displayed through buildings and was expressed through structures. Stone pillars, arches, domes and vaulted roofs were some of the striking features which depicted the glory of the buildings of imperial India. The **neoclassical** style was evident in these buildings. The **neo-Gothic** style was marked by high pitched roofs, painted arches and detailed decoration. An architectural style that was a combination of the Indian and European styles was known as Indo-Saracenic Revival architecture. An example of this is the Gateway of India.

Apply it!

E

Below is an extract from a poem written by Rabindranath Tagore entitled 'Paper Boat'.

Day by day I float my paper boats one by one down the running stream. In big black letters I write my name on them and the name of the village where I live. I hope that someone in some strange land will find them and know who I am. I load my little boats with shiuli flower from our garden, and hope that these blooms of the dawn will be carried safely to land in the night.

1. Shiuli is a name of Hindu baby girl in Assamese. True or false?
2. What does the poet want to express through the poem?

neoclassical: a classical style that has been revived; neo-Gothic: a style of art and architecture which is characterized by the revival of medieval Gothic forms, like pointed arches, vaulted ceilings and mock fortifications

Case Study

Architecture: Mumbai and Chennai

Mumbai

The British built many magnificent buildings. The city of Mumbai consisted of seven islands. It is named after the goddess Mumba Devi and is located near the Chowpatty beach. Some of the important buildings which reflect Indian and European architecture are—The Prince of Wales Museum built to commemorate the visit of the Prince of Wales, the future King of Great Britain. It was designed by George Wittet. The building is three-storeys high with a dome and the balconies and floors depict the Mughal style of architecture. It has rare exhibits of ancient India and art objects of foreign countries. The Victoria Terminus is also known as the Chhatrapati Shivaji Terminus. It is one of the grandest railway stations of the country. It looks like a cathedral and reflects Gothic Architecture. It took 10 years (1878 to 1888) to complete the terminus. It was named after Queen Victoria and its architect was TW Stevans. The Gateway of India was built to commemorate the visit of King George V and Queen Mary to India in 1911. It was designed by George Wittet. It is near the Prince of Wales Museum. It has a high archway and intricate lattice work. Other important buildings are the Secretariat, the Town Hall, University of Mumbai, Elephanta Caves and the Elphinstone Circle.

Chennai

The largest judicial building in Chennai, the High Court, was built in 1892. Its striking features are the elegant domes and corridors. Two of the important buildings located in Chennai are the War Memorial and the Senate House. The War Memorial was built in 1939, in memory of the warriors who gave up their lives during the First World War. The Senate House was once an examination hall of the Madras University, designed by Robert Fellows. Its main features are the dome and stained glass windows. It depicts the Indo-British style of architecture. The Museum houses many old buildings, like a theatre, a library and an art gallery.

Q. In what ways did the British influence the culture of India?

Q. In what ways does this influence prevail in modern times?

Skill Builder

21ST CENTURY SKILLS

Communication skills: Search through the newspaper for the most important stories and photos you see in today's news. Using only five minutes, scan and skim to pick out the best. Fill in the blanks with the story's headline and page number.

1. A story about your community: ....
2. A story of national importance: ....
3. A story of international importance: ....
4. A story about someone local: ....
5. A story you think will matter the most even after ten years: ....

Information literacy: Britishers set up the department of Geographical Survey of India. The institution surveyed villages, cities and made maps of India. In which year was this established?

World Connect

At around the same period, Vincent Van Gogh painted his famous painting *The Starry Night*. This painting is an oil on canvas by the Dutch painter, which displays the view from the east-facing window of his asylum room at Saint-Rémy-de-Provence, just before sunrise, with the addition of an idealized village. It has been in the permanent collection of the Museum of Modern Art in New York City since 1941, acquired through the Lillie P Bliss Bequest. It is regarded among Van Gogh's finest works, and is one of the most recognized paintings in the history of Western culture.

Wind up

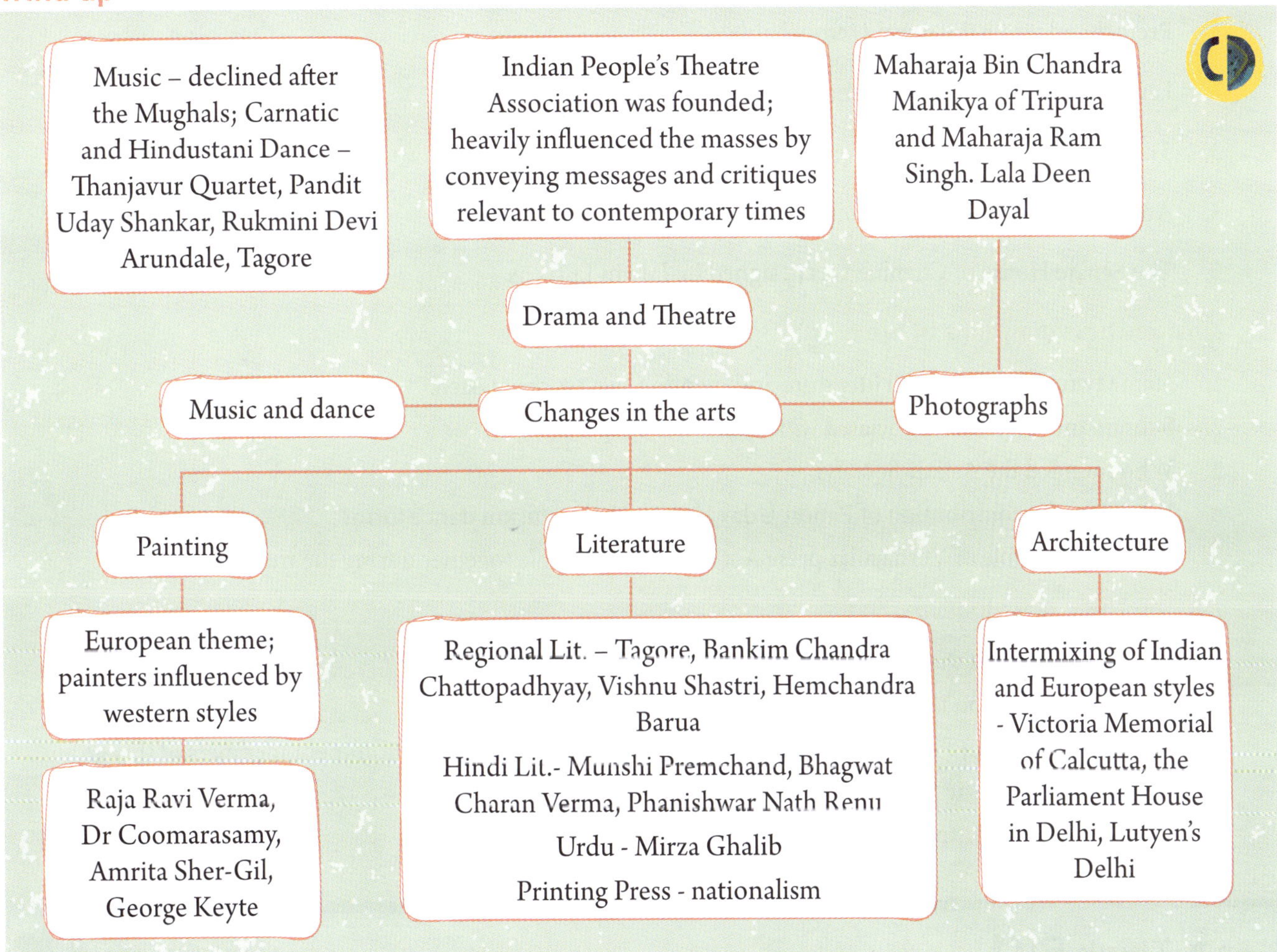

Exercises

A. Choose the correct answers.

1. The founder of the Asiatic Society
   a. William Jones b. James Prinsep
   c. Max Mueller d. Max Mueller
2. Successful in deciphering the Brahmi script used in the Ashokan Edicts
   a. William Bentinck b. William Jones
   c. Mulk Raj Anand d. James Prinsep

3. The *Veda* that is based on music.
   a. *Rig Veda*
   b. *Yajur Veda*
   c. *Sama Veda*
   d. *Atharva Veda*
4. He started the newspaper called *Kesari Maratha.*
   a. Bal Gangadhar Tilak
   b. Raja Ram Mohan Roy
   c. Ishwar Chandra Vidyasagar
   d. Munshi Premchand
5. He drew a lot of inspiration from the paintings of Ajanta and Ellora.
   a. Rabindranath Tagore
   b. Raja Ravi Varma
   c. Dr Coomarasamy
   d. George Keyte

B. Write T for true and F for false.

1. Premchand wrote the novel *Untouchable.*
2. Lala Deen Dayal was a court photographer.
3. The Victoria Memorial is located in Chennai.
4. Architecture was used to exhibit the power of the British.
5. The Senate House of Chennai was designed by Edwin Lutyens.

C. Answer these questions in brief.

1. Name two writers of Hindi literature and mention two works of each.
2. Subramaniya Iyer was associated with which newspaper?
3. Who founded the Asiatic Society?
4. What was the contribution of Pandit Uday Shankar in the fusion dance form?
5. What was the role of Vernacular press Act in bringing people together during the freedom struggle?

D. Answer these questions in detail.

1. What were some of the themes used by authors in their works?
2. Write short notes on the architecture of Mumbai and Chennai.
3. Why was the Indian People's Theatre Association formed? Name a few prominent members of this group.
4. When was the Asiatic Society formed? Why was it formed?
5. What novelty was introduced by Rabindranath Tagore in dance?

Think Big

Integrate with environmental science

Unusual rise in temperature: The unplanned construction of large buildings in urban areas absorbs solar radiation and in the afternoon, these emit heat radiations, increasing the climatic pressure. As a result, year 2019 was the hottest year from last years. Cities often receive more rain than the surrounding countryside since dust can provoke the condensation of water vapor into rain droplets. Suggest ways in which this can be controlled.

13 CLIMATE ACTION

Learning Tools

Create your own study guides by compiling the necessary information for a swift recap.

Main Ideas	Why it matters	Important terms and names
....	....	....
....	....	....
....	....	....
....	....	....
....	....	....
....	....	....
....	....	....
....	....	....
....	....	....
....	....	....

Web links:

https://www.historydiscussion.net/history-of-india/a-study-of-art-architecture-literature-education-and-fine-art/2034

Last accessed on 31 August 2021

12. The Nationalist Movement: Rise and Growth till 1905

Warm up

Akhil asked his teacher, 'Sir, what is patriotism? Does it mean one has to die for the country?' His social science teacher was impressed with the enthusiastic question from Akhil. 'Not necessarily. You can love the culture, preserve and respect its heritage. One example is standing up for the national anthem—we do so to show respect,' said the teacher. 'I still don't understand,' implored Akhil. 'I thought patriotism was all about making a big sacrifice for one's country.' 'Yes Akhil, you are right. It is about big things but also little ones too. And remember, it is not the battlefield alone which produces patriots. You can be patriotic by showing respect to the nation and national symbols, you can feel proud of the rich culture and heritage of the country and of its history too,' said his teacher.

With nationalism gaining **momentum** throughout the country, reformers from different states continued to spread the idea of unity amongst people. Differentiating social practices were abolished and the people saw each other as a united whole—one nation fighting for independence from the colonial rule.

In 1857, a large part of the army rebelled against British authorities. This rebellion started from Meerut but spread to Delhi, Agra, Kanpur and Lucknow. This has been regarded as the First War of Independence. Though it was unsuccessful, it was a defining moment as it paved the way for a united India.

Reasons for Nationalist Movement

There are a number of reasons that sparked the growth of movements around the country. First and foremost, under British administration, India was brought together as one unified nation. The introduction of the railways made the administration of the country much easier, as it took less time to travel from place to place. This benefitted Indians enormously, as reformers could travel from one place to another more quickly to spread the idea of nationalism in different parts of the country. With the introduction of western education, there was a rise of western educated Indian class. This class came in contact with the ideas of equality, liberty and fraternity. The Indians became aware that it was their birth right to be treated as equals and enjoy freedom and liberty. This also became one of the reasons for the rise of nationalism in India. Despite these advantages, British rule was oppressive and cruel towards the Indians. The Queen's Proclamation promised that there would be no discrimination among people and public posts would be given to Indians. However, all these promises were futile and ineffectual. This caused a feeling of discontent among the Indians. The amendment of the Ilbert Bill furthered the discontent and restlessness of the masses.

momentum: the impetus and driving force gained by the development of a process or course of events

Courtenay Ilbert, a British lawyer and a legal advisor to the Viceroy of India's Council, prepared a bill known as the Ilbert Bill in 1883. The bill proposed that the Indian judges would have the right to try Europeans accused of crimes. It was opposed by British residents in India. The violent reaction of the Europeans and Anglo-Indians to this proposal shocked the Indian nationalists. The bill had to be amended in face of the opposition from the British residents living in India.

British control over India led to economic exploitation of the country. British rule brought an end to traditional industries and reduced India to a country that merely supplied raw materials to Britain at extremely low costs. The manufactured products would then be brought to India and sold in the markets at high prices. Heavy taxes were imposed on Indian farmers, leading to the loss of their livelihoods. This caused a sharp decline in farming practices and agriculture, thereby breaking the very foundation which formed the basis of the economy of India.

What's in the picture?

This picture shows victims of the famine in Orissa. Name the many ways that a famine can affect us. Study the photograph and discuss the plight of the people when in the midst of a famine.

In 1866, a famine broke out in Orissa (present-day Odisha). The British Government took no steps or relief measures to control the death toll. One-third of the population died due to this famine. This created feelings of anger and resentment towards the British.

Many acts passed by the British sought to repress Indian actions and thoughts. Lord Lytton's Vernacular Press Act was repressive in nature. At a time when Indians were beginning to unite and rekindle their spirit of nationalism, freedom of expression and speech—the primary mode of communicating with the masses—was curbed. The Arms Act of 1878 forbade Indians to possess arms without a license. The British living in India could possess as many arms as they wanted.

FACT CHECK

The term 'lingua franca' refers to common language.

Lord Lytton reduced the maximum age to sit for the Civil Services Exam from 21 to 19 years. This meant that only a handful of Indians could appear for the exams. By this time, Indians had realized that the British policies were discriminatory and biased. There was no way that the Indians would be treated as equal. This led to the realization that the only way to achieve equality was complete freedom from British rule.

Apply it!

What other policies adopted by the British were repressive in nature?

The introduction of western education created a systematic and uniform mode of communication throughout the country. It also exposed Indians to new ideas of liberty, equality, fraternity, democracy and sovereignty. Events like the French Revolution and the American War of Independence inspired Indians to rise up and fight against the British. Educated Indians emphasized on the glory of India's past. Even European scholars, like Max Mueller and William Jones, considered Indian culture to be far superior to the European culture. This intensified the feelings of nationalism that were already stirring amongst the people. Thus, the need for a political organization arose—one which would unite the masses, foster nationalism and create an awareness amongst the people.

The Founders (predecessors)

A. O. Hume

The year 1855 saw the birth of India's first political association—the British Indian Association. Its main objective was to introduce administrative reforms and spread education. The East India Association came to be set up in 1866 by Dadabhai Naoroji to discuss the issues pertaining to the welfare of the Indians. The Indian Association of Calcutta was set up in 1876 by Surendranath Banerjee. This was a predecessor to India's largest and most prominent political association—the Indian National Congress (INC). In 1885, the Indian National Congress was formed. It was the central and defining influence of the Indian independence movement.

Birth of Indian National Congress

Dadabhai Naoroji

Many Britishers had witnessed the discontent that was on the rise amongst Indians. A.O. Hume, a retired civil servant, played an active role in the formation of the Indian National Congress. He saw the revolt of 1857 as an outcome of misgovernance and took measures to improve the lives of the people.

The first meeting of the Congress was held in Mumbai under the Presidentship of W.C. Bonnerjee, who was a barrister by profession.

There are two distinctive periods associated with the national movement. They are the pre-Gandhian period, which was the period from 1885 to 1919, and the Gandhian era, which was the period from 1919 to 1947.

Pre-Gandhian Era

The pre-Gandhian era is subdivided in two phases. The period between the years 1885 and 1905 is known as the period of moderate nationalism, and the period between the years 1905 to 1919 is known as the period of extremism.

The period from when the Congress was formed in 1885 to the coming of Lord Minto as the Viceroy in 1905 is known as the period of the moderates. Important leaders of the moderate period were W.C. Bonnerjee, Dadabhai Naoroji, Firoz Shah Mehta, Surendranath Banerjee and Gopalkrishna Gokhale. This phase was, however, mostly limited to a handful of educated Indians who were doctors, lawyers, teachers and writers. These early nationalists or moderates had full faith in British governance, justice and fair play. They believed in demanding reforms through constitutional and peaceful means.

Demands of the Moderates

The main objective of the moderates was to train and make the Indians aware about self-governance. To facilitate this, they wanted the civil service exams to be conducted simultaneously in India and England. The resolution held in the annual session made appropriate demands, like larger representation of Indians in both central and provincial legislatures. They demanded for a complete separation of powers between the executive and the judiciary to protect the people from arbitrary acts by the police, as well as by the bureaucracy. The Arms Act, which was repressive, was to be repealed and so was the License Act. At that time, the people were still paying huge amounts of tax to the government and most of their income was spent on the British army or in Britain's expansionist policies abroad. The moderates demanded that expenditure on the army be reduced. To further development in the country, the moderates demanded the spread of primary education among the masses along with investments on developing Indian industries.

Response of the Government

At the beginning, Lord Dufferin encouraged the formation of the INC. However, upon realizing that this party would not become a tool at the hands of the British, he condemned the association and stated that it represented only a minority of the people. Members of the INC realized that the government does not plan to fulfil any of their demands and soon, their tactics became more and more radical. The British government, in its efforts to curb public participation, prohibited government employees from attending any INC deliberations or participating in any event associated with the INC. However, the efforts of the British turned out to be for nothing and achieved the opposite result of what they had previously targeted. With every rebuke and repression, the INC became stronger and stronger.

Achievements

Although not much was achieved during this phase, it was successful in creating a solid political organization which acted as a platform upon which the nationalists of the period could spread their ideas, and make the people conscious about the political scenario of the time.

- 1857 The First war of independence
- 1866 Orissa famine; East India Association set up
- 1876 The India Association of Calcutta was set up
- 1878 Vernacular Press Act and Arms Act passed
- 1883 Ilbert bill
- 1855 British India Association set up
- 1885 Indian National Congress was formed
- 1905 Beginning of period of extremism in the INC

Skill Builder

21ST CENTURY SKILLS

Critical thinking skills: How did the railways, roadways, post and telegraph systems, established by the British, help to unite Indians?

Life skills: It was the irony of history that the Indian congress, which was the brainchild of an Englishman, ultimately decided the destiny of that British rule in India. Do you agree?

Communication skills: "In dealing with Englishmen make up your mind deliberately, speak clearly and work perseveringly. Then and then alone can you hope to be listened to." Who said these words?

World Connect

During the nineteenth century, China was forced to engage in trade activities with European countries, after the Opium wars. This brought in a large number of foreigners from France, Germany, Britain and America to the country. These merchants began to demand large tracts of land in various ports, where they claimed that they were subject to the laws of their own country, and not China. The Chinese were looked down upon, and this created a lot of resentment amongst the people. In the midst of severe drought and disturbances, caused by the growing European influence, the Chinese revolution of 1911 took place, and it overthrew the imperial dynasty. Western influence increased during this time, and this led to the creation of anti-European secret societies called the Militia United in Righteousness (Yihetuan), known in English as the 'Boxers'. The members were pro-nationalists, anti-foreign and anti-Christian. An Eight-Nation Alliance invaded China to defeat the Boxers and took retribution.

Wind up

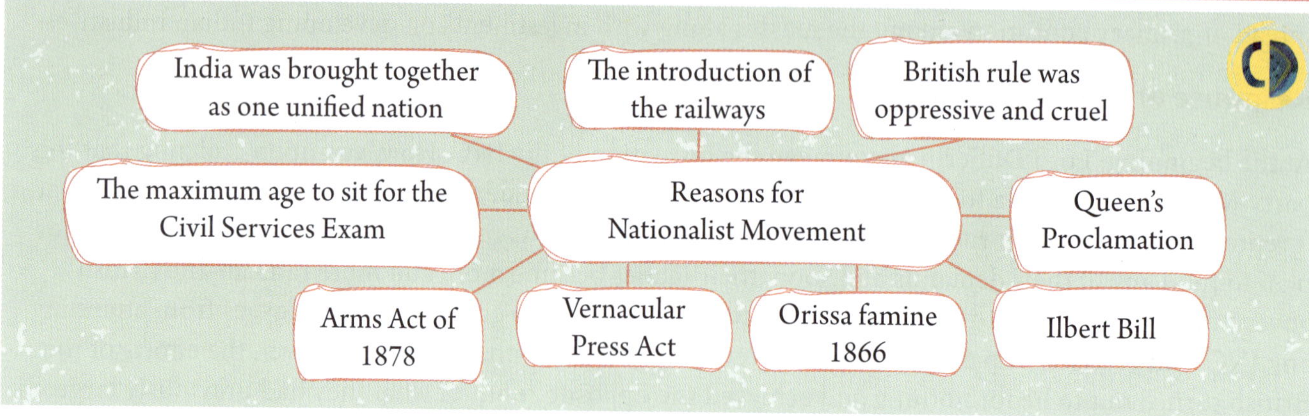

Exercises

A. Choose the correct answers.

1. It was during this person's time that the age limit for Civil Services Exams was reduced from 21 to 19.
   a. Dadabhai Naoroji's b. Lord Mayo's c. Lord Minto's d. Lord Lytton's
2. The founder of the Indian Association of Calcutta
   a. Surendranath Banerjee b. Dadabhai Naoroji c. Justice Ranade d. None of them
3. He was not a leader of the Moderates.
   a. Surendranath Banerjee b. Dadabhai Naoroji
   c. Gopal Krishna Gokhale d. Lala Lajpat Rai
4. A famine broke out in Orissa (present-day Odisha) in the year
   a. 1866 b. 1868 c. 1874 d. 1801
5. The Arms Act was passed in
   a. 1880 b. 1885 c. 1883 d. 1876

B. Fill in the blanks.

1. In 1885, the .... was formed.
2. The first meeting of the National Congress in Mumbai was under the presidentship of ....
3. The objective to disarm the people of India was a step taken by Lord ....
4. European scholars like .... and William Jones, considered Indian culture to be far superior to the European culture.
5. British control over India led to .... exploitation of the country.

C. Write T for true and F for false.

1. The Queen's Proclamation allowed Indians to be appointed in government posts. ☐
2. Industrialization promoted Indian handicrafts in Europe. ☐
3. The founder of the Indian National Congress was an Englishman. ☐
4. Surendranath Banerjee was the father of the national movement in India. ☐
5. The peasants were looked after by the British during the famine. ☐

D. Answer these questions in brief.

1. Name the association that came before the Indian National Congress.
2. Name two important Moderate leaders.
3. What were the main demands of Moderates?
4. What were the main features of the Vernacular Press Act?
5. How did the growth of the press and literature contribute to nationalism?

E. Answer these questions in detail.

1. What was the Ilbert Bill and what did Indians learn from it?
2. Explain the economic policy of the British.
3. Who were the Moderates? Discuss their main objectives.
4. State any factors which resulted in unifying the people of India, with reference to western education and rediscovering India's rich heritage.
5. What was the attitude of the government towards the Indian National Congress?

Think Big

English fun

Imagine you are listening to a speech by Gopal Krishna Gokhale. Write a diary entry about it. Also write about the mood of the audience listening to the Moderate leader.

Learning Tools

Reasons for Nationalist Movement

....

....

....

....

....

....

....

Birth of Indian National Congress

Pre-Gandhian era

Demands of the Moderates

Web links:

https://magadhuniversity.ac.in/download/econtent/pdf/MODERATE%20PHASE%201885-1905-converted.pdf
https://neostencil.com/upsc-modern-history-moderate-phase-and-early-congress

Last accessed on 31 August 2021

13. The National Movement I

Warm up

'I love the Indian people as I love none other and my heart and mind have long been laid on the altar of the Motherland.'

–Annie Besant

Although Annie Besant was European, she fought for India's freedom. What values do we learn from her?

Nationalism reaches the masses of all regions when the people develop a sense of collective belonging. Cultural processes like history, folklore, songs and symbols captures the imagination of the people and brings them together as a collective whole.

The Indian nationalists had realized that the British government was, in no way, willing to give in to their demands. This fuelled their dissatisfaction and discontent.

The Extremists

A faction of the nationalists felt that retaliation was required to get the British to give in to the demands. They adopted radical measures and came to be known as the Extremists. Bal Gangadhar Tilak was the leader of the Extremists. He felt that the people's rights could be gained only by putting pressure on the British government.

There are a number of reasons that led to the rise of extremism in India. Firstly, the Indian Councils Act, 1909, barely met the expectations of the people. No power was given to its members and they existed as a part of the Council only as a means to appease the Indians. During the Bengal famine, the British government did little to provide relief to the dying masses. By this time, western education had spread to the country and news of the revolutions that took place in Italy, Germany, Persia and Egypt greatly influenced the people. The revolutionaries realized that prayers, resolutions, petitions and deputations have no effect on the British government. Under the leadership of dynamic leaders, like Bal Gangadhar Tilak, Lala Lajpat Rai and Bipin Chandra Pal, the struggle for independence took a different turn. They created vehemence and passion in the people who, by this point, wanted complete independence from British rule.

FACT CHECK

The leadership of Bal Gangadhar Tilak, Lala Lajpat Rai and Bipin Chandra Pal was known as Lal, Bal and Pal.

Apply it! E

Name a secret society formed in Bengal during this time.

Geography skills

On an outline map of India, mark the countries that were part of the British empire at its peak.

Objectives and Methods of the Extremists

What's in the picture?

Look at the picture and write what you think is happening.

The extremists wanted to achieve 'Swaraj' or self-rule, but through self-help and self-reliance. They motivated people and reminded them of India's past glory. They also reassured the people to have confidence about the future. They reminded them that in order to achieve freedom, they needed to take drastic action, which would be a blow to the British superiority and confidence. Aurobindo Ghosh, a Hindu philosopher and a nationalist, felt that action and pressure was the best tactic to adopt.

Partition of Bengal

Lord Curzon was against any form of self-government in India. His measures posed immense dissatisfaction amongst Indians. Lord Curzon was responsible for the Partition of Bengal. The main motive behind the Partition of Bengal, according to the British, was administrative necessity. They said that the province of Bengal was too big to be efficiently administered by a single provincial government, whereas the Bengalis saw the partition as a serious attack on the solidarity of Bengali nationalism, tradition and culture. Indian nationalists saw it as a clear plan on the part of Lord Curzon to draw a wedge between the Hindu and the Muslim communities of India. Bengal was partitioned on October 16, 1905. Separate provinces of East Bengal and Assam were created, leaving the province in a state of discontent.

Swadeshi and Boycott Movement

The Partition of Bengal angered the people of India. Mass demonstrations and protests were held all over the country. This is called the Swadeshi Movement. Swadeshi, which literally means 'of one's own country', aimed at the promotion of indigenous industries for strengthening the nation. Swadeshi and boycott were complementary ideas and one would not succeed without the other. British goods were burnt at public places and shops selling them were picketed. The spirit of swadeshi influenced the industries, education, culture and even literature. This movement gave a **stimulus** to Indian industries and handicrafts. Swadeshi factories were set up in many places. The Anti-Partition agitation backfired on Lord Curzon's plans. It gave strength to the national movement. Finally, the Partition of Bengal was revoked in 1911.

Divide in the Congress, 1907

There was always a difference in the ideologies of the Moderates and the Extremists. The Moderates were not happy with the developments regarding the boycott and the Swadeshi movement, which now included the boycott of schools, courts of law, government jobs and legislative councils. While the Extremists wanted to extend their movement beyond Bengal and wanted a strong resolution supporting their programme, the Moderates were not in favour of extending the movement beyond Bengal. They were also opposed to the boycott of legislative councils and associations. There was a group of Extremists who were highly influenced by the revolutionaries of Ireland and Russia, and they targeted police officials and District Magistrates. They even targeted the Viceroys, Lord Minto and Lord Harding. The Extremists were not ready to comply with this. The dispute led to the split between the Moderates and the Extremists in the 1907 session of the Congress held at Surat.

stimulus: a thing that arouses activity or energy in someone or something; a spur or incentive

Steps Taken by British to Control the Extremists

The Prevention of Seditious Meetings Act of 1907 enabled the British government to prohibit any political meetings. The Newspaper Act of 1908 prohibited any article that provoked a rebellion. But the British attitude towards the Moderates seemed to be appeasing. In order to please the Moderates, the Indian Councils Act 1909, which is also known as the Morley-Minto Reforms, was passed. According to this Act, the number of elected members in both the central and the provincial legislature increased. Separate electorates for Muslims were created, which eventually led to the creation of Pakistan and hampered the unity of India as from then on there was no communal harmony.

Formation of the Muslim League

A Muslim organization, called the Muslim League, was formed in Dhaka in 1906. Nawab Salimullah, Aga Khan III and Nawab Mohsin-ul-Mulk were associated with its foundation. The Muslim League laid out demands for special representation and separate electorates for Muslims and was set up to contradict the nationalist demands of the Congress. This gave the British an opportunity to once again implement the policy of 'divide and rule'. While they had earlier conceded to the demands of the moderates, they now focused on satisfying the demands of the Muslims.

Muslim League working committee

Home Rule Movement

Annie Besant was a British socialist who supported the Home Rule Movement for India. She was born of Irish parents and had made India her home since 1893. Annie Besant was pleading India's case of home rule for self-government or Swaraj. In September 1916, a home rule league was started by her. Another home rule league had already been formed by Bal Gangadhar Tilak in Poona in 1916. The movement became very popular and created a lot of enthusiasm amongst the public. Annie Besant became the role model. In 1917, Annie Besant was arrested and there were protests everywhere.

Annie Besant

The Lucknow Pact, 1916

Annie Besant made all efforts to reunite the Moderates and the Extremists. She also made efforts to unite the Hindus and the Muslims. The Muslims who were very disillusioned with the British, made an effort to cooperate with the Congress, especially Muhammad Ali Jinnah and Mohammad Ali Jauhar. In December 1916, the Congress and the Muslim League held their session in Lucknow and both of them decided to be united, especially with the demand for self-government. The Congress agreed that the Muslims would continue to be elected through separate electorates. This agreement came to be known as the Lucknow Pact.

Montagu Declaration

The Home Rule Movement, and the Lucknow Pact, had a great impact on the British government. Indian nationalists were inspired by the Russian Revolution and its philosophy of socialism. In August 1917, Edwin Montagu, Secretary of State of India, declared a change of policy. The aim of the British government, henceforth, would be towards increased participation of the Indians in every aspect of administration with the aim of developing self-governing institutions.

In 1918, a report on Indian Constitutional Reforms was published, which became the foundation for the Montagu-Chelmsford Reforms, Mont Ford Reforms, or the Government of India Act, 1919. However, the act turned out to be highly disappointing as it did not meet the expectations of the people.

- 1905 Partition of Bengal
- 1906 Formation of the Muslim league
- 1907 Divide in the Congress; Seditions Meeting Act
- 1908 Newspaper Act passed
- 1909 Indian Councils Act
- 1911 Partition of Bengal revoked
- 1916 Home Rule League started; Lucknow Pact
- 1917 Montagu Declaration
- 1919 Government of India Act

Skill Builder

21ST CENTURY SKILLS

Critical thinking skills: How can you justify that the formation of the Muslim League was a part of British policy of divide and rule?

Life skills: Why did the extremists demand Swaraj or self-rule?

Communication skills: Imagine yourself to be an extremist having a conversation with a moderate nationalist. Try to explain why you have chosen the extremist policy in order to fight against the British.

World Connect

Between 1873 and 1882, the Home Rule Party in Ireland campaigned for home rule within the United Kingdom and Ireland. It influenced the Home Rule Movement in India.

Wind up

Indian National Movement (1905-1919)

- **Emergence of Extremists**
  - Believed that freedom could only be won by force
  - Lal, Bal and Pal most prominent leaders
- **Partition of Bengal**
  - Bengal partitioned in 1905 by Lord Curzon
  - Swadeshi and Boycott Movement: Protets against the partition of Bengal; boycott of British goods
- **The Muslim League**
  - Demand for separate representation of Muslims
  - Headed by Nawab Samlimullah, Aga Khan III and Mohsin-ul-Mulk
  - Lucknow Pact, 1916: Agreement between Congress and the Muslim League to have separate electorates
- **Home Rule Movement**
  - Demand for self-government of India
  - Spearheaded by Annie Besant

Exercises

A. Choose the correct answers.

1. The growth of the extremists is attributed to
   a. Bal Gangadhar Tilak b. Lala Lajpat Rai
   c. Bipin Chandra Pal d. All of the above
2. Bengal was partitioned in the year 1905, under the viceroyship of
   a. Lord Curzon b. Edwin Montagu
   c. Lord Mountbatten d. Lord Chelmsford
3. The protest and demonstrations against the Partition of Bengal is called the
   a. Home Rule Movement b. Indian Councils Act, 1909
   c. Swadeshi Movement d. Khilafat Movement
4. A divide among the Moderates and the Extremists took place in the Congress session, held at
   a. Nagpur b. Poona c. Bombay d. Surat
5. Two main leaders associated with the Home League Movement
   a. Tilak and Annie Besant b. Tilak and S N Banerjee
   c. Annie Besant and Mahatma Gandhi d. Tilak and Lala Lajpat Rai
6. The spirit of Swadeshi influnced
   a. Industries b. Education c. Culture d. All of these

B. Fill in the blanks

1. Swadeshi means ....
2. A prominent leader of the Muslim League was ....
3. Annie Besant supported the ....
4. Some nationalists followed the examples of the revolutionaries in .... and ....
5. The Indian Councils Act, 1909, was known as the .... Reforms.
6. The Lucknow Pact was signed in the year ....
7. The split in the Congress took place in the year ....

C. Write t for true and f for false.

1. The Congress session at Poona declared the demand for Swaraj. ☐
2. The British allowed the boycott of English goods. ☐
3. The Home Rule League was started by Lala Lajpat Rai. ☐
4. Annie Besant made all the efforts to unite the moderates and the extremists. ☐
5. The British were in favour of establishing the Muslim League. ☐

D. Answer these questions in brief.

1. What was the objective of the Lucknow Pact and where did the members of Muslim League and Congress meet to have their session?
2. Mention the attitude of Lord Curzon towards Indians. Give one example of a measure undertaken by him that caused discontent.
3. Discuss the difference between the Moderates and the Extremists, with reference to their objectives and methods.
4. When and why was the Muslim League founded?
5. What did the Home Rule Movement aim at?

E. Answer these questions in detail.

1. What agreements did the Congress and the Muslim League reach, as per the Lucknow Pact of 1916?
2. What was the argument for implementing the Partition of Bengal? What was the actual reason?
3. Examine the factors that led to the birth of Extremism in the 20th century.
4. Why do we say that the Swadeshi and the Boycott Movement received great response from the public?
5. What were the demands of the Muslim League? How did the British use this to their advantage?

F. Read the passage and answer these questions.

The Prevention of Seditious Meetings Act of 1907 enabled the British government to prohibit any political meetings. The Newspaper Act of 1908 prohibited any article that provoked a rebellion. But the British attitude towards the Moderates seemed to be appeasing. In order to please the Moderates, the Indian Councils Act 1909, which is also known as the Morley-Minto Reforms, was passed.

1. What was the purpose of the Prevention of Seditious Meetings Act of 1907?
2. What did the British government do to appease the Moderates?

Think Big

Integrate with art

Glass candle holder

You will need: a transparent glass, rice in 3 bowls, paint, candles, pallet, spoon

1. Take rice and divide them into 3 bowls. keep the plain rice aside as we will use them as it is.
2. Take one bowl of rice and put the green paint in it and mix it. You can also use food colouring.
3. Take the second bowl repeat the same procedure but with orange or saffron colour. Let the rice dry for a while.
4. Take a glass and put some green rice, then plain white rice and then saffron rice. You can stack rice in as many glasses as you want.
5. After stacking the tri-colours, stand the faux candles on it. The candle holder is ready!

Learning Tools

Use this foldable to recall what you have learnt in the chapter.

1. Fold a sheet of paper in half.
2. Fold this long rectangle in half.
3. Fold both ends back.
4. On the side, make vertical cuts through one thickness of paper, forming four tabs.

Use this book for data occurring in fours.

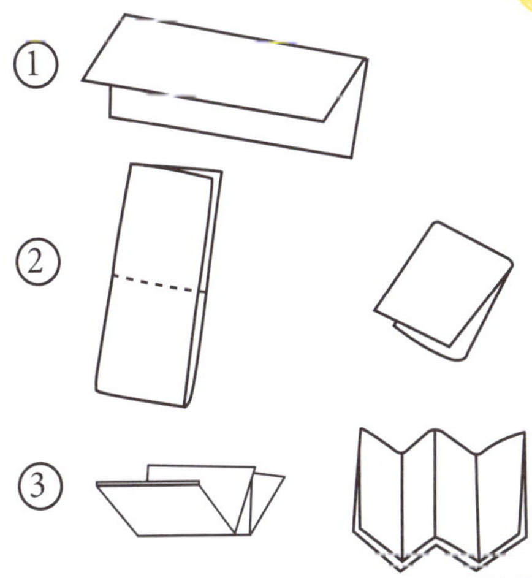

Web links:

https://nios.ac.in/media/documents/secsocscicour/english/lesson-08.pdf

Last accessed on 31 August 2021

14. The National Movement II

Warm up

Batak Mian was a Muslim cook, seldom remembered for his patriotism and heroism in India's struggle for independence. On the eve of Gandhi's first agitation against British rule, this cook was ordered to serve Gandhi with a cup of milk which had been poisoned. As he was serving the milk, he casually spoke to Gandhi in Urdu and told him not to drink it as it had been poisoned. The British could not understand what the cook said to Gandhi and Gandhi too made excuses to not drink that milk. His life was saved by this patriot. However, the British suspected that the cook had leaked this plan, so they had him arrested and brutally tortured him. His house was turned into a crematorium, and later, he and his family were forced out of the village. Later, India got freedom and Gandhiji was murdered. It was the case of a Muslim saving the life of Gandhiji and a communal Hindu rewarding Gandhiji with a bullet for his great services.

As the national movement took the nation by storm, news of World War I broke out and countless Indian soldiers were to fight for the British against Germany. To fund the war, the British **levied** heavier taxes on the people, and towards its end, they enforced harsher restrictions on the people to restrain, what they termed as, 'extremism'. By this time, Gandhi had returned to India from South Africa and had already become a leader of the Congress. During those years in South Africa, Gandhi had emerged as a leader of the anti-**apartheid** movement. There, he advocated the policy of Satyagraha and civil disobedience. Back in India, he practised and taught the people the same principles and **ideologies**, inspiring millions to follow his path. His vision took the freedom struggle to the national level.

Green Earth

Gandhi believed that 'nature has enough to satisfy everyone's needs, but not to satisfy anybody's greed'.

Mahatma Gandhi gave shape and character to the Indian national movement. He urged the masses to adopt non-violent methods of protest or disobedience of the law. Satyagraha, as taught by Gandhi, came to be followed by the people and posed a new challenge to the British. The people looked towards ousting the British through non-violent demonstrations, strikes and protests. Under the leadership of Gandhi, the national movement saw the spirit of nationalism reinvigorated in the people of India.

Apply it!

E

Explain how each of the following factors play a role in your national identity.

- Cultural identity
- Ethnic identity
- Geographic identity
- Linguistic identity
- Religious identity

apartheid: racial discrimination; ideologies: ideas and ideals

The Rowlatt Act, 1919

In 1919, an act was passed which granted the government the right to silence the press, to expel individuals, to set up special tribunals and to imprison political activists or anyone they felt suspicious about without a trial for two years. This act was called the Rowlatt Act. This act was shunned by the nationalists as it was oppressive. It did not allow any lawyer to appeal or consider any argument on behalf of the arrested person.

Jallianwala Bagh Massacre

A mural depicting the Jallianwala Bagh massacre

The Rowlatt Act had created serious disturbances and conflicts. The people were opposed to the Act and demanded its removal. To control the instability and disorder that was brewing, the British imposed martial law. Leaders like Dr Saifuddin Kitchlew and Dr Satya Pal were arrested in Amritsar. On April 13, 1919, a public meeting was conducted in Amritsar to participate in the annual Baisakhi celebrations—both a religious and cultural festival for the Punjabis. General Reginald Dyer, upon arriving at the spot and seeing the large assembly of people, gave an order to shoot at the people to disperse the meeting. This has been considered the most brutal action taken by the British government in India's freedom struggle, killing many people and leaving thousands wounded. It was after this incident that Rabindranath Tagore renounced his knighthood. The Hunter Committee, which reported on this matter, condemned and criticized the actions of General Dyer.

Case Study

The Khilafat Movement

The Khilafat movement originated after World War I as a result of discontent and bitterness of the Muslims against the British. This was due to the ill-treatment of the Turkish Empire in May 1920, when the Ottoman Empire, following its defeat, was partitioned by the victorious countries, including Britain, stripping the Sultan of his powers. The Caliph's authority, which included territorial possession, was reduced. In response to this, Mohammad Ali Jauhar and Shaukat Ali, popularly known as the 'Ali Brothers', started the Khilafat movement, to put pressure on the British government to protect the Caliph. One leader, who joined this movement, was Maulana Abul Kalam Azad. Gandhiji too, joined this movement, as he felt this would bring Hindu-Muslim unity. In 1920, both the Khilafat leaders and the leaders of the Indian National Congress joined hands and led a Non-Cooperation Movement against the British.

Q. Which events lead to the collapse of the Khilafat Movement?

Non-Cooperation Movement

Gandhiji had no faith in the British government, and therefore, he started the Non-Cooperation Movement so that the functioning of the government would come to a halt. The Non-Cooperation Movement included giving up on government titles and boycotting the legislatives, law courts, government schools and colleges. This entire movement was based on the philosophy of non-cooperation and non-violence.

There was a positive response to this movement and people participated in large numbers with great enthusiasm. The Non-Cooperation Movement was one of Gandhi's first organized acts of a large-scale civil disobedience. Lawyers like Motilal Nehru, Chittaranjan Das and Asaf Ali boycotted the courts, students boycotted government-run educational institutions and government employees boycotted their work. Widespread boycott of British-made goods was carried out. People went to the streets wearing khadis and urged the masses to use only swadeshi goods. The British government, confronted with a united India, was, for the first time in Indian history, visibly shaken.

The British government undertook several measures to suppress the movement, but throughout the history of India, there had not been such resilience and spirit, as there was at that phase of the Indian freedom struggle. People were fearless, ready to go to prison, or even die for their nation. While the nation was in fervour, Gandhiji appealed to the people to strictly follow the principle of non-violence. He himself gave up his medals and awards conferred upon by the government. People from all walks of life took part in this movement. However, amidst this chaos, the movement took an ugly turn, when an angry mob set fire to a building in Chauri Chaura, which housed 22 policemen. The 22 policemen in that building were killed. Gandhiji, upset by what had happened, immediately suspended the movement. However, despite his suspension of the movement, he was still imprisoned.

The sudden suspension of the Non-Cooperation Movement led to a difference of operation in the Congress. C.R. Das and Motilal Nehru founded a new party known as the Swaraj Party. The party **propagated** the contesting of election, winning seats and then put a halt to the functioning of the government. Initially, this party met with success, but it failed to meet its objective. Eventually, it lost its importance with the death of C.R. Das in 1925 and Motilal Nehru joined Congress.

The Revolutionary Leaders

Two upcoming leaders now joined the Congress—one was Jawaharlal Nehru, who had completed his education in England. Jawaharlal Nehru realized that the condition of the people in the princely states was wretched. He helped to make the issue of the plight of the people in the princely states a part of the national struggle. Thus started the journey of Nehru, who would one day become the first Prime Minister of an independent India. Subhash Chandra Bose was one of India's most renowned freedom fighters. In 1943, he revived the Indian National Army, which was previously known as the Azad Hind Fauj. Bose had initially appeared for the Indian Civil Services Examination and had ranked fourth among the successful candidates. However, the thought of working under the British government did not appeal to him. He resigned from service and returned to India, to take part in the national freedom struggle.

Jawaharlal Nehru and Subhash Chandra Bose

The Simon Commission, 1927

The government under Lord Irwin was full of unrest and disturbance. The British, therefore, set up a Commission, with John Simon as the chairman in 1927, to investigate the progress of the governance scheme and to suggest new steps for reform. This Commission comprised of seven British Members of

propagated: spread widely

Parliament and not a single Indian member. This enraged the people, as it deprived Indians of their right to participate in the determination of the Constitution of their own country. Protests and demonstrations were held everywhere in the country. People held processions with black flags and posters, on which the words 'Simon, go back' was written. In one of these demonstrations, Lala Lajpat Rai was hurt in a lathi charge. He died soon after.

What's in the picture?

Study the picture and write what you see here.

Purna Swaraj 1929

At the Congress session held in Calcutta in 1928, a decision was made that the Congress would accept **dominion** status as granted to Australia, Canada, New Zealand and many other countries, provided it materializes before the end of 1929. However, this demand was not met by the British government. In the Lahore Session of 1929, which was presided over by Jawaharlal Nehru, it was declared that the objective of the Congress was no longer to achieve dominion status but complete independence, or 'Purna Swaraj', from the British. The flag of India was hoisted in 1929, in Lahore, and across India by Congress volunteers and supporters. The Congress asked the people to observe 26 January as Independence Day.

Revolutionary Movement 1920 to 1930

In the struggle for freedom, the revolutionary movement played a dominant role. This movement began in Bengal. Barindra Kumar Ghosh led many youngsters to revolutionary activities. Many revolutionary societies that believed in armed revolution came up and were engaged in activities that involved bomb-making, robbery and the assassination of British officials. One revolutionary was Chandra Shekhar Azad, who reorganized the Hindustan Republican Association under the new name Hindustan Socialist Republican Association (HSRA). The main function of the association was to work towards an independent India, with equal rights and opportunity for everyone without discrimination on the basis of caste, creed, religion or social status. This group carried out several attacks against British officials. As a retaliation against the British after the Chauri Chaura incident and the suspension of the Non-Cooperation Movement, another prominent leader of the HSRA, named Bhagat Singh, along with other HSRA members, namely Shivaram Rajguru, Sukhdev Thapar and Chandra Shekhar Azad, were involved in a plan to avenge Lala Lajpat Rai. They killed the Assistant Police Superintendent, John Saunders, as he was leaving the district police headquarters in Lahore. Many revolutionaries were arrested after the bombing incident at the assembly chamber in Delhi. Many bomb factories were discovered in Lahore and Saharanpur. Chandra Shekhar, along with a few members, made an attempt to kill the Viceroy. This was in protest of the Lahore conspiracy case, which began in 1929. Chandra Shekhar continued with his activity in Punjab. He died in Alfred Park in Allahabad in 1931, after

Bhagat Singh

FACT CHECK

Inquilab Zindabad, a phrase which translates to 'Long Live the Revoultion' was used by Bhagat Singh in 1929, after bombing the Central Assembly in Delhi.

dominion: sovereignty or contro

being surrounded by the police. He tried to defend himself by firing at the police, but **succumbed** to the bullet injuries and died. Bhagat Singh, Raj Guru and Sukhdev too, were convicted and sentenced to death. This left the country in great distress and anger and cast a shadow on the Congress sessions.

Civil Disobedience Movement and the Dandi March

Gandhiji launched the Civil Disobedience Movement in 1930 with the historic Dandi March or Salt Satyagraha. He began his march from Sabarmati Ashram with seventy-eight followers and reached Dandi, a village situated on the Gujarat coast. Thousands of people joined him on his way. He broke the salt law, by making salt from sea water at the Dandi Beach. This act symbolized the disobedience towards the unjust salt law over which its sale and manufacture was monopolized by the British.

Dandi March

Men, women and children took part in this movement. Peasants, workers, and even the tribals from Central India took part in this movement. Sarojini Naidu actively took part in the freedom movement. The British tried to restrict this movement by imprisoning many of them. Gandhi, along with more than 1,00,000 people were arrested. In the Northwest Frontier Province, the movement was led by Abdul Gaffar Khan who was later known as 'Frontier Gandhi'.

It was during Gandhiji's imprisonment when the First Round Table Conference was held in London in 1930. However, the Congress members decided to boycott the conference, making the whole point of it futile.

Gandhi-Irwin Pact, 1931

It was through the efforts of Tej Bahadur Sapru that the Congress and the government reached an understanding and the Gandhi-Irwin Pact was signed. According to this pact, all political prisoners were to be to be set free with the exception of those involved in violence; harsh orders were to be withdrawn and the salt law was to be abolished. In return, Gandhiji agreed to call off the Civil Disobedience Movement and attend the Second Round Table Conference as the Congress representative.

The Government of India Act 1935

In 1935, based on the discussions concluded at the round table conferences, the British introduced the Government of India Act. The Government of India Act abolished **diarchy** which was to be replaced by provincial autonomy. Governors were given the special power to veto and also had control of the police and civil service. A feudal court was also to be established, which would have jurisdiction over the provinces and the princely states.

The act however, did not satisfy the people, as economic and political power was still in the hands of the British government and Indians still did not have the right to vote. The Congress, however, decided to take part in the elections under the act. The result of the election was that the Congress formed ministries in 6 out 11 provinces in India in July 1937. When World War II broke out in Europe in 1939, the Viceroy announced that India would be involved in the war against Germany, without consulting with the central legislature and the provincial government. This led to the resignation of the Congress ministries in 1939.

succumb: die from the effect of a disease or injury; diarchy: government by two independent authorities

Demand for a Separate Pakistan

The Muslim League, which had not fared well in the 1937 elections, felt very happy with the resignation of the Congress ministers and promised all help to the British in their war efforts. Under Muhammad Ali Jinnah's leadership, a resolution was passed at the Lahore session (1940), declaring Muslims as a separate nation from the Hindus stressing for an independent state. In spite of opposition even from the Muslim Indians, which included Maulana Abul Kalam Azad Kalam, Jinnah was unbending and unshakable on this issue.

Muhammad Ali Jinnah

This was opposed by Gandhiji at the Yerwada jail and he went on a hunger strike. This alarmed both the Harijans and the upper caste Hindus. Eventually, this led to the Poona Pact, signed by the Dalit leader B.R. Ambedkar and Gandhiji, according to which, seats were reserved for the depressed class from the general seats in the provincial legislature.

Quit India Movement (1942)

World War II started in the year 1939. The presence of the British in India made India a target for a Japanese attack. The British government needed the cooperation of the Indian leaders to check the presence of the Japanese army in India. In March 1942, the British government sent a mission headed by the cabinet minister, Sir Stafford Cripps, to break the political deadlock and have a consultation with all the parties. This was called the Cripps Mission. However, the mission was rejected by all the parties, because it did not bring with it the promise of independence in the near future. After the failure of the Cripps Mission, the Congress decided to take active steps to force the British to leave India. The All India Congress Committee met in Bombay on August 8, 1942 and passed the Quit India Resolution. The Congress proposed to start a non-violent mass struggle under Gandhiji's leadership. He demanded complete and immediate independence and gave the slogan, 'do or die'. He said we should either free India from the clutches of the British or we should die in this attempt. Before the Congress could start the movement, the British, in the early morning of August 9, arrested Gandhiji and the Indian National Congress was declared illegal. Riots broke out all over the country. Congress leaders were arrested and taken to unknown prisons. The news of the arrests shocked the nation. There were strikes and demonstrations all over the country. People set fire to police stations, post offices, railway stations and other public buildings. The British came down heavily on the people. Over 10,000 people were killed in firing and the movement was brutally put to an end within a short span of time. The Quit India Movement shook the very foundation of British rule in India. By this time, the British realized that their days in India were numbered.

FACT CHECK

Some leaders, like Aruna Asaf Ali and Ram Manohar Lohia, conducted an underground movement. This movement became very powerful and was a clear message to the British government, that they were not wanted anymore in India.

Netaji and the INA

The British faced utmost danger from Netaji Subhash Chandra Bose, who believed in direct action against the British. After World War II, Japan had taken many Indian soldiers as prisoners of war. In the year 1941, Netaji went to Japan and reached an agreement with the Japanese. The Indian prisoners were released and Netaji organized the Indian National Army. However, the army was not very well-equipped, and in no time, had to surrender. It was after this incident that the British realized that they could no longer depend upon the loyalty of the Indian army.

Advent of Independence

The Shimla Conference

In 1943, Viceroy Lord Wavell tried his best to find a solution to the difference between the Congress and the Muslim League, but Jinnah refused to give in, and raised the slogan 'Divide and Quit'. The war was coming to an end, and the demand for national independence became overpowering.

The Cabinet Mission, 1946

In 1946, the British Prime Minister Clement Atlee sent a three-member group to discuss the transfer of power with the Indian leaders. The members were Patrick Lawrence, Sir Stafford Cripps and A.V. Alexander. The Mission proposed that India be a federation, which included provinces of British India and the princely states, as well as the formation of a Constituent Assembly consisting of 389 members to form the Drafting Committee of the Constitution and an interim government to look after the administration until the Constitution was implemented. However, the Cabinet Mission rejected the demand for Pakistan but proposed autonomy for the Muslim majority areas. In accordance with the Cabinet Mission, elections were conducted in 1946. Congress won with an overwhelming majority. The Muslim League boycotted the election and fixed August 16 as Direct Action Day. This was with an objective to obtain Pakistan. This resulted in violence and arson in Calcutta on a massive scale, which soon spread to other parts of India.

- 1919 Rowlatt Act; Jallianwala Bagh massacre
- 1927 Simon Commission set up
- 1929 Purna Swaraj
- 1930 Civil Disobedience movement and Dandi march
- 1931 Gandhi-Irwin Pact
- 1935 Government of India Act
- 1942 Quit India movement
- 1943 Shimla conference; Indian National Army revived
- 1946 Cabinet Mission
- 1947 India attains independence

Birth of Independent India and Partition

Refugees leaving during partition of India

On February 20, 1947, the British Prime Minister, Clement Atlee, announced that the British would quit India by June 30, 1948. The last Viceroy of India, Lord Mountbatten, who took charge on March 24, 1947, held talks and concluded that partition was the only solution to the problem. On June 3, 1947, Lord Mountbatten announced the partition of India into two independent dominions—Pakistan and India. Each of these would draw up their own Constitution. The choice was given to the princely states either to join India or Pakistan, or remain independent. A Commission was set up, to determine the boundaries. The Indian Independence Act was passed by the British Parliament on July 15 1947, which received the royal consent. Pakistan was to comprise of East Bengal, West Punjab, Sindh, Baluchistan and the North West Provinces. India was to comprise of all the remaining areas included in British India.

India finally achieved its independence on August 15, 1947, but at the heavy cost of partition. Communal hatred reached its peak. Innocent people were killed, houses were burnt, people were forced to leave their home and become refugees. The Indian Independence Act of 1947 made India and Pakistan two separate states.

On August 15, Jawaharlal Nehru was sworn in as the first Prime Minister of India. At midnight of August 14, 1947, Nehru paid tribute to this historic movement with the lines, 'At the stroke of the midnight hour, when the world sleeps, India will awake to life and freedom.' Following the transfer of power, the Constituent Assembly with Dr Rajendra Prasad as its President, prepared the Constitution of India. It came to effect on January 26, 1950, when the Indian republic was born.

Skill Builder

21ST CENTURY SKILLS

Critical thinking skills: Do you think that the non-violent method of protest should work in today's world? Why or why not?

Life skills: Collect rare photographs of the freedom movement and conduct an exhibition of the same during Independence Day.

Wind up

Indian National Movement (1919-1947)

Rowlatt Act, 1919
Draconian British laws to silence the press and detain people without trails; led to the Jallianwala Bagh massacre

Non-Cooperation Movement
Non-violent movement led by Gandhi

Simon Commission
Appointed to look into constitutional reforms; Indians demand for Purna Swaraj

Civil Disobedience
Movement Gandhi marches to Dandi to break the salt law

The Government of India Act 1935
To create the Federation of India

Muslim League
Demand for separate country of Pakistan

Quit India Movement
Full-scale movement against the British; Indians ask British to quit India

India Gains Independence
Lord Mountbatten announces Partition and Indian Independence Act is passed in the Parliament

Exercises

A. Choose the correct answers.

1. This act gave the British the power to imprison politicians without a trial.
   a. Indian Councils Act
   b. Rowlatt Act
   b. Vernacular Act
   d. Indian Press Act
2. Jallianwala Bagh is situated in
   a. Amritsar
   b. Chandigarh
   c. Jalandhar
   d. Bhatinda
3. He renounced his knighthood as a protest against the killing in Amritsar.
   a. Subhash Chandra Bose
   b. Rabindranath Tagore
   c. Jawaharlal Nehru
   d. Lala Lajpat Rai
4. Associated with the Khilafat movement.
   a. Rabindranath Tagore
   b. Subhash Chandra Bose
   c. Mohammad Ali Jauhar
   d. Jawaharlal Nehru
5. Which one of the following began with the Dandi March?
   a. Home Rule Movement
   b. Non-Cooperation Movement
   c. Civil Disobedience Movement
   d. Quit India Movement

B. Match the following

1.	Vernacular Press Act	a.	1915
2.	Arrival of Gandhi in India	b.	1919
3.	Rowlatt Act	c.	1947
4.	Independence of India	d.	1878

C. Fill in the blanks.

1. The Cripps Mission arrived in India in the year ....
2. The last Viceroy of India was ....
3. To break the salt law, Gandhiji marched from Sabarmati Ashram to ....
4. The Shimla Conference in 1945 was called by ....
5. The .... party was formed by Motilal Nehru and C.R. Das.
6. The .... Act gave enormous power to the government to replace the political activities.

D. Answer these questions in brief.

1. Why did Indians boycott the Simon commission?
2. Why did Rabindranath Tagore renounce his knighthood?
3. Give reasons for Gandhiji joining the Khilafat movement.
4. What were the reasons for the emergence of the Non-Cooperation Movement?
5. What is meant by the concept of Purna Swaraj?

E. Answer these questions in detail.

1. What discriminatory powers did the British get as per the Rowlatt Act of 1919?
2. What did the Cripps Mission propose? Why did it fail?
3. Why did Gandhiji start the Civil Disobedience Movement?

4. What was the main objective of the Simon Commission?
5. Describe the important events that took place during the Quit India Movement.
6. Describe the incident in Chauri Chaura causing Gandhiji to call off his Non-cooperation Movement.

F. Arrange the following in chronological order

1. Gandhi began Dandi March ☐
2. Poona Pact ☐
3. Gandhi Irwin Pact ☐
4. Gandhi starts fast unto death ☐

Think Big

Integrate with value education

Below you will find some famous quotes and slogans alongside the names of people who made them popular. Find out what each means and gather few more slogans and quotes from pre-independence.

Famous Quotes and Slogan	Name
Inqilab Zindabad	Bhagat Singh
Jai Jawan, Jai Kishan	Lal Bahadur Shastri
'Do or die' *(Karo Ya Maro)*	Mahatma Gandhi
Jai Hind	Subhash Chandra Bose
Purna Swaraj	Jawahar Lal Nehru

Learning Tools

Create a usable timeline by using an Accordion Book Foldable. List the important point under fours sub-heads: Rowlatt Act and aftermath, Non-Cooperation Movement and Muslim League, Simin Commission and effects, and Civil Disobedience Movement and Quit India Movement. Add characteristics of each group to help you remember the chapter.

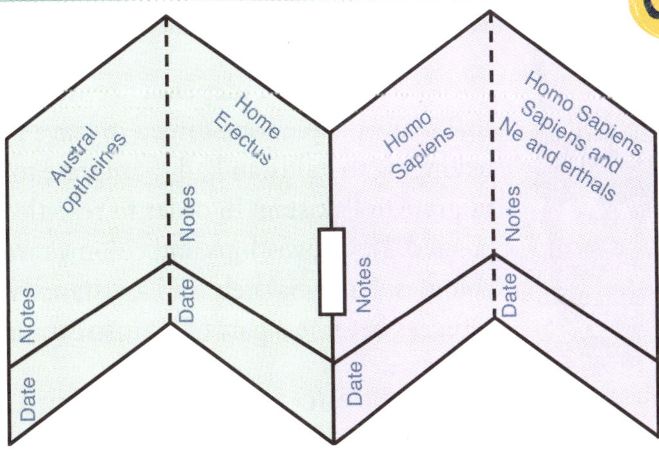

Web links:

http://www.lcwu.edu.pk/ocd/cfiles/History/Maj/Hist-403/The-Rowlatt-Act-Jallianwala-Bagh-Massacre-1919-1.pdf
https://www.britannica.com/event/Quit-India-movement

Last accessed on 31 August 2021

15. The National Movement III

Warm up

At the stroke on midnight, on 15 August 1947, India achieved independence, marking the end of a two-hundred-year long dominion by the British. India and Pakistan were declared independent and now had complete control over the governance of their own countries. The Muslim majority areas were separated from India to create the independent state of Pakistan, which resulted in the relocation of millions of people to either country. This was a period of instability and violence in the country.

Creation of the Union of India

There were tremendous hurdles that challenged the newly-independent India during this period. The people who migrated from Pakistan to India had to be accommodated and a new political system needed to be adopted. By this time, there were more than 500 princely states that had to be assimilated into the Indian nation, many of which wanted to retain their independence, for instance, Junagadh, Hyderabad and Kashmir. The efforts of one man, Sardar Vallabhbhai Patel, India's first Home Minister, also known as the Iron Man of India, were instrumental in absorbing the independent princely states into the Indian fold.

Vallabhbhai Patel

Rehabilitating Refugees

The declaration of independence was followed by communal riots. The result of this was that many people were forced to leave their homes. Many Hindus living in territories belonging to Pakistan had to migrate to India and many Muslims living in India had to migrate to Pakistan. In order to resettle and rehabilitate them, a rehabilitation ministry was created. New townships and colonies were developed. These were known as resettlement colonies. Financial help and assistance were provided in various ways, and gradually, these refugees became a part of mainstream Indian society.

Independence of the French and Portuguese Colonies

In 1948–49, the French administration at Mahe and Chandernagore surrendered. In 1954, the governments of India and France came to an agreement, by which French rule ended in India and all French territories were integrated into India.

Regions such as Goa, Daman, Diu and Dadra and Nagar Haveli were under Portuguese control, but unlike the French, the Portuguese refused to surrender their territories. In December 1961, the Indian army succeeded in evacuating them, leading to the complete assimilation of all Indian territories as one nation.

A Dark Day for India

The seeds of communalism had been sown years ago, but even as India became one united whole, the disunity between Hindus and Muslims continued to plague the society. On January 30, 1948, a grave misfortune struck the nation. Mahatma Gandhi was assassinated by a Hindu fanatic, Nathuram Godse, who believed that Gandhi was tolerant towards Muslims. Till today, 30 January is celebrated as Sarvodaya Day every year.

Democracy and Development

India has always been a **pluralistic** society, with diverse languages, castes, religions and ethnic groups. So, the most challenging job was to integrate the almost 350 million large population and unite them as a single nation state, which was essential to keep the spirit of diversity.

B.R. Ambedkar

At the time of Independence, the greatest issue before India was that of development. The population of India was mainly rural, and therefore, development depended on agriculture, which was the main source of income. This, in turn, was dependent on monsoons. Another issue that India faced was that a major portion of the cultivable fertile irrigated tracts of land had gone to Pakistan. In urban areas, factory workers lived in slum clusters, lacking in health and hygiene.

Therefore, a new set of guidelines and regulations needed to be woven which would keep intact the diversity and democratic vision of India and aim at holistic development. On December 9, 1946, the Constituent Assembly met for the first time and took on the task of framing the constitution. BR Ambedkar was the main architect and he based the ideals of the constitution on those of western constitutions. The Indian Constitution was adopted on January 26, 1950 and India was declared as a sovereign democratic republic.

FACT CHECK

Rajkumari Amrit Kaur was the only woman in the first Cabinet formed after India gained independence.

Now let us examine the unique features of the Constitution and how it enshrines and treasures the rich values of modern and contemporary India.

Parliamentary Democracy

- The parliamentary system of government was adopted by the Constitution of India.
- The Constitution of India guaranteed universal adult franchise, that is, all Indians above the age of 18 would be allowed to vote in all state and national elections, irrespective of gender, class, education or property rights.

What's in the picture?

Identify five leaders of India from this photograph.

pluralistic: relating to or advocating a system of two or more states, groups, principles, sources of authority, etc.

- A federal form of government, that is, two levels of government, was decided to be the best for India. The two levels were to be the state level and the central level and the powers were distributed between the two levels through the union, state and concurrent list.
- According to the Indian Constitution, equality before law and equality of opportunities were guaranteed, and nobody would be discriminated upon on the bases of caste, creed, religion and sex. The right of the poor and marginalized communities was recognized by giving them special privileges. The practice of untouchability was abolished and the **marginalized** communities were allocated special privileges, so that they could be brought into the mainstream. A certain percentage of reservations have been made for them in educational institutions, the legislature and jobs in the government.

Case Study

Identifying a regional language

- Indian leaders were not in favour of creating states on the basis of languages.
- The pain of dividing India on the basis of religion had not vanished from their minds. Therefore, they could not afford another division based on linguistic differences.
- This came as a disappointment for many sections of people, which they expressed through protest marches, hunger strikes and bandhs.

In 1952, a veteran Gandhian Potti Sriramulu demanded the formation of Andhra Pradesh to protect the interest of Telugu-speaking people. He died on the fifty-eighth day of his fast. Soon, the government was forced to reflect on its decision and the state of Andhra Pradesh was formed on October 1, 1953.

The S.K. Dhar Commission was appointed in November 1947 to study the issue of reorganization of states on a linguistic basis. This Commission made many recommendations, and the Central government formed a State Reorganization Committee in 1953 under Fazal Ali. The Committee completed this task in 1955, and according to its recommendations, India was divided into 14 states and 6 union territories. State boundaries were specified and changes were made whenever there was a need.

In 1960, Bombay was divided into two states; Maharashtra for Marathi speaking people, Gujarat for Gujarati speaking people.

In 1966, Punjab was divided into Punjab for Punjabi speaking people and Haryana for Haryanvi speaking people.

More states came to be added over the years. The last three states to be formed were Uttarakhand, Jharkhand, Chhattisgarh and Telangana. At present, there are 28 states and 8 union territories in India.

- The directive principles of our Constitution laid down the formation of Panchayats as one of the goals of the government. This is mandatory for rural areas. This is an effort in creating self-governing bodies at the local level and taking democracy to the **grass roots**.

Jawaharlal Nehru addressing the constituent assembly in 1946

National and Regional Languages

India is a multilingual country, so one common language needed to be adopted. The Constitution of India designates the official language of the Government of India as Hindi as well as English for official purposes. Twenty-two languages have been recognized by the Constitution of India.

The Constituent Assembly decided to adopt a mixed economy, where both public and private sectors would play a prominent and influential role. They would complement each other, and thus, enhance production and generate jobs.

marginalized: (of a person, group, or concept) treated as insignificant; grass roots: the most basic level of an activity or organization

The government set up the Planning Commission in 1950, in order to formulate and execute these policies. The Commission was to promote a rapid rise in the standard of living of the people by using the resources of the country, increasing production and offering employment opportunities to everyone. The government tried to accomplish this task by incorporating Five Year Plans, beginning in 1951. Through these plans, India has been able to advance in different fields such as agriculture, irrigation, industry, transport, communication and social services.

Independent Foreign Policy

India adopted a foreign policy that was so distinctive, the basis of which was on the principles of its own independence, sovereignty and co-existence with other countries. India highly respects the independence and sovereignty of other countries and strongly condemns those countries where a policy of discrimination is based on caste, creed, race or religion. India strongly believes in peaceful dialogue as a solution to even the worst kind of disputes.

Panchsheel Agreement

These are a series of principles considered to be the backbone of the relationship between India and the People's Republic of China. They were shaped in 1954, with reference to decolonization, to assure that the newly formed independent nations co-exist peacefully in a harmonious manner, and the aggressive relationship that they had in the past with the colonizers could be avoided.

The five principles of the Panchsheel Agreement are:

- Mutual respect for each other's territorial integrity and sovereignty
- Mutual non-aggression
- Mutual non-interference in each other's affairs
- Equality and mutual benefit
- Peaceful coexistence

Subsequently, the Non-Aligned Movement was based on Panchsheel.

Non-Aligned Movement (NAM)

Jawaharlal Nehru

After World War II, the powerful countries of the world were divided into two blocs, that is, the Western Bloc led by the USA and the Eastern Bloc led by the former USSR. There emerged a Cold War between the two blocs in the fifties and sixties. In addition to this, there were many military pacts and alliances, which again divided the people of different countries. This period also witnessed the collapse of colonial empires and many countries gaining independence. Some countries, like India, did not want to join any of the two power blocs. It was under these circumstances that the NAM was founded.

The founders of the NAM were Jawaharlal Nehru, President Josip Broz Tito of Yugoslavia and President Gamal Abdel Nasser of Egypt. The NAM urged other countries to be neutral and not join the two major alliances. NAM had only 20 countries to begin with but has now grown in influence to have more than a 100 countries.

India after 60 Years of Independence

India is a huge country and the largest democracy in the world. The democratic values in this country have always been respected. The economy of India has been restructured through new economic policies. Constant efforts are being made to achieve technological advancement, to liberalize the economy of the country and enhance production in various fields.

India has made tremendous progress in technology and human resource development. In 1974, the first nuclear explosion was conducted in Pokhran. It was known as Operation Shakti. In 1975, ISRO built the first satellite, Aryabhata, which was launched by the Soviet Union in 1975. India's first ever Mars probe, the Mangalyaan orbiter, arrived at the red planet in September 2014. The mission was budgeted at 4.5 billion rupees, which was really cheap by Western standards.

However, there are still many challenges faced by the country. Poverty and unemployment continue to be a problem. Housing remains a far-fetched dream for many. Despite constitutional provisions, the practice of untouchability, female infanticide, communal disharmony and rising population continues to plague the nation. However, the onus of solving these problems does not lie with the government alone. People too need to play an active role in dealing with these problems.

FACT CHECK

In January 2015, the Cabinet passed a resolution to abolish the planning commission and constitute in its place the National Institution for Transforming India (NITI AYOG).

World Connect

Sinhala Only Act of 1956

The Sri Lankan Parliament passed an act known as the Sinhala Only Act in 1956, which declared Sinhalese as the official language of Sri Lanka, as it was spoken by 70 per cent of the total population of Sri Lanka. However, the act failed to satisfy the Tamil-speaking population of Sri Lanka, who saw it as an attempt to oppress the minority population of the country. The minority population comprised of the Indian Tamils, Sri Lankan Tamils and Moors.

Skill Builder

21ST CENTURY SKILLS

Critical thinking skills: 'Long years ago we made a tryst with destiny, and now the time comes when we shall redeem our pledge, not wholly or in full measure, but very substantially. At the stroke of the midnight hour, when the world sleeps, India will awake to life and freedom.' Who said these words and on what occasion?

Life skills: What was the role of the Planning Commission after independence?

Communication skills: What did Dr Ambedkar mean when he said that 'In politics we will have equality, and in social and economic life we will have inequality?'

Wind up

India after Independence

- Assimilation of the princely states into the Indian union
  - Assimilation of Junagadh, Hyderabad and Kashmir
- Rehabilitation of refugees
  - Townships, colonies and resettlement colonies
- Independence of French and Portuguese colonies
  - Assimilation of Mahe, Chandernagore, Goa, Daman, Diu, Dadra and Nager Haveli
- Democracy and Development
  - Constitution of India framed
- Non-Aligned Movement
  - India refused to join any power bloc

Exercises

A. Choose the correct answer.

1. The Iron Man of India was
   a. Jawaharlal Nehru
   b. Motilal Nehru
   c. Sardar Vallabhbhai Patel
   d. Mahatma Gandhi
2. The problems that independent India faced at the beginning were
   a. integration of the princely states
   b. to unite the different parts of the country
   c. to rehabilitate the refugees
   d. all of the above
3. According to the Indian Constitution,
   a. equal opportunities should be given to all citizens
   b. untouchability is illegal
   c. there should be a policy of reservation for marginalized communities
   d. all of the above
4. The founders of the Non Aligned Movement were
   a. Jawaharlal Nehru
   b. President Tito of Yugoslavia
   c. President Nasser of Egypt
   d. All of the above
5. The state re-organizing committee was formed in
   a. 1953
   b. 1954
   c. 1955
   d. 1956

B. Fill in the blanks.

1. .... was India's first Home Minister.
2. Junagadh, Kashmir and Hyderabad were .... states.
3. At the time of Independence, Goa was under .... rule.
4. There are .... languages recognized by the Constitution of India.
5. The Planning Commission was set up in the year ....

C. Write T for True and F for False.

1. B.R. Ambedkar based the ideals of the Indian Constitution on those of the western constitutions. ☐
2. In 1975, ISRO built the first satellite, Aryabhata. ☐
3. The French surrendered Mahe and Chandernagore to India. ☐
4. The Western bloc of power was led by the former USSR. ☐
5. Punjab was divided into two states, Punjab and Haryana. ☐

D. Answer these questions in brief.

1. What made Junagadh a part of the Indian union?
2. Write a short note on the Indian Constitution.
3. What role did India play in the formation of the Non-Aligned Movement?
4. Why was the Planning Commission set up in 1950?
5. Name the two blocs of power formed after World War II.

E. Answer these questions in detail.

1. Who was India's first home minister? State one contribution of his which was considered to be a great success.
2. How did the reorganization of Indian states take place?

3. What were the principles of the Panchsheel Agreement? Why were they framed?
4. Who were the founders of NAM and why was it organized?

Think Big

Integrate with Science/Maths

13 CLIMATE ACTION

Teachers and school authorities can take a brilliant step as part of the Independence Day activities- take kids for a tree plantation drive. This is a great way to explain the concepts of the special day through nature. As we enjoy independence, it is also important to preserve our environment. Slogans can be written and pasted on the trees.

The life of trees can be set as an example to convey the ideas of unity and diversity. The growth of trees is remarkable in clusters, which show the significance of unity. Similarly, the concept of diversity can also be seen when different kinds of trees support each other for survival.

Name three problems that the newly-independent nation of India faced.

Learning Tools

Based on what you have studied in the chapter, write your own notes on the following.

Creation of the Union of India

Rehabilitating Refugees

Independence of French & Portuguese Colonies

Democracy and Development

Parliamentary Democracy

Web links:

https://www.epw.in/engage/article/how-did-ambedkar-imagine-india-independence-day-nationalism
https://www.britannica.com/topic/Non-Aligned-Movement

Last accessed on 31 August 2021

1. Resources

Warm up

'Science and technology has made our lives easier. Most of us begin our day by switching on the geyser. We iron our clothes and then eat breakfast. We go to the school by bus. But what makes these things work?' asked Mr. Sharma in class one day. Avni quickly raised her hand and answered, 'From the earth'! Let us learn how the Earth provides all these things to us.

Anything and everything around us is of some use. These things used by us have utility. Food, clothes, furniture, books and medicines—all of them have some usability and worth. This worth is called value. Any element of the environment, which has both utility and value, is called a resource.

Types of Resources

Resources can be classified as natural resources, human-made resources and human resources.

Natural Resources

Naturally occurring substances such as land, air and water that are valuable and necessary in their unmodified form and fulfil our needs in some ways are called natural resources. They are classified based on the level of development and use, origin, stock and distribution.

Based on development: On the basis of their development and use, resources can be classified as—actual resources and potential resources.

Resources that are already being utilized by humans at present are called actual resources. The coal deposits of the Chota Nagpur Plateau and the petroleum oilfield of Mumbai High are examples of actual resources.

Potential resources are the resources that are present around us but may be used only in the future. They cannot be used at present because of lack of infrastructure or **technology** available today. For example, the Gulf of Kutch and the Gulf of Khambhat near the coastline of Gujarat have a huge potential for generating tidal energy. However, India is yet to set up a plant that can harness this energy.

Based on origin: Resources can be biotic or abiotic based on their origin. Biotic resources are living, whereas abiotic resources are non-living. Water, rocks and land are abiotic resources, whereas plants and animals are biotic resources.

Apply it! E

Make a list of three non-renewable resources you use in your daily lives, and state why overusing them would cause their depletion.

5 GENDER EQUALITY

technology: the use or application of latest knowledge and skills available in producing a thing or idea.

Based on renewability: Natural resources can be classified into renewable and non-renewable resources on the basis of their renewability.

Windmills generating wind energy

Renewable resources are not exhaustible. They can be replenished and renewed through various processes. Some renewable resources exist in abundance on Earth and thus being unlimited are not that affected by human activities. Solar energy, tidal energy and wind energy are some examples of renewable resources. There have been tremendous developments in the field of science and technology using which we can harness these resources to generate energy.

Non-renewable resources are exhaustible and are found in a limited quantity on the Earth. Once exhausted, these resources take millions of years to renew. Petroleum, natural gas and coal are some examples of non-renewable resources.

Based on distribution: On the basis of distribution, resources are classified into ubiquitous or localized. Resources found everywhere, such as air and sunlight, are called ubiquitous. Resources found at certain places are called localized resources. Gold and silver are localized resources.

Human-Made Resources

Natural resources have limited uses in their crude form. These resources are changed into useful products. For instance, petroleum was not a human-made resource until human beings found ways to procure petrol, diesel, kerosene and plastics from it. Human beings use their knowledge and skills to convert the natural resources into useful products. Examples of such resources are buildings, roads, machinery and vehicles. These are known as human-made resources.

What's in the picture?

Which source of energy is being used here? How does the consumption of this energy help in the conservation of the environment and energy?

Human Resources

Humans are the most important resource. No substance in nature can be a resource by itself. It only becomes a resource when it is put to use by us through knowledge, skills and technology. Education and good health have helped human beings to become a valuable resource. Therefore, any country that wants to progress must take care of both its natural and human resources. Countries try to develop and improve the quality of skills of its people to produce more resources and progress in a process called human resource development.

FACT CHECK

Sustainable development goals (SDGs) were adopted by the United Nations in 2015. It comprises 17 identified goals that aim to protect the planet Earth. The SDGs are designed to fight poverty, hunger, gender inequality, poor health and wellbeing etc.

Conservation of Resources

Scientific and technological progress has enabled human beings to utilize resources at a much larger scale, leading to the over utilization of these natural resources to the point where they will be exhausted in the near future. Using natural resources carefully, without wasting them in a manner that they get exhausted before being renewed, is called conservation of resources. Development that meets the needs of the present, without compromising on the ability of future generations to meet their own needs, is known as sustainable development. Resources should be utilized judiciously so that after fulfilling our present requirements, they can also be preserved for future generations.

All resources are not inexhaustible; so, they should be used with caution. Many plant and animal species are on the **verge** of extinction. The future of the Earth, therefore, depends on our judicious use of resources.

World Connect

The human race and nature share an inseparable bond, wherein one cannot survive without the other. Yet, with the surge in population, humankind has tapped into nature's resources prodigiously, without giving nature much of a chance to renew herself. A recent UN report states that the amount of resources extracted and consumed by humans has tripled in forty years. The International Resource Panel (IRP), a division of the UN Environment Programme, equates rising consumption to the growing middle class, leading to an increase in the extraction of resources from 22 billion tons in 1970 to 70 billion tons in 2010. This, as specialists agree, is imposing a severe impact on human health and quality of life as it intensifies climate change, increases air pollution and reduces biodiversity. This problem needs to be addressed before the situation becomes irreversible.

Skill Builder

21ST CENTURY SKILLS

Critical thinking skills: Resources should be used judiciously. What would be the consequences that humans will experience if resources are not used judiciously?

Life skills: Air is a valuable natural resource. Find out how air pollution affects our health. List three most common diseases caused by air pollution.

Wind up

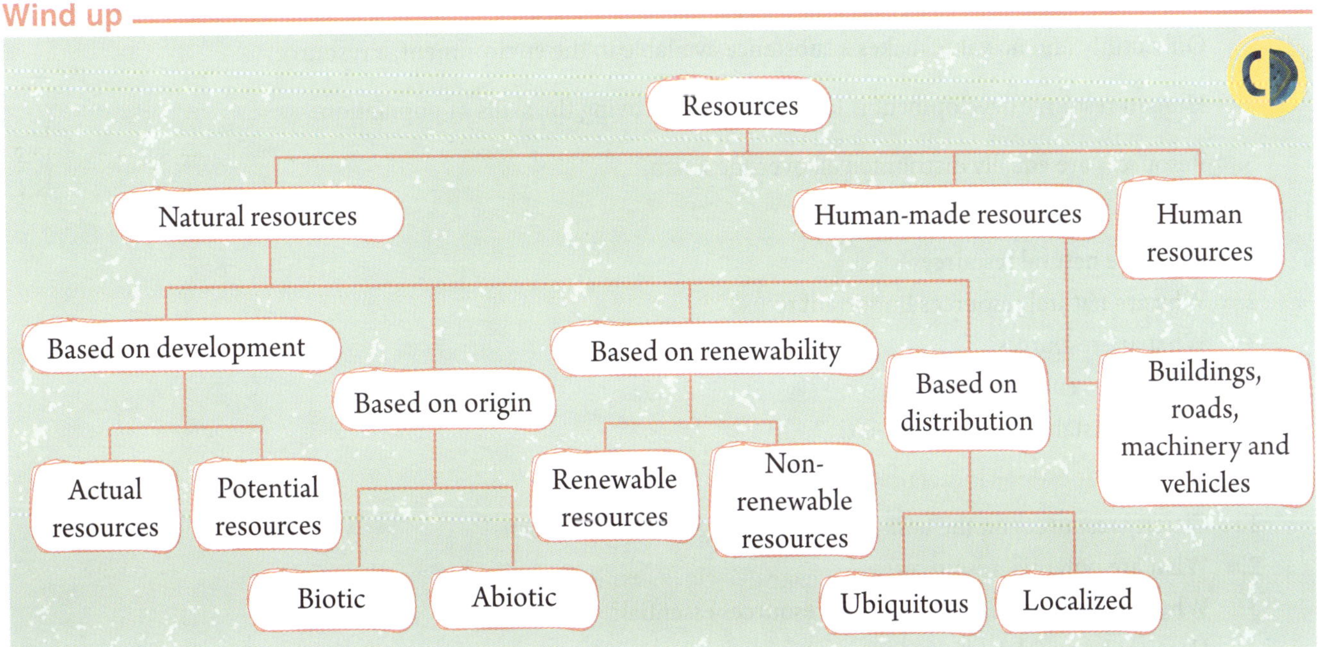

verge: an extreme limit beyond which something specified will happen

Exercises

A. Fill in the blanks.

1. .... resources are derived from living things.
2. .... resources are found only in certain places.
3. Solar energy and wind energy are examples of ....
4. Anything that is used to satisfy a need is called a ....
5. .... are the most important resource.

B. Choose the correct answer.

1. Which of these have some utility?
   a. Water   b. electricity   c. Vegetables   d. All of these
2. Which of the following is an example of a practice associated with sustainable development?
   a. Clearance of forest to build factories
   b. Using petrol in vehicles
   c. Practising farming with no chemical fertilizers
   d. Mining iron from a mine over a period of last 20 years
3. Examples of abiotic resources are
   a. water   b. rocks   c. land   d. all of these
4. Resources drawn from nature and used without much modification are called
   a. human-made resources   b. natural resources   c. cultural resources   d. none of these
5. The basis of classification of resources is
   a. level of development and use   b. origin
   c. stock and distribution   d. all of these

C. Write T for true and F for false.

1. Non-renewable resources have unlimited stock. ☐
2. Ubiquitous resources are found everywhere. ☐
3. Only utility and no value makes a substance available in the environment, a resource. ☐
4. Human resource development is learning and improving the skills of population. ☐
5. Resources are equally distributed all over the Earth. ☐

D. Answer these questions in brief.

1. What are natural resources?
2. Why are natural resources important to us?
3. What are resources?
4. Name two renewable resources.
5. What is sustainable development?

E. Answer these questions in detail.

1. Classify resources on the basis of origin, giving examples of each.
2. What are potential resources?
3. Why is the conservation of natural resources essential?
4. How are human beings an important resource?
5. What are human-made resources? How much important are human beings in producing a resource?

Think Big

Art fun

Make a garbage dump pizza

Collect some small pieces of waste materials such as pieces of cloth, ribbons, buttons, popsicle sticks, chopsticks, paper clips, tin foil, old toy parts, twigs and dried grass. Cut out pizza dough out of cardboard and paste the waste items on it according to the different types of resources. Make sure it looks like a pizza.

Learning Tools

Directions: Our Earth is the source of everything we use and make. Organize the things we use into the proper natural resource categories. Some words may fit in more than one category.

paper tin glass fruits vegetables plastics structures sand natural gas rubber iron clay food clothing aluminium oil companies ceramics medicine

Renewable

Plants

________ ________
________ ________
________ ________
________ ________

Animals

____
____
____

Non-rewable

Minerals

____
________ } ________
________   ________
____
____

Fossil fuels

____
____
____
↘ ________

Web links:

https://www.theworldcounts.com/stories/natural-resources-for-kids

https://www.nationalgeographic.org/topics/resource-types/

Last accessed on 31 August 2021

2. Land and Soil Resources

Warm up

Ninety-five per cent of our food is grown in soil. Soil stores and filters our water and provides a home for the majority of life on the planet, and yet, most of us rarely pay much attention to it. Thousands of years of taking and taking have caught up with us and our soil. Approximately 40 per cent of agricultural soils worldwide are degraded or seriously degraded; we lose an estimated 36 billion tons of topsoil every year. Scientists warn us that we only have about 60 years of productive soil left. What will happen when the Earth has lost all of its soil and can no longer produce food?

Land is one of the most important natural resources. However, land covers only about 30 per cent of the Earth's total surface area; 90 per cent of the world population occupies only 30 per cent of the total land area. The remaining 70 per cent of the land is either sparsely populated or uninhabited because of rugged terrain or harsh climate.

Land Use

The term 'land use' is defined as using land for different purposes, such as agriculture, forestry, mining, building houses, setting up industries and roads and railways. The utilization of land depends on physical factors such as relief, soil, climate, natural vegetation, availability of water and minerals and human factors such as population and technology.

FACT CHECK

In India, around 60 per cent of land is used for agriculture. This is higher than that used in the United States, where 44 per cent of land is used.

Physical factors: Plains formed by rivers provide fertile soil and receive abundant water for agriculture. Mountain slopes are covered with thick forest cover, and the scenic beauty is an attraction for tourists. The plateau region is a storehouse of minerals; so, mining becomes an activity.

What's in the picture?

What do you see in the picture? How does this activity affect the quality of soil?

Human factors: The lifestyle of the people, the location of a place and its accessibility affect land use. Land can be under private ownership or community ownership. Private land is owned by individuals or a group of individuals. Land use of private holdings is according to the need of the land owner. On the other hand, community land is mostly used to serve the purpose of the community, for uses such as fodder, firewood collection and grazing cattle. Such community land is known as common property resource. In some areas, people encroach on community land and misuse it. The Earth's land resources are limited and the land demand is high; therefore, land should be used judiciously.

Soil

Soil is the top layer of the land surface of the Earth composed of disintegrated rock particles, humus, water and air. It is formed by the processes of weathering and erosion. Soil is a combination of **decayed** and **disintegrated** materials.

Soil Formation

Soil formation is a long process and is caused by many factors. It can take up to a thousand years for just an inch of soil to form.

Layers of soil

Parent rock: The original rock from which the soil is formed is called the parent rock. The type of the soil and the minerals present depend on the parent rock it is formed from. The parent rock also decides the colour, texture and chemical properties of the soil. For example, clayey soil is formed from shale.

Climatic conditions: Temperature and precipitation affect soil formation. Greater variations in temperature and moisture in the air increase the rate of weathering.

Relief: Altitude and slope of land play an important role in soil formation. On a steep slope, the soil cover is thin because the weathered rock particles cannot be deposited as they slide down the slope under the force of gravity. On gentle slopes, the soil cover is thicker.

Plant and animal organisms: Plants and microorganisms provide organic matter to the soil and add to its fertility.

Time: It determines the thickness of the soil formed. The deeper layers of the soil are the ones that were formed first.

Soil Profile

A vertical section of soil from the surface to the parent rock is called the soil profile. The process of soil formation creates a **stratified** soil profile. The layers or horizons of soil from top to bottom are as follows:

A Horizon: This horizon is made up of the top layer of soil called the topsoil. It is usually the darkest layer as it has the highest concentration of organic matter called humus. It is also a region of intense biological activity—insects, worms and animals burrow through it and roots of plants grow into it. Some amount of minerals and clay may dissolve in freshwater in this layer and trickle down to the lower layers of soil.

B Horizon: This horizon comprises the subsoil. It is made up of soluble minerals and accumulated clay. Although this layer has less amount of humus, it holds more amount of water compared to topsoil.

decayed: (of organic matter) something that has started to rot through the action of bacteria and fungi; disintegrated: matter that has broken down as a result of decay; stratified: arranged in layers or strata

C Horizon: This layer comprises the deposit on the Earth's surface from which soil is developed. It has small pieces of rocks that are not affected by weathering.

D Horizon: This layer has the unbroken solid rock sheets and is located several feet below the ground surface. It is also called the bedrock. This layer is mostly made of granite, basalt, quartzite, limestone and sandstone.

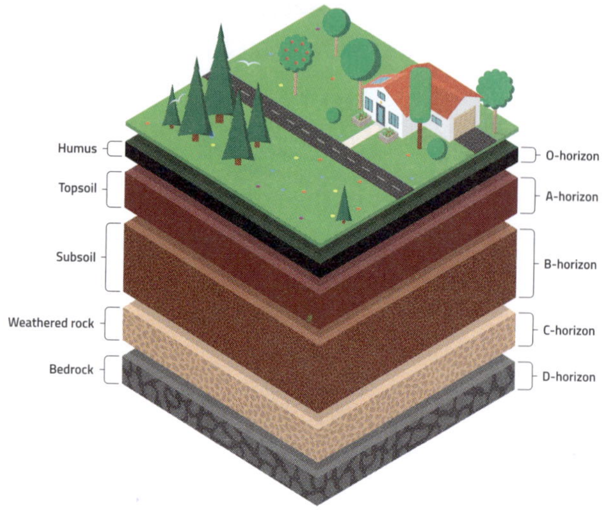

Soil profile

Soil Resources of India

Soil in India varies in composition and structure, from region to region. It is categorized into six types:

Alluvial soil comprises sand, silt and clay brought down by rivers. In India, it is found in the Northern Plains, covering the states of Punjab, Haryana, Uttar Pradesh, Bihar, West Bengal, Assam and in the eastern coastal plains. This type of soil is very fertile and suitable for agriculture.

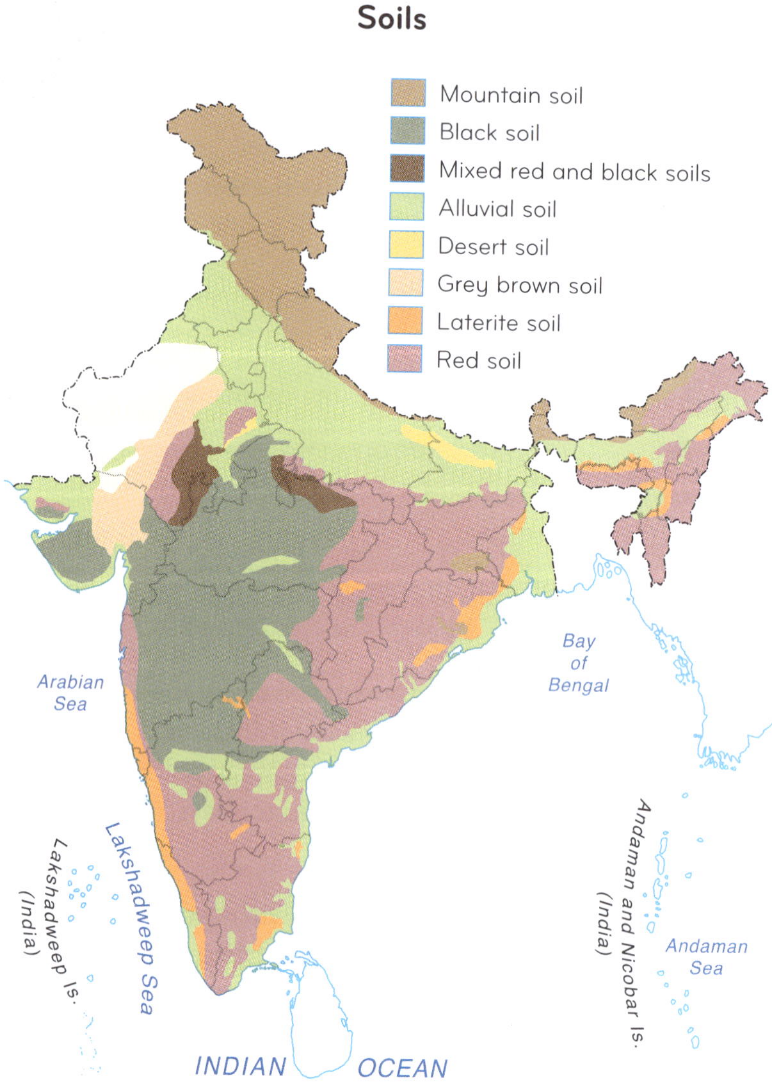

Soils of India

Black soil is formed from the weathering of lava rocks. It is also known as regur soil. This soil is clayey and becomes sticky when wet and cracks when dry. Black soil covers most of the north-west Deccan Plateau and some parts of Tamil Nadu. It is ideal for the cultivation of cotton, and thus, is also known as black cotton soil.

Red soil is reddish in colour because of the presence of iron oxide. This type of soil is found in southern and the eastern parts of peninsular India.

Laterite is rich in iron and aluminium and is commonly considered to have formed in hot and wet tropical areas. It is formed when heavy rains wash away the fertile upper part of the soil. It contains little humus. It is typically found in southern parts of India including Karnataka, Tamil Nadu, Kerala and Madhya Pradesh.

Mountain soil is formed due to the deposition of organic matter and is, thus, rich in humus. This soil is mainly found in Jammu and Kashmir, Uttar Pradesh and West Bengal. Crops such as wheat, soybean and sugarcane grow well in mountain soil.

Desert soil is usually light in colour and sandy in texture. It has sparse vegetation that varies with temperature and elevation. This soil lacks humus but contains a high proportion of soluble salts. It is found in hot and semi-arid regions like western Rajasthan and parts of Gujarat.

Soil Conservation

Soil conservation means protecting topsoil from getting eroded or being washed away. Some of the methods used by the farmers to conserve soil are:

Contour ploughing

Contour ploughing: In this method, the farmer ploughs along a slope rather than up and down the slope. It reduces erosion as the contours of a hill slope naturally obstruct the flow of water down the hill slope.

Terrace farming: Hill slopes are used as cultivable land in this method. The farmer cuts steps or terraces to reduce the speed at which the rainwater flows downhill.

Terrace farming

Crop rotation: It is a system of cultivating different crops on the same land during following years. As different crops need different minerals from the soil, it prevents any one type of nutrient from being exhausted from the soil.

Strip cropping: It is the method of growing different crops—cover crops alternating with cultivated crops—in narrow strips.

Contour barriers: Bunds made using stones, grass and soil can be used to build barriers along contours to restrict the flow of water.

Mulching: The bare ground is covered with a layer of organic matter like straw or husk to retain soil moisture.

Afforestation: It is the process of planting large numbers of trees on land that has few or no trees on it.

Shelter belts: In dry areas, where wind erosion is common, rows of trees and shrubs should be planted to check the velocity of the wind. These rows are called shelter belts.

Soil erosion and the subsequent loss of fertility are serious problems in developing countries. The measures for soil conservation should be planned on scientific lines and implemented with the active participation of farmers.

Skill Builder

21st CENTURY SKILLS

Critical thinking skills: Human beings share an incredible relationship with the nature. We have not only adapted to different natural environments on the Earth but also altered them considerably. Cite some examples, which prove that human beings have adapted to different environments on the Earth.

Life skills: What is a compost? Why is it added to soil?

Information literacy: Make a survey of your neighbourhood and list the various ways in which land has been used.

Case Study

In India, cultivated land is on the brink of desertification. The biggest threat stems from wheat and paddy. Padma Bhushan-awardee agricultural economist Sardara Singh Johl had suggested that wheat and paddy cultivation should be restricted and moved to the Indo Gangetic plains of Uttar Pradesh, Bihar and West Bengal to protect Punjab and Haryana from desertification. However, this is not a sufficient measure as we do not know how to get rid of the agent that is causing this desertification.

Q. Why was the suggestion of moving paddy cultivation to the Indo-Gangetic plains not carried out?

World Connect

Trees and forests are important to us all, as realized by the Guam Soil and Water Conservation Districts, while working towards organizing their fourth annual Educators Symposium on Conservation, from July 28–29 to August 1, at the University of Guam, located on the island of Guam in the Pacific Ocean.

They aim to promote ownership and responsibility amongst students towards nature and the environment. Celebrating for a fourth consecutive year, conservationists in Guam have partnered with local technical experts and companies that care about the environment. This year's theme is 'We All Need Trees.'

Wind up

- Soil
  - Soil formation
    - Factors affecting soil formation
      - Parent rock
      - Climatic conditions
      - Relief
      - Plants and animals
      - Time
  - Soil profile
    - A Horizon, B Horizon, C Horizon, D Horizon
  - Soil conservation
    - Contour ploughing
    - Terrace farming
    - Crop rotation
    - Strip cropping
    - Contour barriers
    - Mulching
    - Afforestation
    - Shelter belts

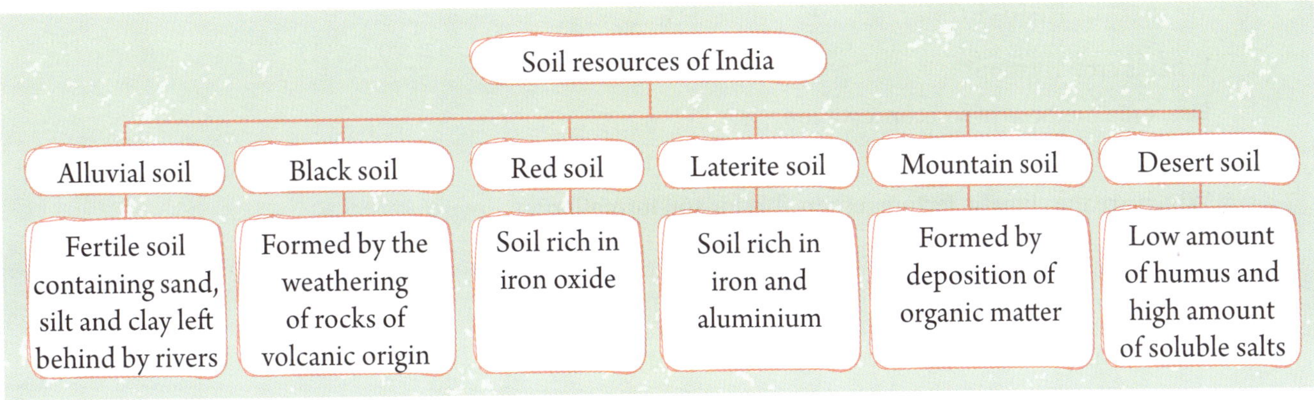

Exercises

A. Fill in the blanks.

1. .... is the process of planting large numbers of trees on land which has few or no trees on it.
2. The formation of laterite soil is due to ....
3. .... is the practice of covering bare ground with organic substances to retain soil moisture.
4. Black soil is ideal for the growth of ....
5. .... soil is found in hot and dry regions.

B. Choose the correct answers.

1. What per cent of the Earth's area is occupied by land?
   a. 45 b. 30 c. 66 d. 70
2. Which of the following steps is a major threat to the environment?
   a. Planting trees b. Desertification
   c. Promoting tourism d. Promoting renewable resources
3. The texture, colour and chemical properties of a soil are largely caused by
   a. climate b. relief c. parent rock d. organic matter
4. As the exposed rock breaks off and starts decaying due to temperature change, this process is called
   a. deforestation b. landslide c. soil erosion d. weathering
5. Soil is made up of
   a. water b. metals
   c. organic materials and rocks d. ice
6. An example of common property resource is
   a. private homes b. land for common usage
   c. agricultural land of individuals d. factories

C. Give reasons for the following.

1. Regur soil is black in colour.
2. Red soil is red in colour.
3. Steep slopes have thin soils.
4. Black soil needs to be tilled after the first rains.
5. Terrace farming is an appropriate way of growing crops in mountainous regions.

D. Answer these questions in brief.

1. What is crop rotation?
2. List some methods of soil conservation.
3. Mention the important factors responsible for soil formation.
4. Which are the climatic factors responsible for soil formation?
5. Briefly explain two measures for soil conservation.

E. Answer these questions in detail.

1. With the help of a neatly labelled diagram, describe the soil profile.
2. Give an account of the various methods of soil conservation.
3. Explain with examples how economic and human factors determine the type of land use.
4. Write two important features of each soil type in India.
5. Explain the distribution of types of soil in India.

Think Big

Integrate with science

Observe how soil is being used in your community, and answer the following questions.

- What type of soil is present?
- What influence does the climate have on erosion?
- What kind of vegetation grows there?
- Is it likely to erode easily?

Learning Tools

Fill up the following table to recap what you learnt in the chapter.

Soils of India	
Type of soil	
Formed by	
Found in	

Web links:

https://geographyandyou.com/soil-erosion-and-conservation-in-india/
https://nios.ac.in/media/documents/316courseE/ch20.pdf

Last accessed on 31 August 2021

3. Water Resources

Warm up

Think about water. It is truly amazing. We use it so much that we cannot live without it; yet, we often take it for granted. If all the Earth's water was kept in a five-litre container, the proportion of water good enough to drink would not even fill a teaspoon. Only a very small amount of water on earth is drinkable.

Human life, as with all animal and plant life on the planet, depends on water. We need water for the many reasons. Water is used for domestic purposes—drinking, cooking, bathing and washing. Water from rivers and lakes is used for irrigation. When water falls from a height, as in waterfalls or dams, it can be harnessed to generate hydroelectricity. Large water bodies like oceans and seas also moderate the climate.

Freshwater Resources

Out of the total amount of water present on the Earth's surface, only about 2.7 per cent is freshwater. About 70 per cent of this freshwater is frozen in the ice caps and glaciers. Only about one per cent of it is fit for our use. It is available as groundwater and as water in rivers and lakes. Rainfall is the primary source of freshwater on the Earth. Rainwater is continuously recycled in nature through evaporation, condensation and precipitation.

Glacier

Human-Made Resources

Dams are large structures built over a river to obstruct the water from flowing freely, thereby creating a reservoir or a lake. Dams are constructed to store water for irrigation, flood control and generation of hydroelectricity. Therefore, dams are also referred to as multipurpose projects. Some important multipurpose projects are the Bhakra–Nangal Project, the Chambal Project, the Damodar Valley Project and the Hirakud Project.

A dam in India

Canals are waterways that connect existing lakes, rivers or oceans. They can be used for transporting goods as well as people and for delivering water to places where water is scarce. There are two types of canals: **inundation** canals and perennial canals. Inundation canals are long canals linked to large rivers. They receive water when the river is high enough, especially during floods. Perennial canals are linked to dams and barrages to provide water throughout the year, they irrigate a large area.

A canal in Amsterdam

Tanks are used to store rainwater for irrigation, drinking, rearing of livestock, fire suppression and food preparation amongst many other purposes in many parts of India. These are efficient means to store clean water. Tanks and canals are used to provide water in both the dry regions and regions scarce of water.

Wells and tube wells: Wells and tube wells are boreholes dug to tap groundwater.

Green Earth

Saving water means saving energy; so, the less water we use, the less energy we waste.

Conservation of Water Resources

There is a shortage of freshwater at present. Hence, utilization of water resources should be planned carefully to obtain the maximum benefit. The distribution of freshwater resources is highly uneven on the Earth's surface. Water scarcity has become a serious problem in the world. Most countries of Africa, West Asia, Australia, the western USA and parts of South America are facing acute water shortages. Water shortage is also caused by misuse, over exploitation and contamination of water resources.

FACT CHECK

Great Pacific Garbage patch is a collection of litter and debris that makes its way from the land to the water bodies around the world. Plastics is one of the main litter found in the garbage patch.

Water scarcity is an environmental concern due to the lack of sufficient water resources to meet the water needs in many parts of the world. In Asia and Africa, this is a prevailing problem, causing a large proportion of the population to become severely affected by it. Climate change, increased pollution and overuse of water are some factors that lead to water scarcity.

An increase in population has put much pressure on groundwater resources for industrial and domestic purposes, thereby over-exerting our existing water resources. If the population of a place is too high, the use of water exceeds the rate at which they receive it. In some places, housing large populations, there has been a sudden, steep decline in groundwater levels.

Apply it! E

What happens to the water if we water plants in the afternoon when the sun is up?

Qualitative Decline

Fertilizers, industrial chemicals, pesticides and many other harmful substances are directly or indirectly discharged into water bodies, without adequate treatment to remove harmful compounds. These are increasingly contaminating the water resources in some developing countries in Asia, Africa and South America. In developing countries, 70 per cent of industrial waste is dumped untreated into the waters where they pollute the usable water supply, leading to a decline in the quality of water.

Water pollution

inundation: an abundance of water or flood-like situation

Ways of Conserving Water

The important methods of conserving water are as follows:

Afforestation: A lot of rainwater is lost through surface run-off. Trees need to be planted so that the roots of trees can slow down surface run-off and improve seepage of water in the soil.

Irrigation: Irrigation methods must be efficiently used so that there is no wastage of water. Excessive irrigation leads to deposition of salts on the surface. Canals and dams need to be repaired to reduce wastage of water. In dry regions with a very high rate of evaporation, trickle or the drip irrigation method is useful, as in this method, underground pipes supply water to the roots of plants. Sprinklers are effective means of irrigation. In this method, **undulating** lands are evenly irrigated.

Industrial water: Water used in industries and factories need not be thrown away. It may be recycled and used for cleaning. Lowering consumption by industries and factories would certainly aid in water conservation.

Domestic use: Taps should not be unnecessarily kept open and wastewater from the kitchens may be used for watering plants.

Rainwater harvesting: This is an effective method of conserving water. Rainwater can be collected in storage tanks and can be used later to fill up wells and tube wells.

Conservation of water resources is possible through planned utilization and protecting the available sources from pollution.

What's in the picture?

What do you see in the picture? How does this help the environment?

World Connect

Two-thirds of the land in Kenya is arid and dry, with very little water resources to meet the needs of the population. The African West Bank, an international non-profit organization, has launched a new form of technology to provide clean water to the people using more economical means. The technology's main focus is to harvest rainwater on a large scale. It has features such as an enhanced collection area, a guttering system, a storage system, filters, water gauges and first flush devices. The rainwater harvesting system launched by AWB collects about 400,000 to 450,000 litres of rainwater, within two to three hours of steady rain. This quantity is enough to supply about 400 people with water for twenty-four months. The largest tank ever constructed is in the Narok County, and it can hold about 600,000 litres of water.

Skill Builder

21ST CENTURY SKILLS

Life skills: In a glass jar, place small stones, sand and soil in layers until half-full. Plant a small plant in the soil and tighten the lid. Place a small bowl of water next to plants. Keep the jar in the Sun for few days. What do you think will happen?

Critical thinking skills: Do you think it is possible to convert saline water of oceans and seas into freshwater for domestic consumption on a large scale? Why or why not? Also, find the names of the countries doing so.

Wind up

- Water resources
  - Freshwater resources
    - Rain, ice caps, glaciers
  - Human-made resources
    - Dams, canals, tanks, wells, tube wells
  - Conservation of water resources
    - Afforestation, drip irrigation, rainwater harvesting

Exercises

A. Fill in the blanks.

1. .... is the main source of freshwater.
2. Waterfalls can be harnessed to generate ....
3. Water covers about .... per cent of the Earth's surface.
4. Large water bodies help to moderate the .... of the Earth.

B. Choose the correct answers.

1. Rainwater is recycled in nature through evaporation, condensation and
   a. photosynthesis b. calcification c. precipitation d. liquidation
2. Excessive .... leads to deposition of salts on the surface.
   a. infall b. irrigation c. flood d. deforestation
3. Underground water reserves have been depleted by
   a. afforestation b. construction of houses
   c. terrace farming d. contour ploughing
4. Human-made waterways for connecting existing lakes, rivers or oceans.
   a. Dams b. Canals c. Tanks d. Wells
5. Which is not an example of ground water?
   a. Water flowing in rivers b. Water through wells
   c. Water through hand pumps d. Water through submersible pumps

C. Write T for true and F for false.

1. Water is a non-renewable resource. ☐
2. Inundation canals are connected to dams. ☐
3. Wells and tube wells are used to extract groundwater. ☐
4. Freshwater makes up only ten per cent of all the water available on the Earth. ☐

D. Answer these questions in brief.

1. What are the various sources of freshwater on the Earth?
2. Why does water scarcity occur?
3. Which are the main pollutants of water?
4. What is rainwater harvesting?

E. Answer these questions in detail.

1. Describe the measures of conserving water.
2. Why is water considered to be a valuable resource?
3. How does planting tress prevent surface run-off?
4. Briefly explain the different ways of conserving the water.
5. Explain how irrigation should be practiced to conserve water.

Think Big — Integrate with science

Take a glass with a little bit of water, some sand and soil, a strainer, bright-coloured paint and some more water. Place the sand on the strainer and top it with the soil. Add two drops of paint on to the soil and sand. Place the strainer on the glass of water. Now, pour a little bit of water on the soil and sand mixture. What do you notice? Does the water colour inside the glass change? Similarly, fertilizers and pesticides can pollute groundwater.

Learning Tools

Our Earth has only a certain amount of water and will never have more. We need to keep our water clean and not waste it. In what ways do you conserve water each day? How can we all conserve water?

How can we conserve water in our homes?	How can we conserve water in our school?
______________________	______________________

How can we keep our rivers and lakes clean?	What should we do to ensure our future has plenty of clean water?
______________________	______________________

Web links:

https://www.britannica.com/science/water-resource
https://www.greenfacts.org/en/water-resources/index.htm

Last accessed on 31 August 2021

4. Natural Vegetation and Wildlife

Warm up

Asia was the cradle for most of the ancient civilizations. The great size of this continent made it possible for different civilizations to flourish. A great range of landforms and diversity of climate allowed the life to grow and bloom in all variety. The continent, thus, has an abundance of biodiversity. Let us learn more about the diversity of natural vegetation and wildlife in the world.

Plants and wildlife are interdependent for their survival. An ecosystem consists of all the plants and animals that live in a particular area together with the complex relationship of interdependence that exists between them and their environment. A biome is a major ecological community, extending over a large area and usually characterized by a dominant vegetation and wildlife.

Natural vegetation on the Earth varies from region to region, depending on many factors. The availability of sunlight, amount of rainfall, type of soil and altitude of a place affect the natural vegetation of the region. Some types of vegetation found in the world are forests, grasslands, deserts, region of almost no-vegetation also called tundra and mountain vegetation. Let us learn about each of them in detail.

Forests

Tropical Rainforest

Tropical rainforests are dense forests found in regions close to the equator. They are also called equatorial rainforests and mostly receive heavy rainfall throughout the year. The vegetation is dense and dominated by trees that do not shed their leaves at one time of the year, and hence, appear to be green throughout. Trees here form a structure called canopy with their overlapping branches and broad leaves, thus preventing the sunlight from penetrating completely.

Distribution: Amazon Basin in South America, Congo Basin in Africa, Malaysia in South–East Asia

In India, equatorial rainforests are found in the Western Ghats, the delta region of West Bengal, parts of Assam, Tamil Nadu and the Lakshadweep islands.

Toucan

Vegetation: Hardwood trees such as mahogany, ebony, rubber, cinchona and rosewood are found in the tropical evergreen forests.

Wildlife: Anacondas, toucans, macaws, gorillas, monkeys, parrots, birds-of-paradise, bandicoots, orb weavers, tarantulas, scorpions

Tropical Deciduous Forests

These forests are also called monsoon deciduous forests. The climate in these forests is marked by alternating spells of warm and dry winters and hot and wet summers. The trees shed their leaves during the dry spell and bear leaves again during the rainy season.

Distribution: Southeast Asia, parts of Africa and Australia

In India, tropical deciduous forests are found in parts of Deccan Plateau, Chota Nagpur Plateau, foothills of Himalayas, north-eastern states and Western Ghats

Vegetation: Teak, bamboo, sal, deodar, sandalwood, fern

Wildlife: Tiger, lion, nilgai, panda, hippopotamus, buffalo, reptiles, deer, chital

Temperate Deciduous Forests

These forests are found in the higher latitudes of the temperate regions of the world, typically on the eastern sides of continents. The leaves of deciduous trees change color or senesce in autumn and fall off in the winter. The climate is characterized by a cold winter season and warm and wet summers. These forests receive precipitation throughout the year.

Temperate deciduous forest

Distribution: Eastern regions of North America, parts of South America, parts of Australia, Japan, parts of China, eastern regions of Canada

Vegetation: Oak, beeches, birches, chestnuts, aspens, elms, maples, basswoods

Wildlife: Rabbits, weasels, foxes, bears, deer, chipmunks, owls, hawks, salamanders, turtles, flycatchers, thrushes, moles

Mediterranean Forests

These forests are found on the western sides of the continents and are mostly concentrated in the regions around the Mediterranean Sea. The climate is characterized by hot and dry summers, while winters are cool and moist. Most precipitation occurs during winters. The plants and trees in these forests adapt themselves to withstand the conditions of long, hot summers with little rain. The trees are of medium height and have waxy or very small leaves. They develop long taproots to draw water from the subsoil.

Olive tree

Distribution: The Mediterranean region (Spain, France, Monaco, Italy, Malta, Greece, Turkey, Albania, Croatia, parts of Syria, Lebanon, Morocco and Egypt), south-central and southwestern Australia, western South Africa, parts of Chile, parts of California in the USA.

Vegetation: Cork oaks, walnut, pine, eucalyptus, rosemary, myrtle, olives, laurels, junipers, cypresses, fig, heather, lavender

Wildlife: Coyotes, roadrunners, scrub jays, foxes, great bustard, Iberian lynx, barbary macaque

Coniferous Forests

These forests found in the higher latitudes are also called taiga or boreal forests. The climate is characterized by long winters and moderate to high annual precipitation mostly in the form of snow. The dominant feature of these forests are cone-bearing evergreen trees. Most of the taiga is concentrated in Eurasian and American cold temperate regions.

Reindeer

Distribution: Sweden, Finland, Norway, Estonia, parts of Scotland, parts of Iceland, Russia, parts of Kazakhstan, northern Mongolia, northern Japan

Vegetation: Pines, spruces, firs, larches, mosses, liverworts, lichens

Wildlife: Reindeer, lynx, wolves, moose, martens, voles, squirrels, shrews, crossbills, warblers, grouse, hawks, polar bears

Grasslands

The location and extent of the grasslands depend on the total amount of rainfall and its seasonal distribution. As the amount of rainfall decreases, the forest cover becomes less dense and grasses grow between the scattered trees. The grasslands of the world are broadly classified into two types.

Tropical Grasslands

Tropical grasslands are found on either side of the equator, in the interior of the continents in the tropical regions. The regions include northern Australia, the Brazilian Highlands and Guiana Highlands (South America) and Sudan in Africa. In such regions, the amount of rainfall is not sufficient for dense trees. Therefore, small trees, shrubs and grasses grow here. The trees that grow in these regions are mostly thorny and stunted, with reduced leaves that help retain moisture.

Temperate Grasslands

Temperate grasslands are the prairies of North America, the steppes of Europe, the pampas of South America, the downs of Australia and the veld of South Africa. These regions have a temperate climate with a moderate amount of rainfall. The temperature ranges from warm to hot during summer with usually cold or freezing temperatures during winter.

Deserts

Hot deserts are found on the western margins of the continents in the tropical regions. The famous deserts are the Sahara Desert and the Kalahari Desert in Africa, the Atacama Desert in South America, the Arabian Desert in West Asia and the Australian Desert in Australia. Rainfall is low and vegetation negligible in these regions. Only drought-resistant plants, or **xerophytic** plants, grow here. Cactus, date palms and acacias are the varieties that grow here. In India, desert vegetation is found in most of Rajasthan (Thar Desert) and in some parts of Punjab and Gujarat.

xerophyte: a plant structurally adapted to growing under very dry or desert conditions

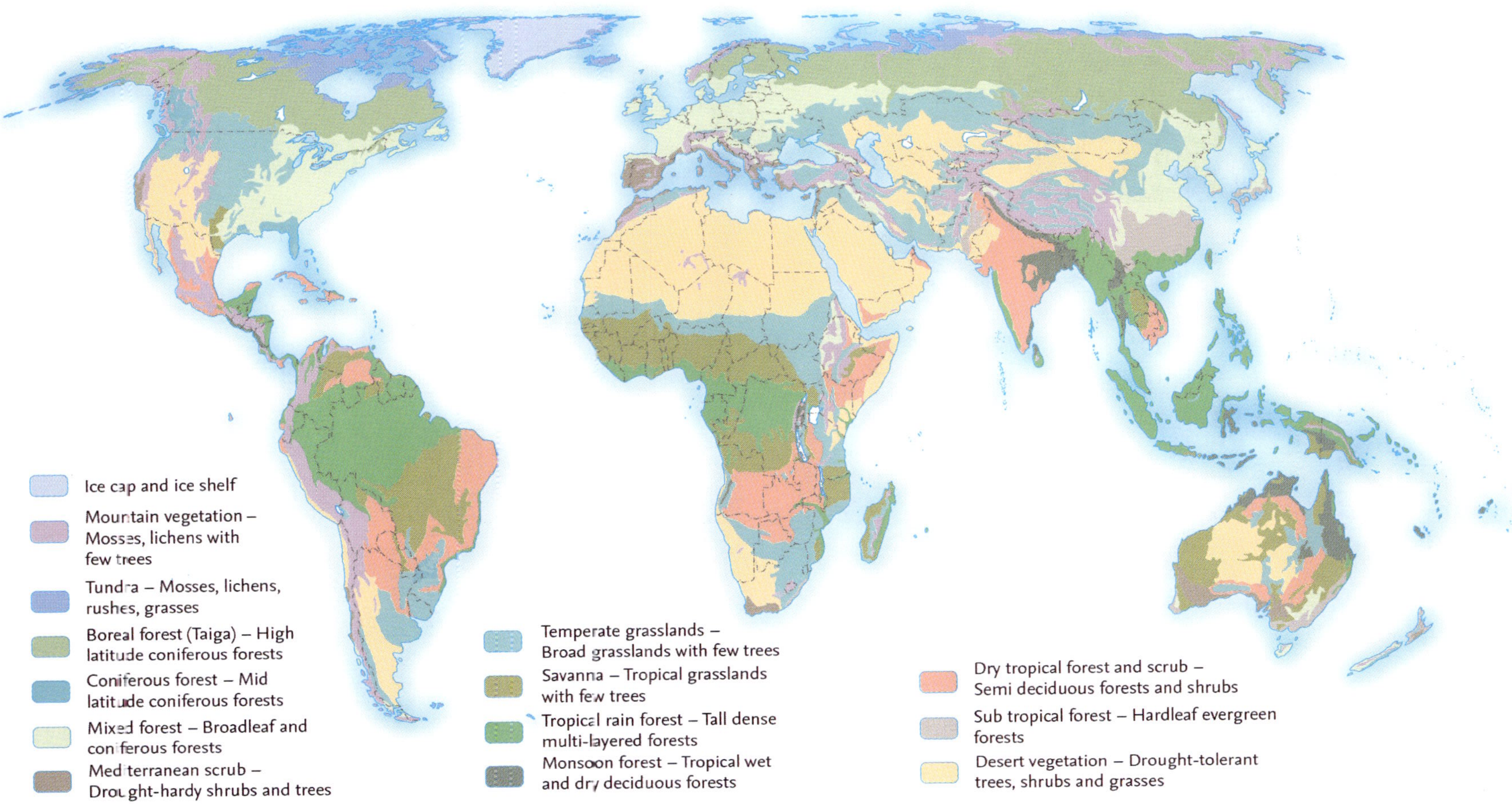

World: Vegetation

Tundra

Tundra vegetation is found in the high latitudes of the northern hemisphere, to the north of the Arctic Circle. Because the region is so cold, the snow cover does not encourage plant growth. Vegetation is sparse and is limited to mosses, lichens and sedges. In the southern parts, some short shrubs grow in the summer season. Short trees such as birches, junipers and willows grow here.

Conservation of Forests

The large-scale cutting of trees during the last few decades has led to ecological imbalances. The removal of forest cover at a large scale is called deforestation. Apart from destruction by humans, other factors such as fire, insects, diseases and storms are responsible for the destruction of natural vegetation. Deforestation has several detrimental effects on our environment, such as loss of habitat for wild animals, loss of fodder for domestic animals and loss of important medicinal plants. The depletion of forest areas has also resulted in excessive carbon-dioxide in the atmosphere, leading to global warming. It is essential to maintain the natural vegetation cover of the planet. Some of the initiatives taken are as follows:

What's in the picture?

a. What do you see in the picture?

b. Prepare a list of products you get from the forests.

c. Do you support the activity shown in the picture? Why or why not?

- Protecting the forest reserves
- Increasing the area under forest cover
- Discouraging the practice of shifting agriculture
- Protection of forest from forest fire

India's bursting population has put a strain on India's forest cover. Most forests are being cleared to accommodate the increasing population, leading to the destruction of habitats and environment in the process. Human activities pose the greatest threat to wildlife and its natural habitat. Hunting and trapping for food by hunters, collectors and poachers has also led to the extinction of many animals. Many species are nearing extinction because of deforestation, destruction of their habitat and indiscriminate hunting. These species include mammals, such as the Indian or the Asiatic cheetah, wild zebu, Indian rhinoceros and Northern Sumatran rhinoceros. CITES is an international body, which stands for the Convention of International Trade in Endangered Species of Wild Fauna and Flora. They prohibit the trade of products made from endangered wildlife. Our government has taken various steps to protect wildlife in the country. National parks and sanctuaries are set up by the government to provide a safe home to wild animals, where they may live and grow in number.

FACT CHECK

World Wildlife Fund (WWF) is an international organization, which promotes the welfare of wildlife. WWF India was established in 1969 to promote the conservation of wildlife in India. The government passed a comprehensive wildlife protection law in 1972, which listed all the animals and birds that are protected.

Apply it!

Hunters occasionally engage in selective hunting of wild animals for recreational purposes. This is called trophy hunting. Do you think this should be allowed? Do some research on the Internet, and write a report on it.

15 LIFE ON LAND

World Connect

Cecil the lion was a major attraction in the Hwange National Park in Matabeleland North, Zimbabwe. In July 2015, he was wounded by an arrow shot by Walter Palmer, an American recreational game hunter. When tracked, it was found that he was killed with a rifle approximately 40 hours later. Two men in Zimbabwe are being prosecuted in relation to the hunt. Since Walter Palmer had a permit, he was not charged with any crime. However, this killing resulted in international media attention and outrage among animal conservationists. This has led to a change in the outlook of the people on the issue of trophy hunting, bringing in more regulations and rules against it.

Skill Builder

21st CENTURY SKILLS

Critical thinking skills: Carbon dioxide is in the air that we breathe. Find out how carbon dioxide helps us and, at the same time, harms us. List the points in your notebook.

Life skills: Climate change is likely to threaten the existence of many animal species; so, preserving habitat for them is very important. Discuss this in class.

Wind up

Natural vegetation

- Forests
  - Tropical rainforest
  - Tropical deciduous forests
  - Temperate deciduous forests
  - Mediterranean forests
  - Coniferous forests
- Grasslands
  - Tropical grasslands
  - Temperate grasslands
- Deserts
  - Sahara, Kalahari, Atacama, Arabian desert, Australian desert
- Tundra
  - Zone of sparse vegetation, high latitudes of northern hemisphere and Arctic Circle

Conservation of forests

- Protecting forest reserves
- Increasing forest cover
- Discouraging shifting agriculture
- Prevention of forest fires

Exercises

A. Choose the correct answers.

1. A tree found in the temperate region.
   a. Mahogany b. Ebony c. Rosewood d. Pine
2. This region in India has equatorial rainforests.
   a. Himalayan region b. Deccan Plateau c. Western Ghats d. Ganga-Brahmaputra Basin

3. The temperate grasslands of North America are called
   a. pampas b. down c. prairies d. veld
4. This plant grows in the desert region.
   a. Beech b. Date palm c. Lichen d. Juniper
5. Coniferous forests are also known as
   a. Taiga b. Tundra c. Mediterranean d. Pampas

B. Write T for true and F for false.

1. A biome is a major ecological community, extending over a large area. ☐
2. Trees in the tropical deciduous forests shed their leaves in the autumn season. ☐
3. Fur-bearing animals are found in the taiga and the tundra. ☐
4. The climate in tropical deciduous forests is marked by alternating spells of warm and dry winters. ☐

C. Give reasons for the following.

1. Tropical rainforests are also equatorial rainforests.
2. Trees of deciduous forests shed their leaves in a particular season.
3. Xerophytic plants are grown in the desert regions.
4. Trees are conical in shape in the taiga.
5. Trees of the Mediterranean region have long roots and have waxy leaves.

D. Answer these questions in brief.

1. What are the different types of natural vegetation found in the world?
2. What type of vegetation and wildlife is found in the coniferous forests?
3. What is tundra?
4. Where is desert vegetation found in the world?
5. What is the full form of CITES?
6. Name the classification of forests depending on when they shed their leaves?

E. Answer these questions in detail.

1. Distinguish between tropical and temperate grasslands
2. What are the initiatives taken to conserve natural vegetation and wildlife?
3. Describe the vegetation and wildlife of Mediterranean forests.
4. Name three animals that are on the verge of extinction because of poaching.
5. Explain what is causing the extinction of animals.

Think Big — Art integration

Prepare a scrapbook containing pictures of natural vegetation and wildlife found in different forests, grasslands and deserts. You may also make use of maps to show the location of each.

Learning Tools

Create your own study guides by compiling the necessary information for swift recap.

Main ideas	Why it matters	Important terms and names
....	....	....
....	....	....
....	....	....
....	....	....
....	....	....
....	....	....
....	....	....
....	....	....
....	....	....
....	....	....
....	....	....
....	....	....
....	....	

Web links:

https://www.vedantu.com/geography/natural-vegetation-and-wildlife

https://edusaint.com/natural-vegetation-and-wild-life/

Last accessed on 31 August 2021

5. Mineral and Power Resources

Warm up

The largest known gold reserve on Earth is the South Deep gold mine in the Witwatersrand Basin in South Africa. Throughout history, it has been subjected to drying out, seawater coverage and flooding and erosion by rivers. In 1852, the first gold deposits were discovered in this basin. This led to the gold rush in South Africa driving many British settlers to lay claim over gold fields in the region. After this discovery, South African gold production went from zero in 1886 to 23 per cent of the total world output in 1896.

Minerals are naturally occurring substances on the Earth. They have a definite and distinctive set of physical properties and chemical composition. Usually minerals do not occur in pure form but are extracted from the earth. The rock or earth from which metal can be obtained profitably is called an ore. Minerals and power resources together form the backbone of industry in any country.

Mining

Minerals rarely occur near the surface of the Earth. They are extracted from deep within the Earth. The process of extraction of minerals from the rocks buried deep inside the Earth's surface is known as mining. A mine is a place where deep holes and tunnels are dug under the ground to obtain a mineral.

Inside a mine

Mining done by excavating the surface to obtain shallow minerals is called opencast mining. Deep bores are dug to obtain minerals deep inside the Earth through shaft mining. Petroleum and natural gas are obtained from the Earth by drilling. Minerals that lie very near to the surface of the Earth are dug out by a process called quarrying.

Types of Minerals

Metals can be metallic or non-metallic based on their physical and chemical properties.

Metallic Minerals

Iron: Iron is the most common and most widely used metal. It is the most important mineral on which industries that require steel depend. Iron and its **alloy**, steel, are used to make machines that run factories, agricultural equipment, transport equipment and items of daily use. Some ores of iron include magnetite, haematite, limonite and siderite.

alloy: a metal that is made by mixing two or more types of metal together

Magnetite has the highest iron content, but haematite is more commonly used. This mineral is widely found in the USA, Russia, China and Sweden. In India, the iron ore is located in Jharkhand, Odisha, Madhya Pradesh, Goa, Karnataka, Maharashtra and Chhattisgarh.

Copper: Copper has often been called the ancient metal as it was the first metal ever to be used by humans. It is one of the most useful and **versatile** metals and conducts electricity better than any other metal, except silver. It is used for tubing and pipes for plumbing and can be made into sheets for roofing. It is also used in manufacturing automobiles, machinery, coins, tools, utensils and even in chemical compounds. Some copper ores include chalcopyrite and covellite. It is also used to make alloys such as bronze, brass and German silver. This mineral is found in Chile in South America, the USA, Russia and Canada. In India, Jharkhand, Rajasthan (Khetri district), Madhya Pradesh and Chhattisgarh are the major producers of copper.

Bauxite: It is the ore of aluminium. Aluminium is a light metal used to make electrical cables and the body of aircraft as it is a good conductor of electricity. It is found in Australia, Jamaica, France and the USA. In India, large deposits of bauxite are found in Jharkhand, Gujarat, Madhya Pradesh, Odisha, Chhattisgarh and Maharashtra.

Manganese: Manganese is obtained from its ores such as manganite and hausmannite. It is used to make steel tougher. It is also used in making alloys to manufacture bleaching powder and electric batteries. It is found in Russia, South Africa and Australia. India's manganese deposits are located in Maharashtra, Madhya Pradesh, Chhattisgarh, Odisha and Karnataka.

Gold: Gold is a precious metal used to make jewellery. It is also used in dentistry and medicine, in coins and medallions and it also acts as a store of value. Gold backs the international monetary system. About half of the world's gold is found in South Africa, with significant amounts distributed in Canada, Japan and the USA. In India, Karnataka (Kolar), Tamil Nadu and Andhra Pradesh are the leading producers of gold.

Uranium: It is a radio-active mineral used in the generation of nuclear power, manufacturing bombs and agriculture in small quantities. It is found in North America, Africa, Australia and India. In India, uranium deposits are found in Jharkhand, Andhra Pradesh and Meghalaya.

Non-metallic Minerals

Diamond: Diamonds are used to make jewellery, abrasives, tools and microelectronic devices. These minerals are found in large quantities in South Africa and Australia. In India, diamonds are mined in Panna, Madhya Pradesh.

Mica: Mica is used in electronic insulators, paint plastics, rubber, and welding rods and as joint cement. It is found in Russia, Finland, South Korea, France and Canada. In India, mica is found in Jharkhand, Rajasthan and Andhra Pradesh.

> **Apply it!** E
>
> Prepare a list of minerals that you use in your everyday routine.

Power Resources

Power is needed for the growth and development of agriculture, industry, transport and communication. Power resources are of two types—conventional and non-conventional. The sources of power, such as coal, petroleum, natural gas and **hydel** or hydroelectric power, are called conventional energy resources. They have limited reserves and are likely to get exhausted. On the other hand, solar energy, wind energy, geothermal energy, nuclear energy, tidal energy and biogas energy are called non-conventional energy sources. They have unlimited reserves.

versatile: able to adapt or be adapted to many different functions or activities; hydel: related to harnessing of energy using the flow or motion of water

Conventional Resources

These traditional resources have been used for a long time. Some resources are non-renewable as they take a long time to be formed. Fossil fuels are energy resources formed within the earth from the remains of plants and animals from millions of years ago. Coal, petroleum and natural gas are examples of fossil fuels.

Coal: Coal is formed from the decayed remains of land plants that were buried under the earth. The coal we are using today was formed millions of years ago. It is used for generating thermal power. Coal is available extensively and acts as an efficient source of electricity. However, it causes pollution and is bulky to transport.

Based on the carbon content, coal is divided into four types:

- Anthracite, which contains more than 90 per cent carbon and emits or gives out little smoke on burning.
- Bituminous, which contains nearly 70 per cent carbon and is the household coal.
- Lignite, also known as brown coal, which contains only 40 per cent of carbon owing to its high moisture content.
- Peat, which consists mainly of vegetable matter and emits a lot of smoke.

The USA, Russia, China, Germany and France are leading producers of coal in the world. Neyveli in Tamil Nadu has vast lignite deposits. Coal is also found in Jharkhand, Chhattisgarh, West Bengal, Assam and Meghalaya.

FACT CHECK

Almost all synthetic fabrics and materials like nylon, polyster, rayon, acrylic that are used today are made from petroleum or natural gas.

Petroleum: Petroleum is a black, greenish liquid found in porous sedimentary rocks or is sometimes trapped between two layers of sedimentary rocks. Compared with coal, petroleum is easier to transport, and the refining of petroleum allows for the extraction of derivatives called

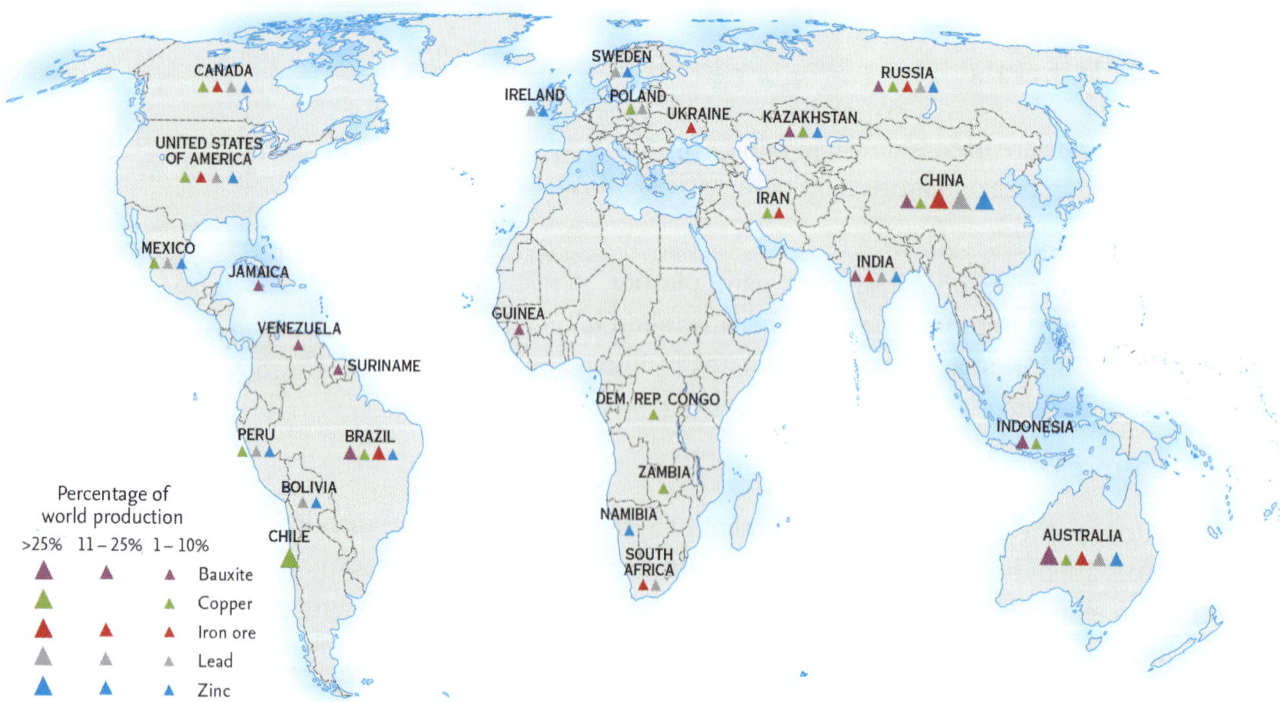

World: Ore Production

petrochemicals like petrol, diesel, wax, plastics and other lubricants. However, petroleum has also been a cause of environmental pollution through oil spills. Petroleum is often referred to as 'black gold'. It is found in large quantities in Iran, Iraq, Kuwait, Saudi Arabia, Qatar, Venezuela, Algeria and the USA. In India, petroleum deposits are found in Mumbai High, Digboi in Assam and Ankeleshwar in Gujarat.

Natural Gas: Natural gas occurs along with petroleum. By-products are used in the agricultural and industrial sectors. Natural gas is advantageous as it is easier to transport, cleaner than coal and cheaper than oil. The main source of natural gas is the relatively shallow stretch in the North Sea, from Lincolnshire to the Netherlands. Gas is transported over great distances by pipelines.

Hydroelectric Power: River water or rainwater stored in dams is made to fall from heights. The falling water flows through pipes inside the dam, over turbine blades placed at the bottom of the dam. The moving blades then turn the generator to produce electricity. This is called hydroelectricity. It is a non-polluting and renewable resource. However, hydroelectric power also has its disadvantages as it causes the displacement of local communities and **inundates** lowlands. The leading producers of hydroelectric power are Paraguay, Norway, Brazil and China.

India: distribution of coal, petroleum and hydroelectric power		
Coal	**Petroleum**	**Hydroelectric Power**
West Bengal, Odisha, Jharkhand, Madhya Pradesh, Chhattisgarh, Andhra Pradesh, Tamil Nadu, Rajasthan, Gujarat	Assam valley, Arunachal Pradesh, Gulf of Khambhat, Mumbai High, river basins of Godavari, Krishna and Kaveri	Himachal Pradesh, Uttarakhand, Punjab, Uttar Pradesh, Maharashtra, Tamil Nadu, Karnataka

Non-conventional Sources of Energy

Conventional energy sources are depleting quickly as there is an increasing demand for energy. Non-conventional energy is abundant, renewable, pollution-free and eco-friendly.

A geothermal region in Iceland

Solar Energy: The Sun is the greatest source of energy for us. Solar water heaters, street lighting, cookers, pumps and solar ponds are becoming popular all over the world. Solar energy is beneficial as it is inexhaustible non-polluting. However, it is expensive to generate.

Wind Energy: Wind is an important source of non-conventional energy. High-speed winds rotate the windmills that are connected to a generator to produce electricity. Construction of wind farms requires a place experiencing constant and steady winds. Wind farms are found in Netherlands, Germany, Denmark, the UK, the USA and Spain.

Geothermal Energy: The energy derived from hot springs and emission of steam, from hot rocks at great depths, is called geothermal energy.

It provides clean electricity and is always available. The major producing countries are the USA, New Zealand, Iceland, Philippines and Central America.

Nuclear power plant

Nuclear Energy: Radioactive metals like uranium and thorium are

inundate: to cover an area of land with a large amount of water used to produce nuclear energy. It is obtained by splitting the nucleus of an atom of a heavy radioactive element. This process is called nuclear fission and releases tremendous energy. The greatest producers of nuclear power are the USA, France, Germany, Sweden, Belgium and Canada.

Tidal Energy: The rise and fall of water in oceans and in the coastal areas is called tide. Tidal energy can be harnessed by building dams at narrow openings of the sea. During high tide, the energy of the waves is used to turn the turbine installed in the dam to produce electricity. The leading producers are France, the UK, Russia, Canada and India.

Biogas: It is generated by using biomass, farm waste such as rice husk and **bagasses**, animal and poultry waste. These have been set up in some villages in the northern plains to fulfil various power needs. It is cheap, easy to operate and makes use of bio waste, which makes it a very efficient source of power.

India: Non-Conventional Sources of Energy			
Nuclear power	**Geothermal energy**	**Solar energy**	**Wind energy**
Tarapur in Maharashtra, Rawatbhata in Rajasthan, Kalapakkam in Tamil Nadu, Narora in Uttar Pradesh, Kakrapar in Gujarat, Kaiga in Karnataka	Manikaran in Himachal Pradesh, Puga in Ladakh	Himachal Pradesh, Ladakh, Rajasthan	Tamil Nadu, Andhra Pradesh, Karnataka, Gujarat, Kerala, Maharashtra, Lakshadweep

Conservation of Mineral and Power Resources

Continuous mining and wasteful use of minerals and power resources may lead to their exhaustion. Therefore, it is necessary to use them economically and save them for the future generations.

Some of the methods of conserving power resources are as follows:

- Minimize the use of fossil fuels
- Save electricity
- Emphasize on the increased use of the renewable and alternative sources of power.

Everything we have, and everything we use, comes from our natural resources. We must use them wisely and treat them with respect.

What's in the picture?

Identify the picture and write point-wise views on it.

World Connect

Niyzanei Eshkol, an elementary school in Gaza, began operating an electrical system powered by solar energy, to completely meet the school's needs. Months were taken initially, for planning and construction, after which the installation was successful. This follows after the worst fuel shortage experienced by the region in history. Cross-border tunnels, which were used for fuel supply into Gaza, had been destroyed due to the ongoing conflict in this region. Today, solar panels is the only solution to Gaza's population.

bagasse: the leftover dry residue after the extraction of juice from sugarcane

Skill Builder

21st CENTURY SKILLS

Critical-thinking skills: What is the gold rush? What do you think gives way to gold rush?

Life skills: Make a list of the features found in a house and write down which material these features are made of.

Information literacy: Find out and name three minerals that are an important part of our daily diet.

Wind up

- Conservation of natural resources
  - Minimizing the use of fossil fuels
  - Saving electricity
  - Using alternative energy
- Mineral resources
  - Metallic minerals: Iron, copper, bauxite, manganese, gold, uranium
  - Non-metallic minerals: Diamond, mica
- Power resources
  - Conventional sources: Coal, petroleum, natural gas, hydroelectric power
  - Non-conventional sources: Solar energy, wind energy, geothermal energy, nuclear energy, tidal energy, biogas

Exercises

A. Fill in the blanks.

1. Iron is a .... mineral.
2. Uranium is a .... mineral.
3. .... is the best quality coal.
4. All minerals have a definite .... composition.
5. Wind farms require winds that are .... and ....

B. Choose the correct answers.

1. Minerals found here are not accessible.
   a. Greenland b. Serbia c. Antarctica d. Japan
2. Natural gas occurs along with
   a. manganese b. limestone c. coal d. petroleum
3. An example of a mineral fuel is
   a. coal b. bauxite c. iron d. gold
4. Minerals found near the Earth's surface are taken out by the process of
   a. quarrying b. drilling c. digging d. weathering
5. Extraction of minerals is carried out by the process of
   a. weathering b. clearing forests c. clearing land d. mining

C. Give reasons.

1. Copper is a versatile metal.
2. Conventional resources are depleting fast.

3. Manganese is used in iron and steel industry.
4. Petroleum is referred to as black gold.
5. We need to conserve the conventional sources of energy.

D. Answer these questions in brief.

1. What are minerals?
2. What is the advantage of using non-conventional resources?
3. Name two methods of conserving power resources.
4. What is mining? Mention the types of mining.
5. What is tidal energy?

E. Answer these questions in detail.

1. How is coal formed? Explain the properties of each type of coal.
2. Give a brief account of the mineral resources of India.
3. What is meant by non-conventional source of energy? Explain why there is a need to switch from conventional to non-conventional sources of power.
4. How is hydroelectric power generated?

Think Big

English fun

Not all of our clothes are made of organic materials. Think about some of your clothes items and list down the materials that are used to make them. You can take help from the labels on your clothing. What materials are your buttons or zips made of? List at least five of these.

Learning Tools

Mineral and power resources

Mining
....
....

Conservation of mineral and power resources
....
....
....

Types of minerals
→ ....
→ ....
→ ....
→ ....

Power resources

Conventional	Non-conventional
....	....
....	....
....	....
....	....

Web links:

https://www.nios.ac.in/media/documents/316courseE/ch23.pdf
https://www.britannica.com/place/India/Resources-and-power

Last accessed on 31 August 2021

6. Agricultural Practices

Warm up

Rajiv stays in a small village in Punjab. He owns two hectares of land on which he farms and has two cows. The land he owns is very fertile and he grows both wheat and paddy. He grows vegetables in between the cropping seasons. Various schemes offered by the government and trainings regarding new developments in agriculture are occasionally conducted. Wells and canals are available to irrigate the field. He, along with his farmer friends, has bought a tractor with which he ploughs his land. He also uses a few traditional methods mainly during the harvesting time. He sells only a small part of his produce in the nearby field called mandi. The rest is used for his family consumption. He also needs to take care of his cow as he sells the milk in the nearby milk cooperative. A municipal cooperative worker told him about the ways he can take care of his cattle. The government helps Rajiv and all his farmer friends in many ways.

Agriculture is the most important and the oldest occupation of human beings. It involves farming and the methods used to raise and look after crops and livestock. Agriculture is a combination of two Latin words, *ager* meaning field and *cultura* meaning cultvation. In India, agriculture is a predominant occupation for a large percentage of the population.

Different economic activities can be broadly grouped as primary, secondary and tertiary. Primary activities involve obtaining and procuring raw materials from the natural environment, for example, fishing and farming. Secondary activities involve the processing of raw materials, for example, manufacturing of steel and cloth weaving. Tertiary activities include all the services that provide support to primary and secondary activities, for example, transport and banking.

Factors Affecting Agriculture

There are a number of factors that affect agricultural practice, or farming, in different parts of the world.

Relief: This includes the physical features of an area of land, especially its rivers and mountains. Arable land is a land used for farming. Crops that need thick layers of soil, for example, rice and wheat, cannot be grown on mountain slopes. Mountain slopes are good for tea and coffee cultivation.

Climate: Hot and humid climate favours agriculture. Thus, in the equatorial and tropical regions, crops are cultivated almost throughout the year. In the temperate regions, the temperature is too low for plant growth.

Soil: Soil acts as a medium to supply moisture and nutrients to the plant. Each soil type with its variety of nutrients and minerals is suitable for the production of particular crops. Alluvial soil is the most fertile soil. Rice grows best on clayey alluvial soils, while black lava soil is suitable for cotton.

Human factors: In addition to these natural factors, several human-made factors, such as infrastructure, availability of capital and governmental policies decide the type of agriculture practised in an area.

Types of Farming

Farming can be classified into subsistence farming and commercial farming on the basis of geographical conditions, demand, labour and technology.

Subsistence Farming

When the produce is consumed by the farmer and his family, or exchanged and sold amongst a small group, it is known as subsistence agriculture. Farms are small in size, and yields are low. Subsistence agriculture can be sedentary, that is, practised in one place or shifting, that is, moving from place to place. Subsistence farming is further classified as primitive subsistence farming and intensive subsistence farming.

What's in the picture?

What do you see in the picture? Write a note on the type of farming practice that you see there.

Primitive subsistence farming: This type of subsistence farming involves shifting cultivation and nomadic herding. It is largely dependent on rainfall and natural fertility of the soil.

Shifting cultivations is a primitive method of farming. It is also known as slash and burn agriculture. It is practised by tribes living in regions near the equator and the tropics. The people clear the forest by cutting and burning an area. The ash produced by burning vegetation increases the fertility of the soil. Crops are grown in these forest clearings with primitive tools such as digging sticks and hoes. Mostly, tuber crops such as tapioca, cassava, manioc and yams are grown along with maize, millets, beans and bananas. Crops are grown in the same patch of land for two to three years after which the land becomes infertile. Shifting cultivation leads to deforestation and soil erosion.

Nomadic herding is mainly practised in the semi-arid and arid regions of Sahara in Africa, Central Asia and in some parts of India, like Rajasthan and Jammu and Kashmir. Herders move from one place to another along the defined routes with their animal for fodder and water. The movement is in accordance to the climatic conditions and terrain presented by a particular region. The animals reared are sheep, goats, camel and yaks. These animals provide food such as milk and meat. They also provide wool and hide, which are used to make clothes and shelter. Nomadic herders do not have permanent dwellings, they mostly live in tents, which can be dismantled and carried from place to place.

Intensive Subsistence Agriculture: In intensive farming, the farmer tries to get the maximum possible output from a small plot of land. The farmer uses simple tools and abundant human labour. Some chemical inputs and irrigation methods are also used to increase production. This type of farming is mostly practised in the densely populated countries of the monsoon region. Due to a long growing season and fertile soil, the farmer can grow two or three crops annually on the same land. The most important crop is rice. The other cultivated crops are wheat, maize, sugarcane, pulses and oilseeds.

Geography skills

Working from this map, use different colours and shade the regions practising the different types of farming on an outline map of the world.

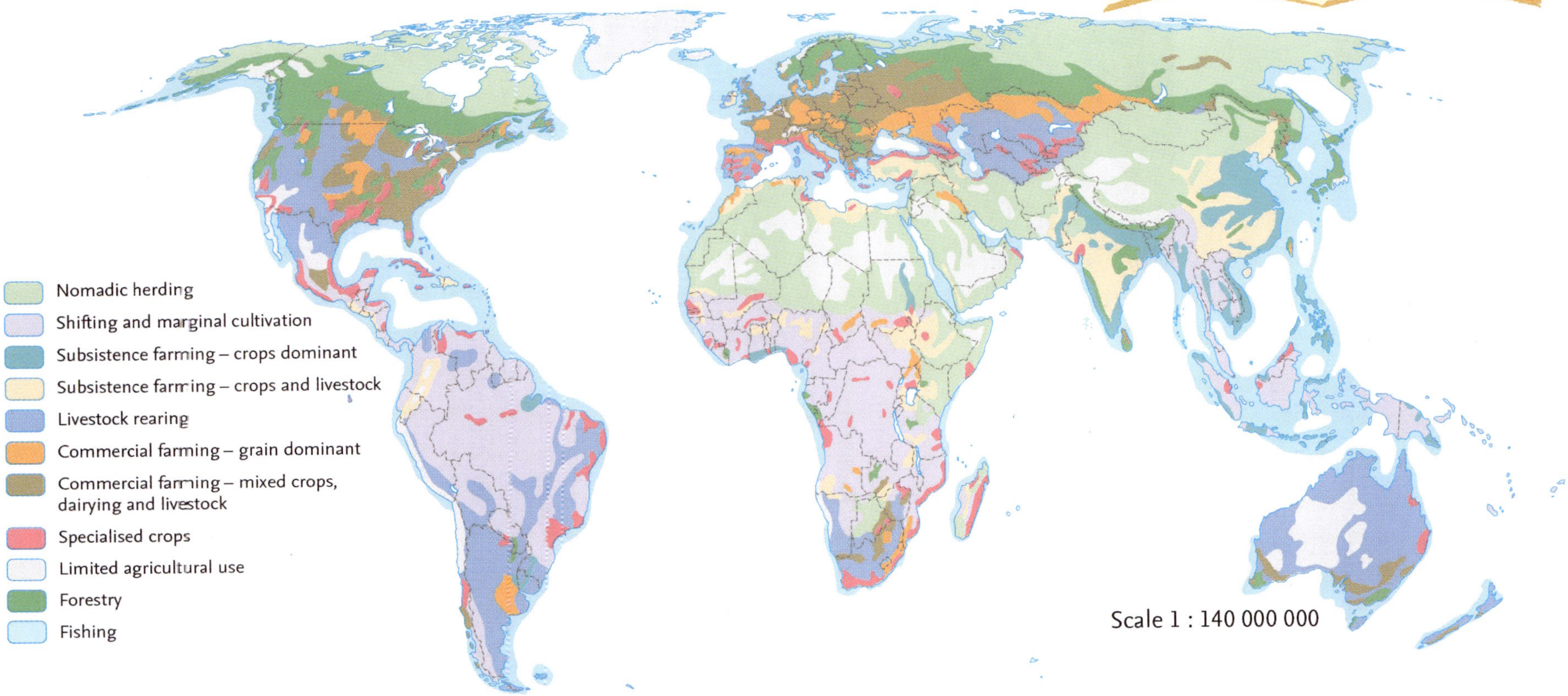

Types of agricultural practices around the world

Commercial Farming

When the scale of farming operations are large and the products are grown in large quantities and sold to larger and far-off markets, it is known as commercial agriculture. There are different types of commercial agriculture practised in the world. Some of them are extensive commercial agriculture, plantation agriculture, mixed farming and dairy farming.

Extensive Commercial Agriculture: This type of agriculture is practised on a commercial scale, and crops are grown for sale in the market. It is common in regions where there is abundant land but very sparse population, particularly in the mid-latitude temperate grasslands—the prairies of North America, the pampas of Argentina, the steppes of Eurasia and the downs of Australia. The main crops grown are wheat and maize, corn, barley, oats, rye and cotton.

Plantation Agriculture: This is a type of commercial agriculture with specialization in one single crop. This is mostly practised in the tropical and sub-tropical regions. The farms, called estates, are very large. Cheap and skilled labour and huge capital investments are required. This method ensures that high-quality crops will be produced. The crop is processed before being sent to the market for sale. The estates are well connected to ports and railroads. The entire agricultural system is scientifically managed, like a factory. Plantation agriculture involves cultivation of crops like banana, coffee, tea, cashew and rubber.

A tea plantation in Assam

Mixed Farming: In this type of farming, crops are grown and animals are reared on the same farmland. Various crops, such as cereals and vegetables are grown and the farmers keep dairy animals to obtain milk. The farm size is moderate, and farming is done intensively. The use of modern machinery and improved seeds ensure a high yield. Crop rotation is practised to retain soil fertility. Cereal crops like wheat, maize and barley, along with root crops like potatoes and turnips and legumes like peas and beans, are grown. Fodder crops, such as alfalfa and lucerne, are grown for animals, and sometimes, poultry is kept. Efficient methods of farming, quick means of transport and a ready market in the nearby populated areas ensure good returns for the farmers. This is mostly practised in the thickly populated areas of Europe, eastern USA, Argentina, south-east Australia, New Zealand and South Africa.

Dairy Farming: The farming practice where cattle are reared for milk and milk products, which are sold to the urban centres, is known as dairy farming. The farms are scientifically maintained and machines perform all activities. Manual labour is limited as machines perform the daily task of milking cows and bottling the milk. The countries known for their dairy products are Australia, New Zealand, Denmark, Switzerland and the Netherlands.

Cattle ranches rear cattle and sheep for meat. A ranch is an area of land developed for the practice of grazing and raising of livestock. Western USA, Canada, Latin America and South America are known for such ranches. Ranches are known as 'stations' in Australia and 'runs' in New Zealand.

FACT CHECK

According to the FAO world agriculture statistics, 2010, India is the world's largest producer of many fresh fruits and vegetables, milk, major spices, select fibrous crops such as jute, staples such as millets and castor oil seed.

Truck Farming, Market Gardening and Horticulture

Large populations in big cities leave no space for traditional cultivation of fruits and vegetables within their boundaries. Market gardens are usually located outside towns and cities, where the soil and climate are favourable and land is available. Besides a market, this form of agriculture requires an efficient transport system for quick movement of the perishable produce. Refrigerated trucks with storage facilities are often used. This type of farming is called truck farming. Horticulture is the term used for special farming of fruits and flowers in the city outskirts. All densely populated urban centres get their daily needs fulfilled through this type of farming.

Dairy farmers, India

World Connect

According to the Brazilian Association of Collective Health, about 70 per cent of the food consumed by Brazilians is contaminated by agrochemicals. At least one-third of the agrochemicals used in Brazil have been banned in the European Union and the United States as these have detrimental impacts on human health. These are said to cause birth defects and hamper the immune system of large populations in Brazil. This came after a study conducted by the World Health Organization, which discovered that glyphosate, which is a key ingredient in pesticides and fertilizers, causes cancer.

Skill Builder

21st CENTURY SKILLS

Life skills: Imagine yourself as a worker in one of the dairy farms of Australia. Write an article stating how you spend every day in the same.

Information literacy: What is sustainable agriculture? Name the methods of sustainable agriculture.

Critical thinking skills: What are the various agricultural techniques that are environment friendly?

Wind up

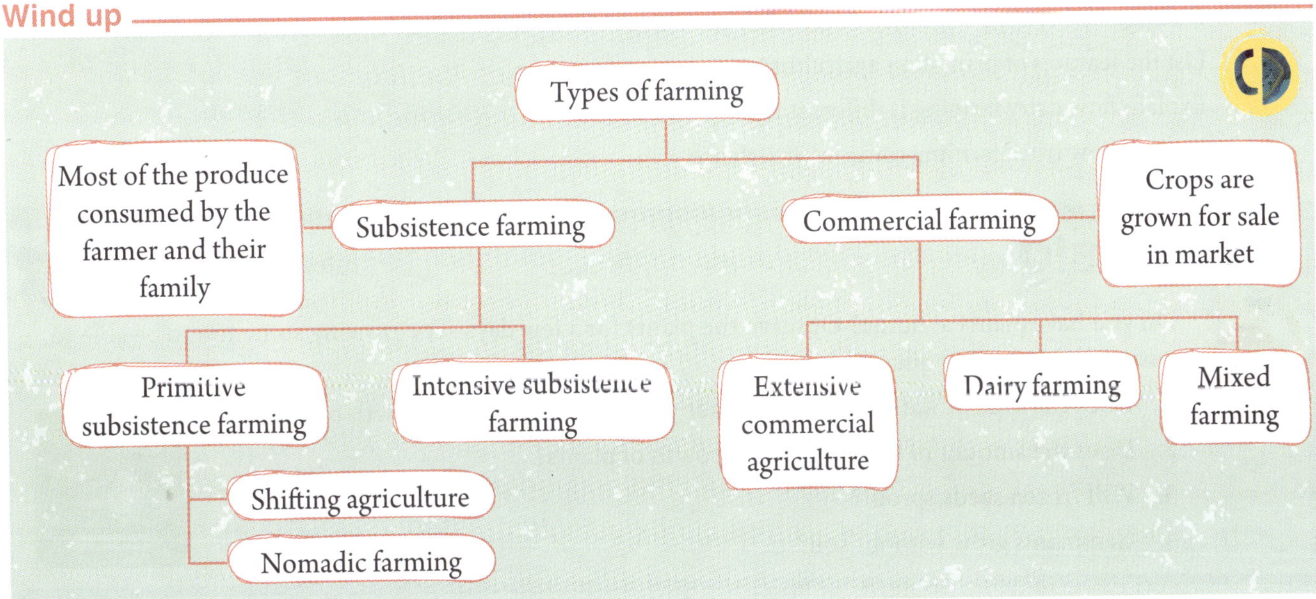

Exercises

A. Fill in the blanks.

1. Cattle ranches are features of .... farming.
2. .... activities involve the processing of raw materials.
3. When the scale of farming operations are large and the products are grown in large quantities, it is known as .... agriculture.
4. Shifting cultivation is a .... method of farming.

B. Choose the correct answers.

1. A factor that affects agricultural practice is
   a. slope b. relief c. irrigation d. machinery
2. Extensive commercial agriculture is practised in
   a. High-latitude grasslands b. Tropical grasslands c. Temperate grasslands d. Temperate deciduous forest
3. An example of tertiary activity is
   a. banking b. hunting c. agriculture d. fishing
4. Fishing is an example of
   a. primary activity b. secondary activity c. tertiary activity d. agriculture activity
5. The word 'agriculture' has been derived from the Latin word
   a. *ageri* b. *ager* c. *agri* d. *agar*

C. Answer these questions in brief.

1. What is agriculture?
2. What is mixed farming?
3. What is truck farming?
4. What is horticulture?
5. Classify the types of farming.

D. Answer these questions in detail.

1. Distinguish between intensive and extensive farming.
2. Distinguish between subsistence agriculture and commercial agriculture.
3. List the features of plantation agriculture.
4. Explain how dairy farming is different from mixed farming.
5. Explain how truck farming came into existence.

Think Big Integrate with science

Do you have plants at home? Observe the plants for a few days. Try growing some too to be able to answer the following questions.

1. Does the type of water you use to water your plants affect the growth of plants?
2. Does the amount of light affect the growth of plants?
3. Will frozen seeds sprout?
4. Can plants grow without soil?

15 LIFE ON LAND

Learning Tools

Use this foldable to recall whatever you have learnt about in the chapter.

1. Fold a sheet of paper in half.
2. Fold this long rectangle in half.
3. Fold both ends back.
4. On the side, make vertical cuts through one thickness of paper, forming four tabs.

   Use this book for data occurring in fours.

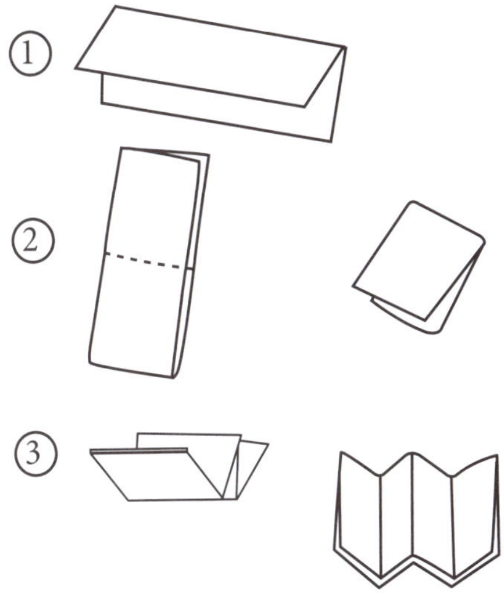

Web links:

https://www.tractorjunction.com/blog/types-of-farming-in-india-procedure-benefits-and-role/

Last accessed on 31 August 2021

7. Major Crops

Warm up

The Mesoamericans collected rubber latex from the sap of trees in a bucket and then dried it. To make shoes, they would dip their feet in the latex and allow it to dry. After several dips and dryings, they could peel a shoe from their feet. Next they smoked their new rubber shoes to harden them. The process was used to make rubber items around the 1800s. Let us learn more about not only rubber but also other important crops that help us satisfy our hunger, nutritional requirements, clothes, bags, etc.

We have studied in the previous chapter about how climatic factors influence agriculture. Every crop needs a particular set of climatic conditions to grow well. In this chapter, we will learn about the major crops, their physical requirements and regions where they grow.

Crops are classified as food crops, cash crops, beverage crops and fibre crops.

Food Crops

The crops grown as food to feed people are called food crops. They include vegetables, cereals, legumes, seeds and nuts. They are cultivated on 60 per cent of world's agricultural land.

Rice is one of the major food or cereal crops of the world. It is the staple diet of people living in the tropical and sub-tropical regions. Rice requires a temperature of about 25°C at the time of sowing. An annual rainfall of more than 100 cm is ideal for its growth. It requires plenty of water; hence, alluvial clayey soil is best suited for growing rice as it holds stagnant water.

A farmer spreads fertilizer in a rice field

Wheat is the staple crop of the western world and the cooler regions. This crop is grown in areas located in the temperate regions of the world, where extensive farming is practised. It requires a temperature of 10°C at the time of sowing and around 15°C at the time of ripening. Places that receive rainfall of between 50 cm to 75 cm are ideal for growing wheat. The weather should be cool and moist at the time of growing, while bright sunshine is required at the time of ripening. Wheat generally grows in well-drained loamy soils. Most work in the wheat growing regions of the mid-latitudes is carried out with machines. In the tropical regions, manual labour is mostly needed.

Maize was first grown by the Incas and the Aztecs, the civilizations of Americas. It is still the staple food of the people of Latin America. It is also known as corn. Maize requires a temperature of about 20°C during the growing period, with an average rainfall of about 50–75 cm. Fertile and well drained soils such as loam, alluvium and red soils are ideal for growing this crop.

Millets is a collective name given to coarse grains such as jowar, bajra and ragi. These are grown in regions with moderate to high temperatures, low rainfall and less fertile soils. The three major millets grown in India are jowar, bajra and ragi.

Millets

Cash Crops

Also known as commercial crops, they are grown for the sole purpose of selling the produce in the markets. They are not grown as a source of food but mainly as raw material for industries.

Sugarcane is a tropical crop and is a major source of sugar. It grows well from the cuttings of a healthy sugarcane stem, and the same root is used for getting more than one crop.

Sugarcane is grown at a temperature of 21°C–27°C and requires an approximate amount of produce in the markets. It grows well in loamy or alluvial soil as these are fertile and well drained. There should be adequate supplies of chemical fertilizers and insecticides as sugarcane is a soil-exhausting crop. It also requires labour from sowing to harvesting season.

Rubber is prepared from the sap of the rubber tree. It is used in the manufacture of tyres and tubes for vehicles, waterproofing and insulating. Rubber is a plantation crop that grows well in places with a temperature of about 30°C. About 200 cm or more of rainfall, which is evenly distributed throughout the year, is ideal for this crop. It requires bright sunshine, humid climate and the absence of strong winds to grow well. The plant generally requires well-drained, weathered soil, like laterite or alluvial soils. Rubber is obtained from the milky fluid called latex obtained from rubber trees. Latex is collected in small cups as it trickles down slowly from the cuts made in the bark of a rubber tree. This juice is later purified, dried, made into rubber sheets and then taken to the factory.

A rubber tree

Fibre Crops

Cotton is the most important fibre crop as it the most widely used fibre in clothing. Cotton is grown in places with high temperatures of about 27°C during the growing period, with 210 frost-free days. Rainfall should be around 75 cm. There should be bright sunshine during the growing period. This crop grows well in well-drained loamy soil, which is capable of retaining moisture, and black cotton soil. A lot of labour is required for picking cotton.

Jute is known as 'the golden fibre' because of its yellow colour and versatile use. It is widely used in the agricultural and manufacturing sectors. This crop grows well at a temperature of 25°C or more, with an average rainfall of over 150 cm. Alluvial soils, rich in salts, are ideal for growing jute. The fertile alluvial soils of the flood plains and deltas are ideal as they are renewed by the annual floods.

Apply it! E

List some of the problems faced by farmers in India during the lockdown imposed in 2020 due to the COVID-19 pandemic.

Beverage Crops

Tea, the most popular beverage, is a tropical crop. It is obtained from the leaves of the tea plant, which is basically a tropical bush. It grows at a temperature of about 25°C and requires an annual rainfall of 150–200 cm well distributed throughout the year. Tea cannot withstand stagnant water and frost. Hence, it requires deep, well-drained, fertile loamy soil. Hill slopes are ideal sites for tea gardens, which are known as tea estates. Tea cultivation requires manual labour for the plucking of tea leaves. China is the largest producer of tea in the world.

What's in the picture?

a. Which crop do you see in the picture?

b. Find out the uses of the crop shown.

Coffee is endemic to Africa and the Ethiopian Highlands. Brazil is the largest producer of coffee in the world. The coffee brew is made from coffee beans, after they are picked, roasted and ground. There are three main varieties—arabica, robusta and liberica. Coffee grows well in places with an average temperature of 14°C to 26°C, with rainfall not exceeding 150 cm. Rich porous soils, and even volcanic soils, are ideal for growing coffee as they are well drained, with no stagnant water and have a high degree of fertility.

Distribution of Crops

Crops	Leading Producers in World	Leading Producers in India
Food Crops		
Rice	India, China, Japan, Sri Lanka, Indonesia, Philippines, Egypt, eastern USA	Ganga valley, hill slopes of north-eastern states, West Bengal, Andhra Pradesh, Tamil Nadu, Bihar, Odisha, Assam, Uttar Pradesh, Punjab and Haryana.
Wheat	The USA, Canada, Russia, Australia, China, Argentina, India	Punjab, Haryana, Uttar Pradesh, Madhya Pradesh, Bihar
Maize	The USA, Canada, China, Russia, Brazil, Mexico, Argentina, South America	Bihar, Uttar Pradesh, Karnataka, Madhya Pradesh, Andhra Pradesh and Telangana
Millets	India, China, the USA, Niger, Argentina, Nigeria	Karnataka, Maharashtra, Rajasthan, Uttar Pradesh, Tamil Nadu, Madhya Pradesh
Cash Crops		
Sugarcane	Brazil, India, Cuba, China, Thailand, Mexico, the USA	Uttar Pradesh, Maharashtra, Tamil Nadu, Andhra Pradesh, Karnataka Bihar, Punjab and Haryana
Rubber	Malaysia, Thailand, Sri Lanka, Indonesia, Brazil, India	Kerala, Karnataka, Tamil Nadu, Kerala, Andaman and Nicobar
Cotton	The USA, Egypt, Mexico, China, Pakistan, Brazil, Uzbekistan, India	Maharashtra, Gujarat, Andhra Pradesh, Karnataka, Tamil Nadu
Jute	Bangladesh, India, Thailand, Brazil, China	Ganga-Brahmaputra delta, West Bengal, Assam, Bihar, Odisha, Meghalaya, Tripura
Beverage Crops		
Tea	China, India, Sri Lanka, Kenya, Uganda, Japan, Indonesia, Bangladesh	Assam, West Bengal, Kerala, Tamil Nadu, Himachal Pradesh, Uttarakhand
Coffee	Brazil, Colombia, Venezuela, Ecuador, Peru, Mexico, El Salvador, Jamaica, Ivory Coast, Kenya, Uganda, India	Tropical highlands of Karnataka and Tamil Nadu, Kerala

Agricultural Development

Most of the countries in the world are making sincere efforts to increase crop production to meet the needs of the increasing population. This can be achieved through increasing land under cultivation, growing more than one crop in a year, improving irrigation facilities, using high-yielding varieties of seeds and using organic and chemical fertilizers.

World Connect

The European Union, along with the Indian government, has started a new project called Water4Crops. The research shows that using treated wastewater for irrigation increases yields in crops such as okra and brinjal. Wastewater from domestic and industrial sources can be recycled to provide assistance to farmers, industries, researchers and government organizations. Eleven Indian, and twenty-one EU organizations, collaborated to develop domestic wastewater treatment technologies suitable for rural areas. Over a period of four years, since the initiation of the project, these organizations are looking forward to scaling up the project by integrating it with the Mahatma Gandhi National Rural Employment Guarantee Scheme and corporate social responsibility schemes of companies.

Skill Builder

21ST CENTURY SKILLS

Critical thinking skills: What are the major causes of farmer suicides in India?

Life skills: Find out the difference between the lifestyle of farmers in the USA and India on the basis of pictures collected from magazines, books, newspapers and the Internet.

Information literacy: We all love chocolates. But, do we know where it comes from? Do some research and find out which plant chocolate is made from, which countries are its major producers and the climatic conditions under which it grows well.

Wind up

Major crops

- Food crops
  - Crops grown as food to feed people
  - Rice, wheat, maize, millets
- Cash crops
  - Grown for sole purpose of selling in the markets
  - Sugarcane, rubber
- Beverage crops
  - Crops that are used to make beverages
  - Tea, coffee
- Fibre crops
  - Crops that are used to make beverages
  - Cotton, jute

Exercises

A. Choose the correct answers.

1. Golden fibre refers to
   a. tea b. cotton c. jute d. maize
2. Leading producer of coffee
   a. Brazil b. India c. Russia d. Mexico
3. Which of the following is not a variety of coffee?
   a. Liberica b. Arabica c. Inca d. Robusta
4. Name the staple diet of tropical and sub-tropical regions.
   a. wheat b. rice c. jute d. coffee
5. Which of these is not a cash crop?
   a. rubber b. coffee c. rice d. tea

B. Fill in the blanks.

1. Cotton cultivation requires .... number of frost-free days.
2. Hill slopes are ideal sites for .... gardens.
3. .... and .... are fibre crops.
4. Tea is a major .... crop in India.
5. Wheat thrives best in well-drained .... soil.
6. The three major millets in India are ...., ... and ....

C. Give reasons.

1. Tea gardens are grown on hill slopes.
2. Coffee is grown on tropical hills.
3. Jute is known as 'Golden Fibre'.
4. Millets are known as 'Dry Crops'.
5. Wheat is grown in temperate regions.
6. Clayey soils are best for rice cultivation.

D. Answer these questions in brief.

1. What are millets?
2. Name two beverage crops.
3. What type of soil is suitable for cotton cultivation?
4. Where is rice cultivated in India and the world?
5. What climatic conditions are required in to grow wheat?
6. What are food crops? Give two examples

E. Answer these questions in detail.

1. What are the conditions necessary for rice cultivation?
2. Briefly describe the conditions required to cultivate fibre crops.
3. Name the two major beverage crops. Give an account of their geographical requirements and world distribution.
4. What are the conditions necessary for sugarcane cultivation?
5. What is latex? How does it lead to the production of rubber?

Think Big

English fun

A number of cotton cultivating farmers in Maharashtra and other farmers in India die by suicide every year. Write an article to be published in the newspaper highlighting the difficulties faced by farmers in our country.

Learning Tools

Fill up this table to recap what you have learnt in the chapter.

Food crops (definition):	**Crops and requirements for growth**	**Distribution in the world**
Cash crops		
Fibre crops		
Beverage crops		
Agricultural development		

Web links:

http://www.fao.org/india/fao-in-india/india-at-a-glance/en/
https://farmer.gov.in/M_cropstaticswheat.aspx
Last accessed on 31 August 2021

8. Manufacturing Industries

Warm up

Have you ever wondered where the goods that you use in your everyday routine come from? How do industries manufacture car equipment? It is intriguing if you wonder how industries manufacture all this! In this chapter, we will discuss the manufacturing industries in our country. We will look at the different aspects of manufacturing and the contribution and classification of the industries.

Manufacturing industries are considered the backbone of economic and social development in today's world. Export of manufactured goods expands trade and commerce, which significantly helps in the modernization of agriculture and reduces the heavy dependence of people on agricultural income by providing jobs. Also, manufacturing industries produce such a range of goods that allow us to lead comfortable lives. Everything that we use today has been manufactured in some part of our country and the world.

Classification of Industries

Industries are classified on the basis of their size, raw materials, end products and ownership.

Basket-weaving

On the Basis of Size

Based on size, industries can be classified into three types—cottage, small scale and large scale.

When an industry employs people in small family set-ups, using hereditary craftsmanship, the industry is termed as cottage industry. It is usually a family or a household unit where a special skill helps create products for household use, and sometimes, for use in some other industry. They invest very less capital, use local raw materials and simple tools with practically no power. Most products are produced by hand, and the craftsmen involved are called artisans. They sell their products in the local markets. Products of cottage industries largely include pottery, baskets, textiles and jewellery.

Small-scale industries use power-driven machines. Raw materials are obtained from outside, and goods are sold through traders. They are generally owned by an individual and employ a small number of labourers. They use less capital and technology. Small-scale industries play an important role in the developing countries. They produce paper goods, toys, furniture and machine parts.

Large-scale industries use heavy, power-driven machines, huge capital investment, thousands of labourers and have a complex management system. They bring in raw materials from far-off places and send the finished products to distant markets. Examples are iron and steel industry, textile mills, transport equipment and petrochemicals.

On the Basis of Ownership

On the basis of the nature of ownership, industries can be classified into public sector, private sector, joint sector and cooperative sector.

Public sector industries are owned and managed by the central or state governments or their agencies. Bhilai Steel Plant and Bharat Heavy Electricals Limited are examples of public sector industries. Private sector industries are owned and managed by an individual or a group of individuals. Reliance Industries, Tata Steel and Hindustan Motors are private sector industries. Joint Sector industries are owned and managed jointly by private firms and government agencies. Examples are Oil India Limited and Gujarat Alkalies. Cooperative sector industries are owned and managed by a group of people who form their own cooperative society. They are generally producers of raw materials. Such organizations keep in mind the interest of the producers of raw materials and keep the middlemen away. Examples are Anand Milk Union Limited (AMUL), Karnataka Milk Federation, Nirmal Ujjwal Credit Cooperative, Indian Farmers Fertilizers Cooperative Limited, etc.

On the Basis of Raw Materials

According to the source of the raw materials, industries can be classified into five types.

Packed coils of steel sheet in a steel mill

Agro-based industries obtain materials from agriculture. Examples are cotton and jute textiles, sugar and food processing industries. Mineral-based industries obtain raw materials from rocks and minerals. Examples are iron and steel, aluminium and cement industries. Pastoral-based industries obtain raw materials from animals such as sheep, goats and cows. These industries make use of skin, bones, milk, flesh and horns of the livestock. Woollen textiles, leather goods and dairy products are pastoral-based industries. Marine-based industries obtain raw materials from seas and oceans. Examples are processing of sea food and manufacturing fish oil. Forest-based industries obtain raw materials from plants, trees and bushes. Some examples are paper, cardboard, pharmaceuticals and furniture.

On the Basis of Output or End-Product

According to the nature of the end-products, industries are classified into two types.

Paper and pulp mill

The industries whose finished products are used as raw materials for other industries are basic industries. Iron and steel is a basic industry as its products are used for manufacturing machines or parts of machinery, automobiles, etc. Consumer goods industries are the ones where finished products are directly used by consumers. Examples are sugar, paper, cosmetics and automobiles.

Factors Influencing the Location of Industries

There are specific factors that are assessed in detail, before locating and establishing an industry. These factors are vital for the existence and success of any industry.

Availability of raw material: It is an important factor in deciding the location of an industry. If the raw material is heavy and bulky and cannot be transported easily and cheaply over long distances, then the industry is located closer to the raw material. For example, in iron and steel industries, iron ore and coal are both bulky materials. Therefore, steel plants are located near iron ore and coal mines. In India, most steel plants are located in the coal and iron ore belt of Chota Nagpur Plateau.

Availability of power: Energy is a critical input for industries. Energy can be thermal, hydel or nuclear. A constant and steady supply of electricity is necessary to run the machinery. Electricity can be easily transmitted to long distances. Hence, the industries that require abundant electricity are located near the source of power. For example, the aluminium industry, which requires a lot of electricity, is located near a power-generating unit.

Green Earth

Human consumption of natural resources per annum has increased from around 1 tonne in hunter–gatherer societies to 15–30 tonnes in modern industrialized nations.

Labour: Industries require both manual labour (unskilled) and skilled (qualified and trained) workers. Unskilled labour is usually cheap and easily available in the densely populated regions. Agro-based industries are labour intensive. Skilled workers include technicians, engineers and managers. Certain industries have developed primarily based on the presence of skilled labour as the watch-making industry of Switzerland.

Transport: Raw materials and finished products both require an efficient means of transportation. Roads, railway junctions and port towns are major industrial centres. Mumbai and Kolkata in India and Osaka in Japan are good examples. Also, the northern plains of India have good roads and railways. Therefore, they have many industrial towns.

Market: Nearness to the market is essential for the quick sale of manufactured goods. For example, woollen goods do well in cold climates, in places like Ludhiana in Punjab, which are closer to Kashmir. Perishable goods like dairy and food items also need to be located near the market.

Capital: To establish an industry, one needs a large amount of capital investment. Individuals, banks, financial organizations and government agencies usually provide the capital.

Water supply: Industries, such as textiles, iron and steel and paper, require huge amounts of water for washing, cooling, etc. Therefore, they are located near rivers, lakes or other sources of water.

Land: Industries require large lands for setting up. Low and flat lands are usually ideal for setting up such industries.

Climate: Industries tend to be located in areas of moderate climate. The importance of climate in setting up an industry has diminished these days. Initially, the cotton textile industry was started in Mumbai due to its humid climate and because the surrounding regions had suitable climatic conditions for cotton cultivation.

Government policy: Governmental support is needed in the development of industries in the modern times. In the backward areas, the government gives subsidies to the entrepreneurs to start industries.

Industrial Input and Output

Apply it! E

Governments around the world have introduced laws to protect the rights of factory workers. Find out what the government has done to protect the rights of the factory workers, including children. Despite these laws, what is the condition of these workers till date?

An industrial system comprises inputs, processes and outputs. The inputs are raw materials, power, land and transport. The processes are the economic activities that convert these raw materials into finished products. Outputs are the end products, with value added to them. In the case of chocolate, the raw materials are cocoa beans, labour and transport cost. The processes involved in the creation of cocoa beans includes cleaning and roasting of the beans and then removing their husks. They are then ground into a powder called cocoa powder. To transform cocoa powder into chocolate, the powder is ground further and mixed with milk powder, sugar and emulsifying agents. The end product is a bar of chocolate.

Industrial Regions

Industries are unevenly distributed all over the world due to varied locational factors. Industries tend to concentrate in a few pockets due to certain favourable factors. Areas with a dense concentration of industries are called industrial regions.

The eastern part of North America, western, central and eastern Europe and eastern Asia are four major industrial regions of the world.

The major industrial regions of India are shown on the map.

What's in the picture?

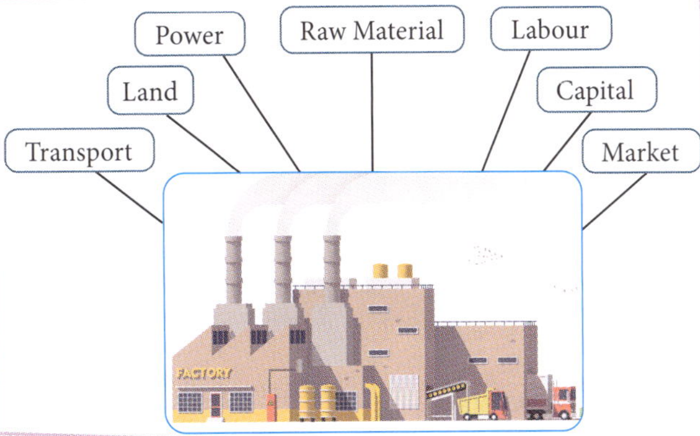

Study the picture and explain the factors affecting location of an industry.

Geography skills

Working from this map, mark the major industrial regions of India on an outline map

India: Industrial regions

World Connect

Today, robots, which were previously mostly imaginary, have become a reality in many industries worldwide, assisting humans in various responsibilities. The World Economic Forum released a report estimating that by 2025, 85 million jobs may be displaced by a shift in labor division between humans and machines. The current global leader in industrial robotic automation is South Korea, followed by Japan. In China, robots are increasingly interacting with customers.

Skill Builder

21ST CENTURY SKILLS

Critical thinking skills: Why is there a shift from the raw material-based locations to market-based locations.

Life skills: Some believe that the next revolution would be the era of sustainability. Do you agree with the statement, and if yes, then what would be the consequences for industries?

Creativity: Design a poster to spread awareness about the way industries pollute the environment.

Wind up

- Types of industries
  - On the basis of size
    - Small-scale
    - Large-scale
    - Cottage
  - On the basis of ownership
    - Public sector
    - Private sector
    - Joint sector
    - Cooperative sector
  - On the basis of raw materials
    - Agro-based
    - Mineral-based
    - Pastoral-based
    - Marine-based
    - Forest-based
  - On the basis of output
    - Basic
    - Consumer goods

Exercises

A. Choose the correct answers.

1. These industries have been considered to be the backbone of economic and social development in today's world.
   a. Manufacturing b. Mineral resources c. Wood industry d. Insurance
2. Which of the following is not an agro-based industry?
   a. Petroleum b. Textile c. Sugar d. Food processing
3. Marine-based industries are based on
   a. minerals b. forest products c. agricultural products d. oceanic products

4. Fish is a product of
   a. mineral-based industries
   b. agro-based industries
   c. marine-based industries
   d. forest-based industries

B. Fill in the blanks.

1. Reliance Industries is an example of a .... industry.
2. .... industries obtain their material from rocks and minerals.
3. Iron and steel plants in India are concentrated in the coal and iron ore belt of the .... Plateau.
4. Osaka in Japan and .... in India are important industrial centres.

C. Distinguish between the following.

1. Agro-based and mineral-based industries
2. Public sector and cooperative sector
3. Private sector and joint sector
4. Small scale industries and cottage industries

D. Answer these questions in brief.

1. Mention the type of industries based on raw materials.
2. How are basic industries necessary for consumer goods industries?
3. Give two examples of mineral-based industries.
4. Name the major industrial regions of the world.

E. Answer these questions in detail.

1. Discuss the factors that decide the location of an industry.
2. What are industries? In what ways are industries important to us?
3. Classify industries on the basis of size and ownership, giving one example for each.
4. Explain cooperative industries with the help of examples. Why do you think there is need to have cooperative industries?

Think Big

Art integration

Industrial waste is one of the biggest causes of pollution on the Earth. Build a waste sorting system by sorting the following items:

- Glass
- Metal
- Paper
- Cardboard
- Batteries
- Soft plastic
- Hard plastic

If you get together with your friends or classmates, you can make sets and donate to local factories or restaurants.

Learning Tools

Make a multi-page pocket book and record notes about the types of industries based on size, raw materials, ownership and output. Organize the notes in the appropriate pockets.

1. Fold a sheet of paper (8 1/2" _ 11") in half.
2. Open the folded paper and fold one of the long sides up two inches to form a pocket. Refold along the fold so that the newly formed pockets are on the inside.
3. Glue the outer edges of the two-inch fold with a small amount of glue.
4. Make it a multi-page booklet by gluing several pockets side-by-side. Glue a cover around the multi-paged pocket book.

Web links:

https://www.hq.nasa.gov/iwgsdi/Manufacturing.html

https://www.toppr.com/guides/geography/manufacturing-industries/what-are-manufacturing-industries/

Last accessed on 31 August 2021

9. Industries: India and the World

Warm up

According to a survey conducted by United Nations Industrial Development Organization (UNIDO), after the lockdown was imposed in 2020, manufacturing in India had stopped, except for the rice-milling sector, where production reportedly dropped by half. In manufacturing, some of the most affected industries have been metals and chemical products, motor vehicles, machinery and equipment, textiles, etc.

Industrialization has followed different patterns in different parts of the world. Some countries have progressed far more than others because of abundant natural resources and trained human resources. Some have progressed less because they have not been able to take optimum advantage of their natural resources as they lack a trained workforce. Some countries have taken fast strides towards development because they have been able to make up for the lack of natural resources by developing skills and technologies. Minerals and power resources together form the backbone of an industry in any country.

Iron and Steel Industry

The iron and steel industry is the backbone of the modern industry. An overall development can take place if there is enough steel available within a country to establish other industries. The USA, Germany, Russia and Japan are the leading steel manufacturing countries in the world.

World: Major Industries		
Industry	**Leading Producers in the World**	**Leading Producers in India**
Iron and Steel Industry	Pittsburgh and Detroit in the USA Ruhr and Saar in Germany Ukraine	Chota Nagpur plateau region Durgapur, Bhilai, Bokaro, Rourkela
Textile Industry	Georgia, North Carolina and South Carolina in the USA Moscow in Russia Osaka and Nagoya in Japan Manchester and Liverpool in the United Kingdom Hong Kong South Korea	Mumbai–Ahmedabad region Madurai–Coimbatore region

Chemical Industry	USA Moscow and St Petersburg in Russia	Mumbai, Delhi, Bengaluru, Chennai and Kolkata
Information Technology	Silicon Valley in California	Bengaluru in India

Tata Iron and Steel Company Limited (TISCO)

Jamsetji Tata

The availability of raw materials required for setting up a steel plant is the most important factor that determines its location. As the raw materials are heavy and bulky, the location has to be in close proximity to the available raw materials. This is what Jamsetji Tata thought when setting up a steel plant at Sakchi (now Jamshedpur) Jharkhand, in 1907, which is now known as the Tata Iron and Steel Company Limited. The locational advantages enjoyed by the steel plant are as follows:

- Good quality iron ore (haematite) was available easily from the nearby districts of Singhbhum in Jharkhand and Mayurbhanj in Odisha.
- High-quality coking coal was brought from the Jharia mines in Jharkhand and Raniganj mines in West Bengal.
- Limestone and dolomite could be brought from Sundergarh in Odisha.
- Manganese was brought from Keonjhar in Odisha.
- Sakchi is situated at the confluence of two rivers—the Subarnarekha and the Kharkai, which supply enough water for washing and cooling.
- The states of Jharkhand, Odisha and West Bengal are densely populated so there is a ready supply of skilled and unskilled labour.
- Kolkata is about 280 km away from Jamshedpur. It is an important port and can easily handle the import and export of goods.
- Jamshedpur is well connected, with metropolitan cities like Kolkata, Mumbai and Chennai by efficient road and rail networks.
- The region around Kolkata is industrially very developed. This provides a good market for the products of the Jamshedpur steel plant.
- The capital required for investment was provided by Tatas as well as by others.

Jamshedpur started producing steel in 1912. TISCO is a private sector plant that has served the country very well for decades now. It is now known as Tata Steel. The growth and development made Jamshedpur a hub of economic activities. Many factories, technical institutes and metallurgical laboratories were set up in the city. Jamshedpur is now manufacturing locomotives, trucks, agricultural machinery and electronics. Today, it is a thriving industrial town, which is well connected by rail, road and air.

Pittsburgh, Pennsylvania, United States

The USA is the world's largest producer of iron and steel. It accounts for about one-fourth of the world's total iron and steel production. The important centres of production are the Mid-Atlantic seaboard and the Pittsburgh-Youngstown district. Pittsburgh is an important city in south–west Pennsylvania (USA).

The city is located at the confluence of Allegheny and Monongahela rivers. Pittsburgh is an important inland port and lies on the path of the trade routes between the east and the west.

The process of extracting a metal from its ore by heating is known as smelting. It takes place in a blast furnace. The first blast furnace was set up here in 1872. Pittsburgh enjoys the following locational advantages:

- Fairly cheap and efficient transportation of high grade coking coal, in large quantities, from the nearby Appalachian coalfields.
- Fairly cheap and efficient transportation of high-grade iron ore from the northern fields. The iron ore comes from Minnesota, which is 1500 km from Pittsburgh.
- Sufficient water supply from the rivers.
- Great Lakes provide easy and cheap inland water transport.
- Availability of labourers, both skilled and unskilled, from the countries of Europe and other parts of the USA, due to high wages paid in the steel mills there.
- Most furnaces and steel plants located along the river banks readily receive and dispatch heavy freight.
- Thousands of factories in this region provide a ready market for the finished products.

Today, many steel old steel plants have closed down due to the high cost of operation, while some steel plants have shifted their location to the adjoining areas.

What's in the picture?

What is a blast furnace used for?

Apply it!

The Bhopal Gas Tragedy that occurred on 3 December, 1984, was one of the worst industrial disasters. Find out how the disaster took place and how it affected the environment and lives of the people. Prepare a report and a timeline to explain the course of the events.

Cotton Textile Industry

The cotton textile industry is an important industry, providing human with the most basic need—clothes. In India, cotton textile was made as far back as 3000 years ago. Very fine fabric was manufactured on handlooms by Indian weavers. The muslin of Dhaka, the chintzes of Masulipatnam and calicoes of Calicut were famous worldwide. The first modern cotton mill in India was set up in 1818, at Fort Gloster near Kolkata, but it closed down. Production in India actually started in 1854 at the Bombay Spinning and Weaving Company Ltd. Today, textile exports and garment exports are large foreign exchange earners in our country. Let us take a close look at this industry in India and Japan.

Ahmedabad, India

Ahmedabad is situated in Gujarat on the banks of the Sabarmati River. After Mumbai, it is the second largest cotton textile centre of India and is referred to as the 'Manchester of India'. The first cotton mill was established here in 1861.

The cotton textile industry in Ahmedabad enjoys a number of advantages because of its geographical location. These are as follows:

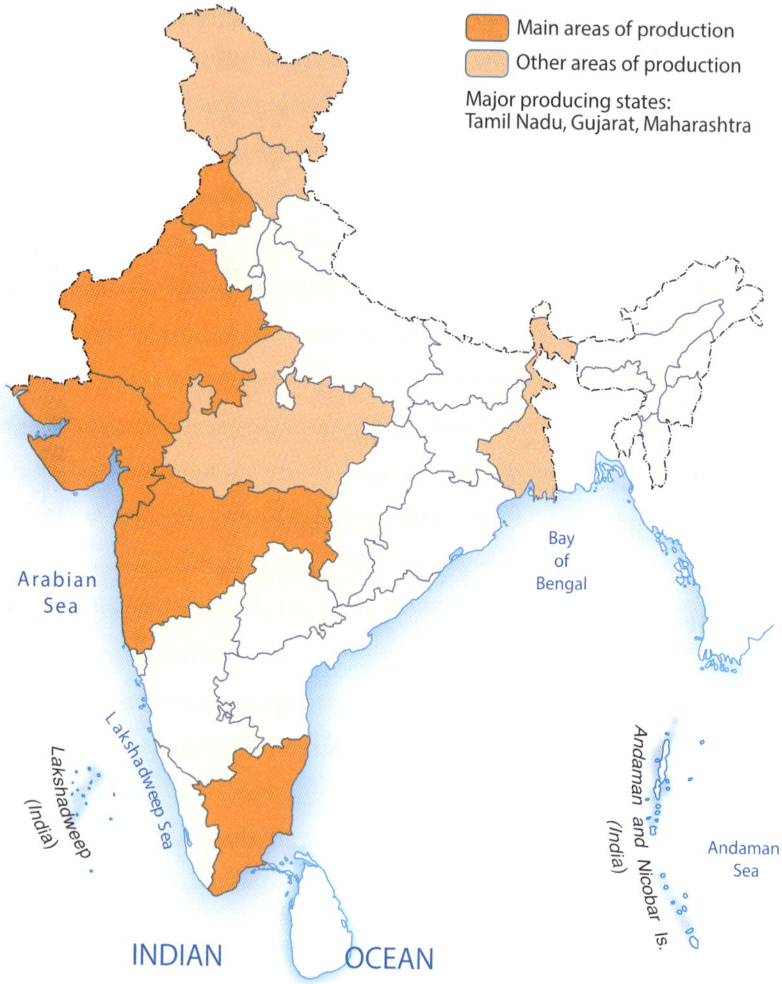

India: Textiles

- Ahmedabad is located in proximity to the cotton belt of India. The soil in the region is mainly black soil, which is suitable for growing cotton Thus, it is easier to transport cotton to the manufacturing site.
- The water required for the industry is readily available from the Sabarmati River.
- Gujarat and Maharashtra have a dense population. Ample labour, both skilled and unskilled, is also available for working in the mills.
- Hydroelectricity is available in abundance.
- Land for setting up cotton mills was available at Ahmedabad, at much cheaper rates than at Mumbai.
- The climate of Ahmedabad is humid, which is suitable for textile manufacturing.
- Ahmedabad is well connected to other parts of the country, by road and rail.
- Being close to the Arabian Sea, Ahmedabad can also export its textiles to the Middle East, Africa and Europe through the port of Kandla in Gujarat.

In the past 20 years, the cotton textile mills in Ahmedabad have been facing many problems, which have led to the shutting down of several mills. These problems are caused by outdated machinery, increasing demand for synthetic fabrics, lack of funds to upgrade technology and stiff competition from the opening of new textile centres in the country.

Osaka, Japan

Japan is situated in the eastern hemisphere and is considered an industrial giant. This country has limited natural resources, and its industries rely heavily on imports. Solely because of the dedicated and disciplined workforce, Japan has flourished as an industrial nation.

Osaka is a big industrial town situated in the southern part of the Honshu Island at the head of the Osaka Bay. Osaka has become the chief cotton textile producing centre of Japan because of the following advantages:

FACT CHECK

Osaka is the largest metropolitan area of Japan.

- Situated near the sea, Osaka has a humid climate, which is suitable for spinning and weaving textiles.

- Osaka is one of the busiest ports of Japan. It can easily import raw cotton from countries such as India, China, the USA and Egypt. Export of cotton goods is also handled by this port.
- Most parts of Japan are mountainous in nature. There is ample hydro-electricity available for running the mills. Some thermal power is also generated by coal, from Kyushu and Hokkaido.
- The river Yodo supplies enough water to use in the cotton mills.
- Osaka is situated on a flat stretch of land. Therefore, there is enough land to set up cotton mills.
- Road and rail network is also excellent, linking Osaka to other parts of Japan.
- Cheap and highly skilled labour is available.
- Cheap hydroelectricity is available as Japan is a mountainous island.
- The USA, China, Vietnam, Hong Kong, Middle-east, North African and other Asian countries provide a very good market for the Japanese cloth industry.
- The cotton textile industry of Osaka is efficiently organized, with suitable government support.

Because of these advantages, Osaka has often been called the 'Manchester of Japan'.

Information Technology (IT) Industry

The information technology industry is one of the fastest growing service industries in the world. It includes the processing, storing and transferring of information in a digital form. It includes manufacturing computer software, hardware, discs and different telecommunication systems that help in information storage.

Bengaluru, India

In India, the fastest growth of IT occurred in Bengaluru, the capital of Karnataka, in the Deccan Plateau. Bengaluru has certain specific advantages for the development of information technology.

Infosys headquarters, Bengaluru

- Bengaluru has a pleasant climate throughout the year that makes it an ideal place for working.
- Karnataka has numerous educational institutions and software training centres.
- It is the home to technically efficient personnel.
- Bengaluru has been attracting a lot of foreign and domestic IT firms, which opened their centres there. Software parks encourage people to work with the latest techniques, gadgets and favourable government policies. Foreign firms, like Dell Technologies, IBM, Intel, Motorola, Hewlett Packard and Sun, have set up their work centres here.
- Indian companies have established their centres in Bengaluru. IT giants, like Infosys, TCS and Wipro, have employed highly trained people to work on projects for the domestic and foreign markets.

Many US, European and Japanese firms have accepted Indian talent and are outsourcing work to Indian firms, which are mostly centred in Bengaluru. Therefore, Bengaluru has been rightly given the name 'Silicon Valley of India'.

Silicon Valley, California, USA

The name Silicon Valley was first used by Don Hoefler, referring to the semi-conductor industry around Palo Alto. The term 'Silicon Valley' was used to describe the Santa Clara County in the state of California in the USA. Frederick Terman, the 'Father of Silicon Valley', encouraged graduates to start their own companies to perform research. The Silicon Valley region is a part of Santa Clara Valley, located next to the Rocky Mountains of North America.

Headquarters of Hewlett Packard, Silicon Valley

Later on, Bill Hewlett and Dave Packard founded Hewlett-Packard (HP), a big name in the IT industry. Similarly, others made their centres in the Silicon Valley, for more developments in IT. Companies such as IBM, Xerox, Sun, Cisco and Intel set up development projects. All a huge capital base, technically skilled personnel, power facilities, government support and a pleasant climate have favoured the growth and development of the IT industry in the Silicon Valley.

World Connect

Environmental impact is amongst the biggest concerns in today's age. Solar energy, which is a clean alternative to fossil fuels, is being utilized around the world to better manage resources and control pollution. However, new studies indicate that production of solar panels could actually undercut the ability to combat climate change and reduce environmental toxins through the use of solar energy. Manufacturing these products in itself uses tremendous amounts of water and electricity. Building these panels also involves using harmful chemicals such as sodium hydroxide and hydrofluoric acid, which would eventually emit greenhouse gases. Not only this, the creating of solar panels also creates waste. There is hope, however, that in the near future, solar companies will adopt stronger sustainability measures.

Skill Builder

21ST CENTURY SKILLS

Critical thinking skills: Why has there been a shift from integrated steel plants to mini steel plants in all countries?

Information literacy: Industries provide employment to many people in a country. The employees of such industries form labour unions to protect their rights in terms of wages, hours and other working conditions. Find out more about labour unions, and write a report on it.

Life skills: How does noise pollution affect our ears? Study the structure of the ears to understand the effects of loud noise to our ears.

Wind up

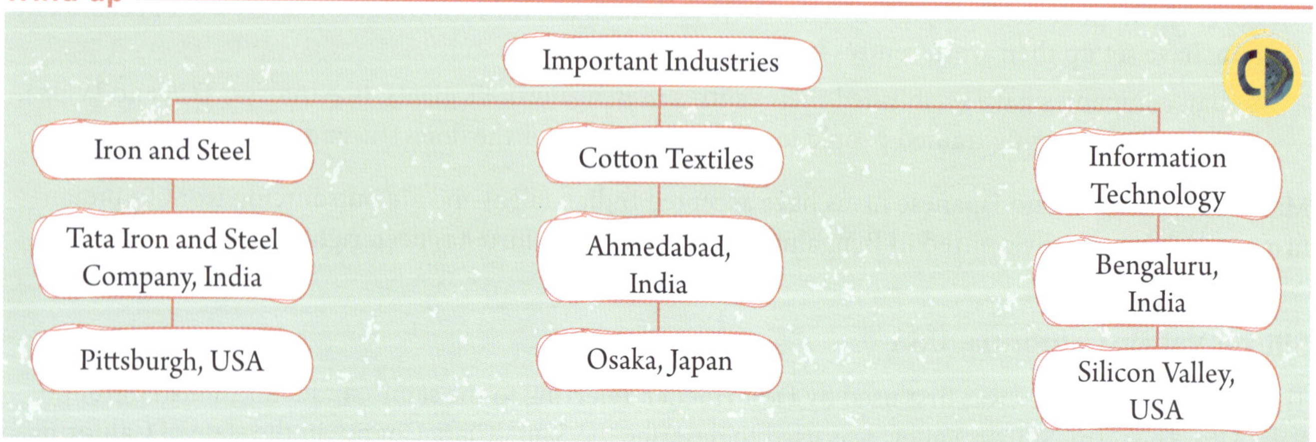

Exercises

A. Fill in the blanks.

1. The river that provides sufficient water to Osaka's textile industry is ....
2. The process of smelting is done in a ....
3. The four steel centres of India are ...., ..., ... and ....
4. The first cotton textile mill was established in ....
5. Silicon Valley is located near the .... Mountains.

B. Choose the correct answers.

1. From where did the Silicon Valley get its name?
   a. From the meaning of the word silicon
   b. From a computer software
   c. From a valley by the same name that existed in California, US
   d. From the silicon that was used to make chips for computers
2. The leading steel manufacturing countries in the world
   a. USA   b. Japan   c. Germany   d. Bangladesh
3. Name the major industry that provides the primary needs of humans like clothing.
   a. chemical industry   b. transport industry   c. textile industry   d. iron and steel industry
4. A smooth network of inland transport for Pittsburgh was provided by
   a. Sakchi   b. Great seas   c. Great Lakes   d. Ohio river
5. Mumbai, Delhi, Bengaluru, Chennai and Kolkata are centres of
   a. Chemical industry   b. Iron and Steel industry
   c. Jute industry   d. none of these

C. Write T for true and F for false.

1. Osaka is known as 'Manchester of Japan'. ☐
2. Osaka has a dry climate that is suitable for weaving and spinning. ☐
3. The chintzes of Dhaka were world famous. ☐
4. There are a number of foreign-based IT companies in Bengaluru. ☐
5. The name Silicon Valley was first used by Don Hoefler. ☐

D. Answer these questions in brief.

1. Why is Ahmedabad called the 'Manchester of India'?
2. What is India's biggest advantage in the IT industry?
3. Where does the iron and steel industry of Pittsburgh obtain its raw materials from?
4. What are the challenges faced by the cotton textile industry of Ahmedabad?

E. Answer these questions in detail.

1. What are the advantages of Osaka as the centre of cotton textile industry?
2. List the factors that made Sakchi an ideal location for setting up TISCO.

3. List the advantages that helped Bengaluru become an IT hub.
4. What are the factors that helped Ahmedabad to become a textile centre?

Think Big

Art integration

Make a cartoon strip, of dialogues between the cotton mill workers of Ahmedabad and that of Osaka.

Learning Tools

Create your own study guides by compiling the necessary information for swift recap.

Iron and steel industry	Cotton textile industry	Information technology industry
....	....	....
....	....	....
....	....	....
....	....	....
....	....	....
....	....	....
....	....	....
....	....	....
....	....	....
....	....	....
....	....	....
....	....	....
....	....	....
....	....	....

Web links:

https://www.toppr.com/guides/general-knowledge/resources-of-india-and-world/industries-of-india-and-world/

Last accessed on 31 August 2021

10. Human Resources

Warm up

Lakshita is a semi-skilled worker in a cement factory. She is very efficient. Her husband is a household worker. They have two kids and live in the worker's colony where living conditions are not good. Recognizing Lakshita's capabilities, the company plans to train her to increase her potential and improve her living conditions. Her organization has certain schemes to impart education to those workers who are efficient but lack proper skills. Lakshita, like many other workers employed by the factory, is a human resource whose skills are being utilized to manufacture cement.

Natural resources have always been the material basis of societies. While these resources are useful to us, without humans making use of them, they would be of little value. Human resources comprise the people who have a certain skill to provide services. A worker in the factory, a doctor, a teacher, an engineer, a milkman and a plumber, are human resources. They produce or facilitate in producing resources.

Population Distribution

The population of the world is not distributed evenly. There are approximately seven billion people in the world spread unevenly across the globe due to several physical and human factors such as quality of land, climate, availability of natural resources and socio-economic development. The way in which people are spread across the surface of the Earth is known as the pattern of population distribution. The continents of Asia and Europe have the maximum concentration of population. The number of persons living per unit area is known as population density. Asia has the highest population density in the world and India and China are the most populous countries in the world. The average density of the population in the world is 51 people per square kilometre.

Regions of High Population Density

Some of the highly populated regions of the world are as follows:

- Eastern Asia and south-eastern Asia: Japan, China, North and South Korea, the Philippines in the east and the Indian subcontinent (India, Pakistan and Bangladesh) account for nearly half of the total world population.
- Western Europe: This region has a high density of population as it has achieved a high level of industrialization. Countries such as Great Britain, France, Belgium, the Netherlands, Italy, Ukraine and European Russia are densely populated.
- Eastern and central part of North America: This area around the Great Lakes in the USA and Canada has a high density of population. It is highly developed both agriculturally and industrially.

FACT CHECK

According to the latest UN estimates, the population of the world is predicted to reach around 11 billion by the end of the 21st century.

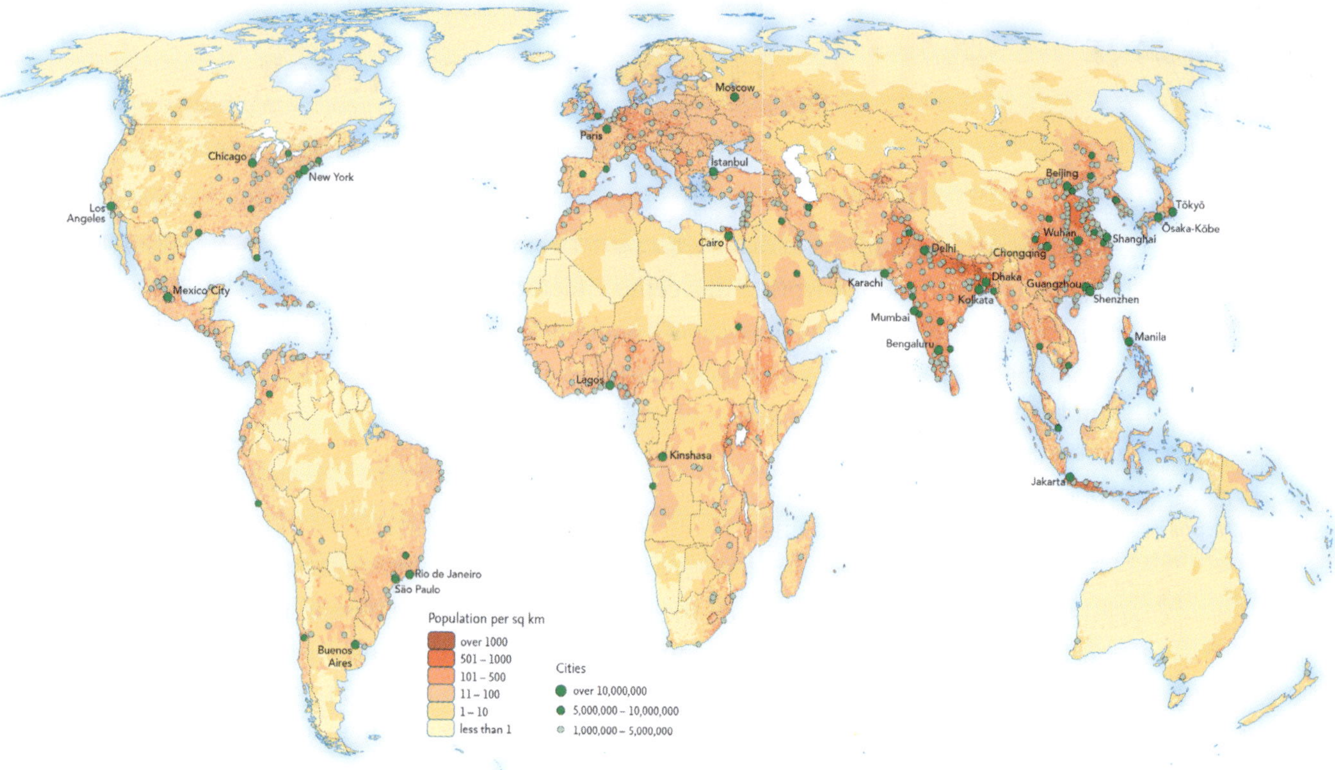

World: Population Distribution

- Regions of low population density include the polar region, tropical deserts, high altitude mountainous regions and equatorial forests.

Geography skills

Working from this map, colour the regions that are densely populated with red and those that are scarcely populated with blue on an outline map of the world.

Population Distribution in India

India is the second most populous country in the world, with its population amounting to more than a fifth of the world's population. The highest population is found in the northern plains of India and in the coastal strips. Uttar Pradesh, Bihar and West Bengal have level land, fertile soil and suitable climate for agriculture, and hence, have a high density of population. Density of population is also high in industrial towns and cities like Durgapur, Kulti, Burnpur and Batanagar, business centres like Kolkata, Mumbai and Chennai and mining centres like Raniganj. In Rajasthan, the population density is very low, due to the hot climate.

Factors Influencing Population Distribution

The distribution of population over the world, is the result of various factors. They are as follows:

Climate: People prefer to stay in places with moderate climate. Life becomes difficult where the climate is either very hot or very cold. The temperate regions of the world and the sub-tropical areas are densely populated. The north-east USA and the northern plains in India are thickly populated. On the other hand, the Arctic regions, Ladakh in India and the Sahara Desert are sparsely populated due to the prevalent extreme climatic conditions.

Relief: Density of population is very high in the vast plains of the world. The Ganga Valley, the Nile Delta and the Mississippi Delta have dense populations, whereas the plateaus and the mountain regions have less people. In mountainous regions, transportation and cultivation are not at all easy, and life is difficult.

The mountainous regions of the Rockies and the Andes are sparsely populated. In India, the north-eastern mountainous regions and the Himalayas have very few people.

Availability of water: Most settlements tend to develop along sources of water like rivers and lakes. Therefore, the valleys of the Ganga, the Yangtze Kiang and the Rhine are densely populated.

Soils: Regions with fertile soils have always attracted people because of their ability to support agriculture. The fertile plains of Ganga–Brahmaputra in India, Yangtze Kiang in China and the Nile in Egypt are densely populated.

Social factors: The ease of living and social policies of a place also determine its population distribution. Places with affordable living standards have higher population. Basic amenities such as housing, sanitation, healthcare and educational facilities attract many people. This is the reason why cities and suburban areas are densely populated and villages are sparsely populated. London, New York and New Delhi are good examples of such cities.

Economic factors: Population distribution and density of an area also depend on the type and scale of its economic activities. Factors such as availability of jobs and high wages can contribute to high population density through migration. Growing commercial activities, along with improved transport and infrastructure, lead to a considerable change in the population distribution of a region. For example, Osaka in Japan, Detroit in North America, Guangzhou in China and Mumbai, Bangalore, Chennai in India are major economic hubs, and hence, are densely populated.

Cultural factors: Places that are the centres of religious activities or have any other cultural significance attract numerous people. Haridwar, Varanasi, Jerusalem, Vatican City are some examples.

Population Growth

Population growth is the change in the number of people living in a particular region over a period of time. The rate at which population grows is expressed as a percentage. Population growth can be natural or induced. Natural growth of population can be measured by birth rate and death rate. Birth rate is the number of live births per 1000 people and death rate is the number of deaths per 1000 people. The difference between the birth rate and death rate of a country is called natural growth rate. Induced growth in population is attributed to the inflow and outflow, that is, migration of people. Emigration is the movement of people out of a country. Immigration is the movement of people into a country.

Population Composition

The population of a country does not only refer to its size and growth rate but also the distribution of members according to age, sex, literacy and occupation, which are important characteristics of population. These attributes define the structure of the population.

Age Composition: This refers to the number of people in different age groups in a country. The population may be divided into three main categories. They are

- Persons below 15 years
- Persons between 15 and 65 years
- Persons above 65 years

What's in the picture?

Dubai is surrounded by desert, yet the population thrives. What could be the reason for this?

The people in the age group of 15–65 years are the productive population that makes the country prosperous or developed as the people in this group make up the working population. The other two groups are the dependent population, and it indicates greater expenditure on the care of the aged (elderly dependent) or the children (young dependent).

Sex Ratio: The ratio between males and females is known as the sex ratio. It is represented as the number of females per 1,000 males. In underdeveloped countries, the sex ratio is often unfavourable to females. In India, the ratio is 940 females per 1000 males. High **maternal mortality, female infanticide**, sex-selective female abortions, neglect of the girl child lead to a higher mortality among girls at a young age, resulting in a large number of deaths of young girls in India.

Literacy: The word 'literate' refers to persons who can read and write. The higher the level of education or skills acquired by the population of a country, the more developed it is. More than 80 per cent of the world's population is literate. In India, the literacy rate has grown to 74 per cent according to the census of 2011. There is also a gender disparity in India's literacy rate, with men achieving higher levels of education compared to women.

Population Growth and Economic Development

Population growth directly affects the economic development of a country. It obstructs the development of a country by putting pressure on the existing natural resources of that country, bringing about significant increases in the demand for food, water and energy. This stress and shortage of resources lead to poverty and destitution and hinders development. In India, population has grown steadily at about 2 per cent. While population explosion can be detrimental to the growth and development of any economy, there have been instances where population growth has led to greater productivity. The economic history of the USA and the European countries shows that population growth contributed greatly to the increase in their national output. However, population growth should be in accordance with the availability of natural resources and basic amenities in a country.

Population Pyramid

A population pyramid illustrates the age and sex structure of a country's population. The population is distributed on a bar graph, with males shown on the left and females on the right. The male and female populations are broken down into 5-year age groups represented as horizontal bars, with the youngest age groups at the bottom and the oldest at the top. The shape of the population pyramid can change over time based on fertility, mortality and international migration trends. A country having high birth rate and death rate will have a population pyramid with a broad base which narrows towards the top. Thus, population pyramid helps in learning about the nature of population of a country. It tells us not only about sex composition but also the age structure, that is, how much proportion of the population falls in working and dependent categories.

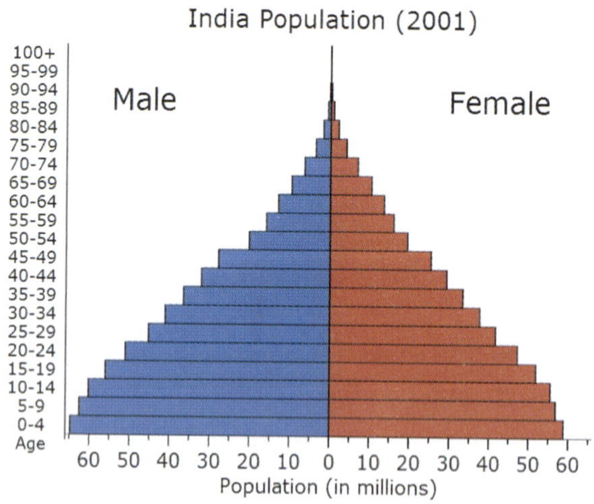

Population pyramid

Apply it!

'Population growth leads to starvation.'

Write what you understand by these lines.

maternal mortality: death of a woman while pregnant; female infanticide: the deliberate killing of newborn female infant

World Connect

In 2015, migrants from Western and South Asia, Africa and the Western Balkans travelled across the Mediterranean Sea to seek refuge in European countries, away from their war-torn countries. Thus began the European migrant crisis, which took place as the result of the ongoing conflicts and refugee crises in many Asian and African countries. Since then, countries of the Eurpoean Union have been making great efforts to manage the crisis. Funding for border patrol operations in the Mediterranean has been increased, and plans to combat migrant smuggling and the relocation and resettlement of asylum seekers have been drawn up. While some countries have been willing to accommodate these asylum seekers, many are resisting their arrival. More than a million migrants entered Europe in 2015, and about 135,000 people arrived in the first two months of 2016. Thousands of people lost their lives in the journey to Europe.

Skill Builder

21ST CENTURY SKILLS

Critical-thinking skills: In what ways have population pressures contributed to the degradation of agricultural lands?

Life skills: With a population of more than 7 billion, the world population is bound to increase exponentially by 2100. What advancements do you think would have to be made in education, medicine, environmental issues and food and water supply to support a global community of 10 billion people? What about 15.8 billion? Discuss this in class.

Information literacy: Coronavirus disease 2019 (COVID-19) is a current new virulent disease whose transmission and fatality is rising with each passing day worldwide. Find out how it is affecting the population of a country or a region.

Wind up

Human resources

- Population distribution
  - Factors affecting population distribution
    - Climate
    - Relief
    - Availability of Water
    - Social Factors
    - Economic Factors
- Population density
  - Regions of high population density
  - Eastern Asia, south-eastern Asia, western Europe, eastern and central North America
- Population growth
  - Birth rate
  - Death rate
  - Emigration
  - Immigration
- Population composition
  - Age composition
  - Sex ratio
  - Literacy

Exercises

A. Fill in the blanks.

1. .... has the highest density of population in the world.
2. Japan is .... populated.

3. Natural growth of population can be measured by .... rate and .... rate.
4. .... is the process of people moving out of the country.
5. Industrial towns such as Durgapur and Batanagar are .... populated.

B. Choose the correct answers.

1. Which of the following cities is densely populated due to its religious significance?
   a. Pune b. Chennai c. Varanasi d. Chandigarh
2. The average density of world's population is
   a. 10 persons per square kilometre b. 80 persons per square kilometre
   c. 20 persons per square kilometre d. 51 persons per square kilometre
3. The highest density of the population in the world is in
   a. Europe b. South America c. South central Asia d. none of these
4. Which of the following is not the region where very few people live?
   a. High altitudes areas b. Plains c. High mountains d. Equatorial forest area
5. The population of the world is
   a. 77 billion b. 7.0 billion c. 0.77 billion d. 0.077 billion

C. Write T for true and F for false.

1. India has an unfavourable sex ratio. ☐
2. The region around the Great Lakes is densely populated. ☐
3. South Asia is a region of high population density. ☐
4. Lower the literacy rate, higher the level of economic development of a nation. ☐

D. Answer these questions in brief.

1. Why are people called 'human resource'?
2. What is population growth?
3. What is population distribution?
4. Which areas of the world are densely populated?
5. Write a short note on sex ratio as an indicator of economic development of a country.

E. Answer these questions in detail.

1. What does the population pyramid tell us about dependents of a country?
2. Population is unevenly distributed in the world. Explain the different factors that affect the pattern of population distribution with the help of examples.
3. How crowded a country is has little to do with its level of economic development. Give an example to show its validity.
4. What is natural growth rate? What leads to a change in population?
5. Explain the distribution of population in India.

Think Big — Maths integration

With the help of your geography and maths teacher, make the population pyramids for Japan, India and the USA.

Learning Tools

Make your own study guide by following these steps.

MAIN POINTS (*Note down the important headings and the main ideas*)

→ ....

→ ....

→ ....

→ ....

→ ....

→ ....

→ ....

→ ....

Keywords

....

....

....

....

....

....

Assess yourself (Use the questions at the end of the chapter to assess how much you have learnt and understood)

Web links:

https://censusindia.gov.in/census_and_you/age_structure_and_marital_status.aspx

Last accessed on 31 August 2021

11. Disaster Management

Warm up

The World Health Organization (WHO) defines pandemic as an outbreak of disease across a wide area and many countries, even continents. Some of the worst pandemics humanity has witnessed are the Black Death, the Great Plague of London and the Spanish Flu. In the 21st century, we have had major outbreaks like SARS, Ebola and coronavirus (COVID-19).

What do you do when the ground suddenly starts shaking? The trees seem to be wobbling and there is complete chaos everywhere you look. Disasters are sudden events, such as floods, earthquakes, cyclones, accidents, droughts, epidemics and events of disruption or blasts caused by the use of weapons of mass destruction, that cause deaths and damage to property. These events often occur unexpectedly. While we cannot prevent most of them from happening, we can prepare ourselves and take steps to reduce their impact. Implementing awareness programmes to educate people about natural disasters and the steps to take to survive in the midst of one and while recovering from one; improving capabilities of personnel and implementing concrete measures, such as proper and functioning communication systems for warnings are important steps to reduce the impact of such disasters.

The human endeavour to lead a peaceful and comfortable life is often threatened by disasters—natural and human-made. Examples of natural disasters are floods, cyclones, earthquakes and droughts, which occur with little or no human intervention. Human-made disasters include train accidents, plane crashes, industrial or nuclear accidents, biological disasters, terrorist attacks and the use of weapons of mass destruction.

Disaster Management

Disaster management is the proper and efficient handling of disaster-affected regions, disaster-affected people and overall preparedness in case of a disaster. It comprises plans and actions taken before, during and after a disaster to reduce the impact, suffering and the damage caused by it. Disaster management aims to manage a disaster and tries to mitigate its impact. In the occurrence of a natural disaster, the community is always the first to provide help. Young students are an important part of the community. They should play an active and helpful role in such times.

Natural Disasters

Earthquakes

The sudden vibration of the Earth's crust, causing a part of the Earth's surface to shake, is called an earthquake. The point inside the Earth where the vibrations originate is called seismic focus. The point on the Earth's surface that is directly above the focus is called the epicentre of the earthquake. The instrument that records and measures the vibrations of an earthquake is called a seismograph. The magnitude or intensity of an earthquake is measured by the Richter Scale. The numbers on this scale range from 0 to 9. Earthquakes of magnitude 7 or above are very destructive and cause severe damage to life and property. Earthquakes are caused by the internal forces of the Earth, like the movement of molten rock beneath the Earth's crust and the movement of the tectonic plates. They may also occur at the time of volcanic eruptions. The seismic zoning divides India into four zones, namely Zone II, III, IV and the most vulnerable Zone V.

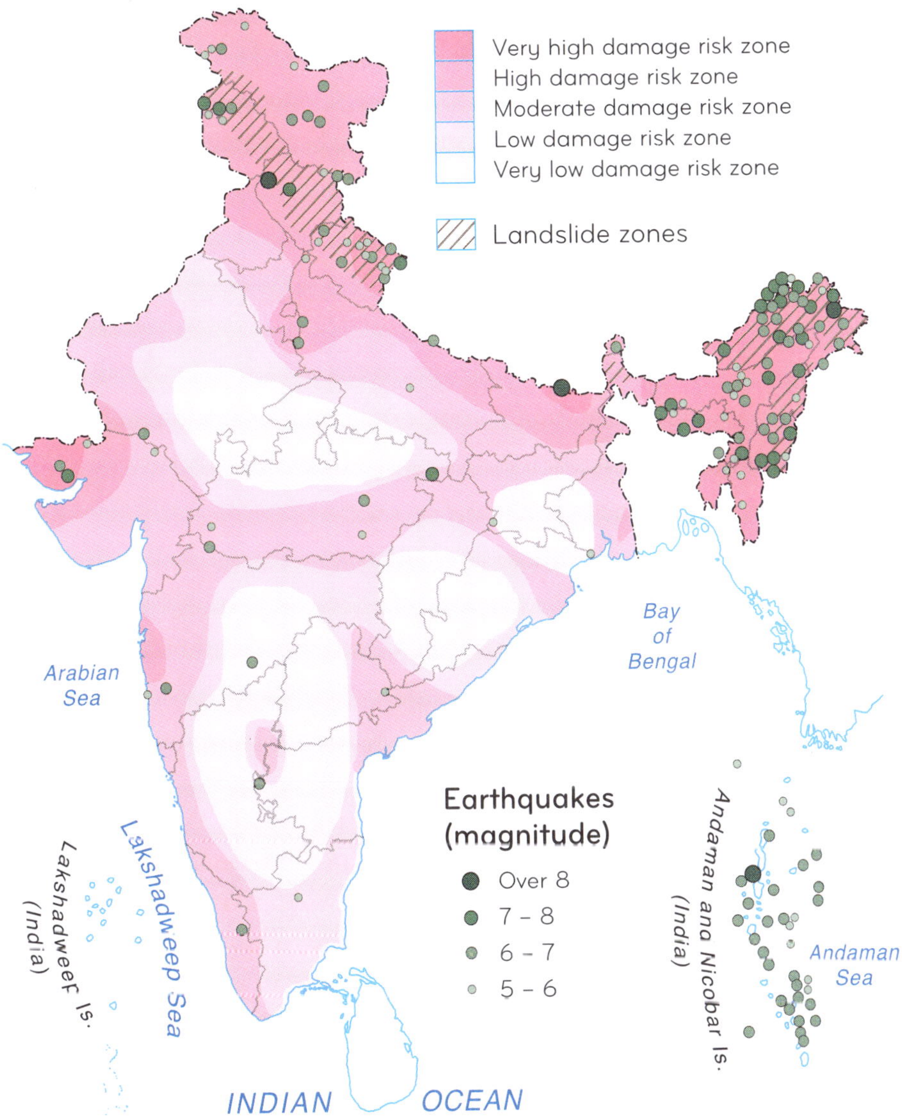

India: Seismic zones

Measures to Minimize the Risk

Short-term predictions of earthquakes are not possible, and earthquakes always strike suddenly, catching people unaware. However, certain measures can be taken to prepare the public from earthquake, thereby reducing the damage caused by them.

- Leave your home or school building and move into an open area.
- Learn the basic first-aid functions.
- All buildings and other structures, such as bridges, flyovers and dams, should be made as per the building by-laws to withstand the shaking of the surface depending on the seismic sensitivity of their location.

- Vulnerability assessment for old buildings should be carried out in hazard prone zones. Old buildings should be strengthened through the process of retrofitting.
- Community sensitization programmes must be organized to prepare people to face the disaster.
- After an earthquake, one must first check for any injuries that others might have received, provide first aid to the injured, move out in the open area and prepare for an aftershock, avoid broken wires, glass windows and check for gas leaks.

Cyclones

A cyclone is a large rotating storm that forms over warm waters. Strong winds blow from all directions towards the centre, in a spiral motion. When a cyclone hits, it brings along heavy rains, winds and **storm surges** strong enough to destroy buildings and uproot trees. India has a coastline of about 7,500 km, which is very prone to very severe cyclonic formations in the Bay of Bengal and Arabian Sea. West Bengal, Odisha, Andhra Pradesh and Tamil Nadu are the most vulnerable states. However, as has been witnessed in the last few years, the western coastal states of Maharashtra, Karnataka, Kerala, Goa and Gujarat too have become vulnerable.

Precautions

- Keep track of the latest weather information through radio and television and act accordingly.
- Move to a stronger building, in case it is a hut or a semi-pukka house.
- Keep an emergency kit ready and pack food items in a waterproof bag.
- After the cyclone, one should be careful about gas leaks, fallen electric wires and damaged or weakened structures that might collapse.
- To prevent the impact of storm surges and strong winds, sand mounds should be created on coastal areas.
- Trees should be planted to reduce the impact of winds.
- Specifically designed halls should be kept ready in advance for community shelter during the disaster.

Floods

Floods occur when a sudden influx of water submerges areas of land, causing danger to life and property of people in that area. The most common type of flood occurs when a river overflows its banks and the water spreads on the surrounding land. It can also be caused due to blocking of river channels due to landslides, strong tides and storms in the sea, change in the course of a river, deforestation, etc. Floods may occur gradually, within few hours or even suddenly at times. Most floods are seasonal, occurring during the rainy season. In India, floods frequently occur in the Ganga plains, in the Brahmaputra basin in Assam and in the deltas of the rivers Mahanadi, Godavari, Krishna and Kaveri.

Precautions

- Know the safest and fastest routes to reach safe shelters located at higher grounds.
- Learn about flood warnings and weather reports on TV and radio.
- Turn off the main power switch of the house when the flood water enters to prevent short-circuiting and shock hazards
- Place furniture and other belongings higher up so that they do not get immersed under water.
- Keep waterproof bags for packing food articles, first aid kit, some clothes and mosquito repellent.
- Drink only boiled water and eat only fresh cooked food.
- Be watchful of snakes as snakebite is common during floods.

storm surge: rise of the sea level when the sea experiences changes in wind and atmospheric pressure.

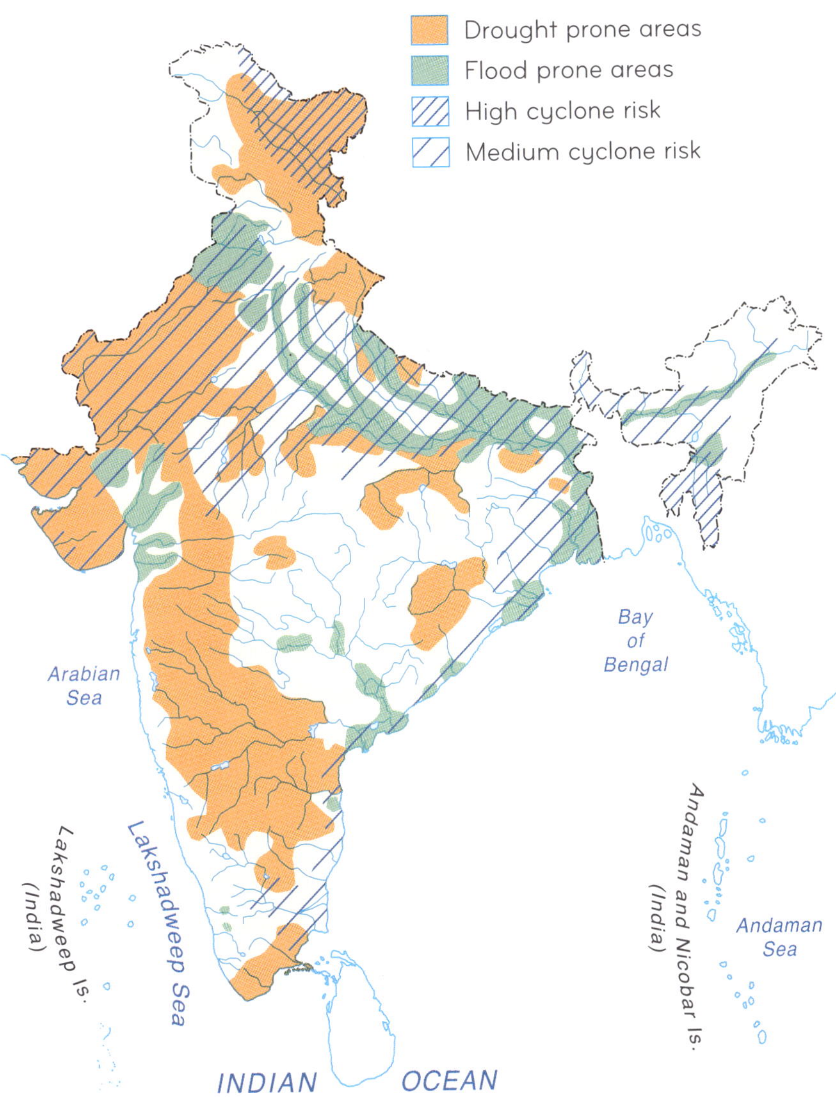

India: Flood and drought prone areas

Droughts

Droughts occur when a region receives deficient or no rainfall over a long period of time. Shortage of water in drought-prone areas results in the falling of groundwater table, crop failure, shortage of food, fodder and employment. The drought-prone areas of India are Rajasthan, Gujarat, parts of Andhra Pradesh, Chhattisgarh, central Maharashtra, Tamil Nadu, Odisha, Punjab and Haryana.

What's in the picture?

Study the picture and in your own words, write a report on the living conditions of people here.

Precautions

- Develop rainwater harvesting systems.
- Promote drip and sprinkler irrigation.
- Increase forest cover through afforestation schemes.
- Encourage crop insurance schemes.
- Plant drought-resistant crops.

Human-made Disasters

Two world wars have been fought in the history of the world, and they have caused immense death and destruction—each war causing more destruction than any natural disaster. In some cases, most of the countries involved in these wars continued to face the consequences years after the wars ended. Human-made disasters are a result of human actions or inaction and cause immeasurable loss and suffering to human lives and destruction to the environment around them. These disasters are also called anthropogenic disasters.

Fire-related Disasters

Fire accidents are mostly caused by faulty electrical wiring, gas leakage or human negligence. Electricity wires and gas pipelines in homes and buildings should be checked regularly to avoid short-circuit in case of the wires and leakage in case of gas. Human negligence usually refers to the carelessness on the part of the humans to not get electrical switches or gas stoves checked, or most importantly, to carelessly throw matches and cigarettes without putting them off first.

Precautions

To cope with such disasters, the following steps should be followed:

- Fire extinguishers should be kept in homes and buildings.
- Basic training should be provided on how to extinguish the fires of different origins—there are different methods to extinguish a fire caused by a gas leak and an electrical fire.
- Evacuate the building immediately if it catches fire. Remember not to use elevators during fires, instead use the stairs.
- Remember never to throw water on fire. Make use of sand to cut the oxygen supply.
- If the clothes you are wearing catches fire, roll over on the ground to extinguish the fire.
- Call the fire services department immediately, in case if any fire breaks out in the building.

Nuclear Disasters

Nuclear radiation is the energy released from radioactive elements such as uranium and plutonium. While nuclear energy is used as a resource to produce power and electricity, exposure to nuclear radiation can be extremely dangerous and can cause irreversible harm to the body. While all possible precautions are taken, accidents occur, and these are considered the most devastating disasters that cause widespread loss of life and property. Nuclear accidents occur when a reactor core gets damaged and a significant amount of radiations is released into the atmosphere. In 1986, there was an explosion at the Chernobyl nuclear plant, releasing a large quantity of radioactive particles into the atmosphere, killing a large number of people—about thirty people died immediately inside the plant in Ukraine and more afterwards. More than 20,000 people had to be relocated, and over half a million people suffered from the long-term effects of radiation, through diseases such as cancer, which is currently still being investigated. The area near the plant remains uninhabitable till date.

> **Apply it!** E
>
> Research and write a paper on the moral and ethical implications of war on civilians.

Precautions

- Evacuate the affected place when alarmed.

- Wearing a mask and staying indoor is necessary. Avoid touching any object outside.
- Take shelter in a building with hard walls, and close doors and windows to cut off ventilation.
- Do not drink tap water anywhere within the affected area.
- Government should supply drinking water by tanks and other suppliers.

Chemical Disasters

The accidental release of one or more hazardous or toxic substances, which could harm human health or the environment, is called a chemical accident. Chemical accidents could occur due to fires, explosions, leakages or releases of toxic or hazardous materials from factories or industries. The most significant chemical accident recorded in history was the 1984 Bhopal disaster in India, where more than 3,000 people were killed after a highly toxic vapour was released at a Union Carbide Pesticides factory. The after-effects of this disaster have left over 300,000 people with serious medical conditions, including nerve damage, growth problems, gynaecological disorders, respiratory issues, birth defects, and elevated rates of cancer and tuberculosis till date.

Precautions

- Preventing chemical industries from operating in populated areas.
- Regular safety checks and pollution checks should be conducted by government agencies.
- Relief measures should be laid out to reduce the consequences.

Terrorism-related Disasters

Terrorism is a serious problem in the modern world. It has been defined as the illegal or unauthorized use of violence, intimidation and exploitation of human fear of political groups, which are driven by their own political, social and religious interests, to help them achieve these goals. Bomb blasts, mass shootings and use of sheer violence are their method of operation.

Precautions

- Staying updated with the current affairs and follow the instructions of the local emergency police officials.
- Reporting suspicious persons to the authorities.
- Reporting unattended bags or articles in public places to the authorities, without first touching them.

World Connect

Considered by many to be one of the most devastating natural disasters that the world has seen in the last 50 years, Ethiopia is facing one of the worst droughts it had ever faced. The drought has led to limited agricultural production, strained livelihoods and aggravated food insecurity among poor and susceptible households. At least six million Ethiopians are facing critical food shortages. In an effort to fight the devastating drought, many measures have been taken to restore the land. The government has allocated 16.5 billion Birr to buy wheat and distribute human and animal feed, water and other assistance to the drought victims. A commission was set up to identify ways to cope with any disaster phenomena. The Early Warning, Alert and Response System (EWARS) approach, developed with development partners, can be used to conduct public health surveillance, detect disease outbreak and cases of severe acute malnutrition during emergencies in flood-prone areas of the country.

Skill Builder

Life skills: In the event of a cyclone or a flood, what will you take with you, if you had to evacuate your home and go to the nearest shelter?

Critical-thinking skills: Identify potential hazards in the classroom that may cause damage or injury during an earthquake. List, and if possible, make changes in the classroom to reduce potential hazards. Do the same at home as well.

Form groups of four in the classroom. Each group can make a project on any one of the topics given below.

1. Hazards likely to come across during evacuation.
2. Ways of helping others who are injured during earthquakes.

Wind up

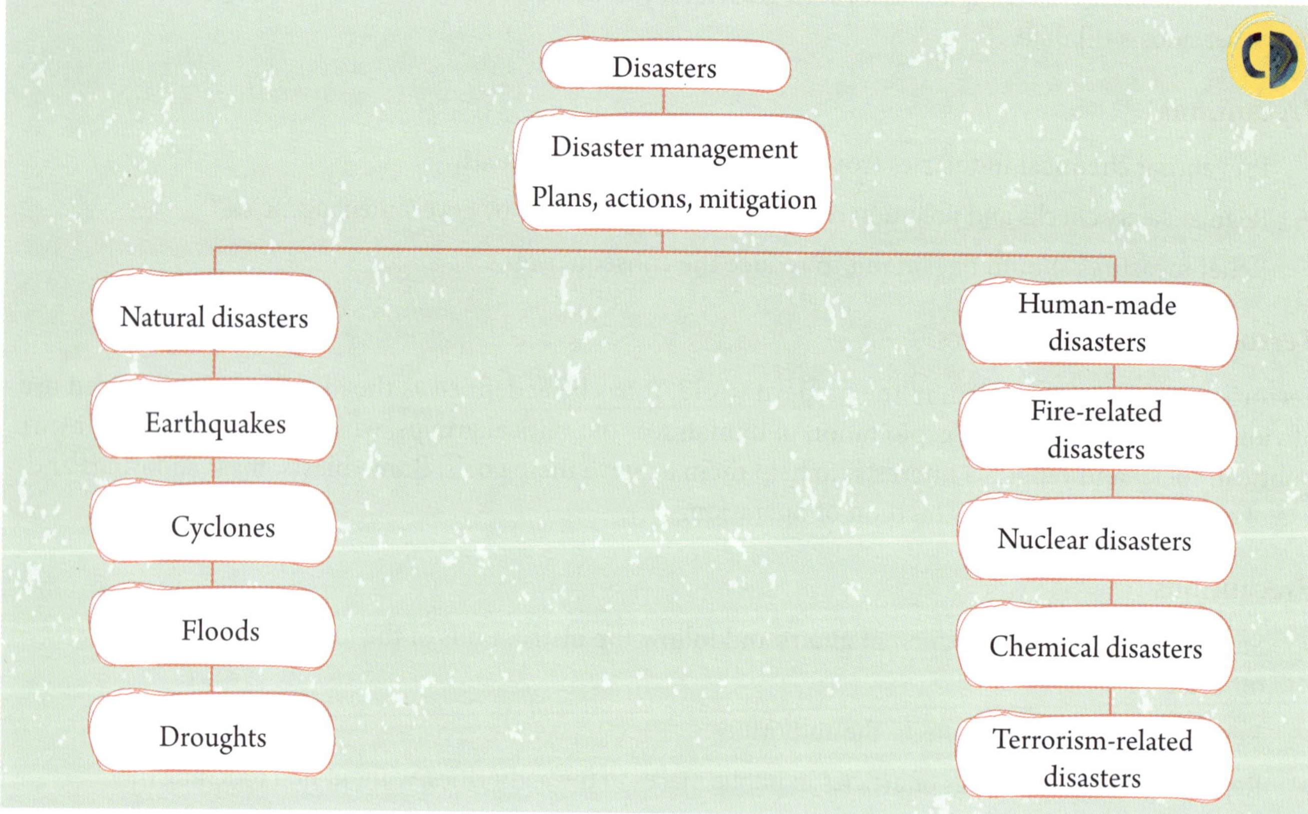

Exercises

A. Fill in the blanks.

1. The point on the Earth's surface, which is directly above the focus is known as ....
2. The most important cause of drought is scarcity of ....
3. .... are events of destruction that cause loss of life and damage to property.
4. .... is the proper and efficient handling of disaster-affecting regions.
5. The toxic gas release at the Bhopal gas tragedy occurred in the year ....

B. Choose the correct answers.

1. The point inside the Earth where vibrations originate is called
   a. epicentre b. seismic focus c. seismograph d. magnitude
2. The Chernobyl disaster was a
   a. fire-related disaster b. nuclear disaster c. chemical disaster d. biological disaster
3. This can prevent drought.
   a. Rainwater harvesting b. Deforestation c. Wasting water d. none of the above
4. A large rotating storm.
   a. Cyclone b. Flood c. Earthquake d. Tsunami
5. The range of a Richter Scale is
   a. 0 to 5 b. 0 to 7 c. 0 to 9 d. 0 to 11

C. Distinguish between the following.

1. Nuclear disaster and chemical disaster
2. Flood and drought
3. Focus and epicentre
4. Cyclones and floods

D. Answer these questions in brief.

1. What are the possible consequences of a chemical disaster?
2. What precautions need to be taken, when we are indoors during an earthquake?
3. What is a nuclear disaster?
4. What are the causes of drought?

E. Answer the following in your own words.

1. What is a cyclone? Mention the steps of precaution required to minimize the impact of cyclones.
2. Prepare a chart showing 'do's and dont's' at the time of earthquake.
3. Explain how human beings too are responsible in creating disaster-like situations. Give examples.
4. What are the effects of droughts? Which regions in India are prone to droughts?
5. Explain what causes nuclear disaster. Also, mention the steps required to be taken during the nuclear disaster.

Think Big

Integrate with science

Give scientific reasons:

- It is safer to find shelter under things like a bed and table at the time of earthquake.
- In Monsoons, do not take shelter near hillside.
- Do not use lifts at the time of earthquakes.
- The foundation of an earthquake-proof building is separated from other land.

Learning Tools

A. Complete the following chart:

Natural disasters

Human-made disasters

B. Make a folded chart and record notes about the eight types of disasters studied in the chapter. Organize the notes in the appropriate pockets.

1. Fold the number of vertical columns needed to make the chart.
2. Fold the horizontal rows needed to make the chart.
3. Label the columns with the names of different disasters.

Chart

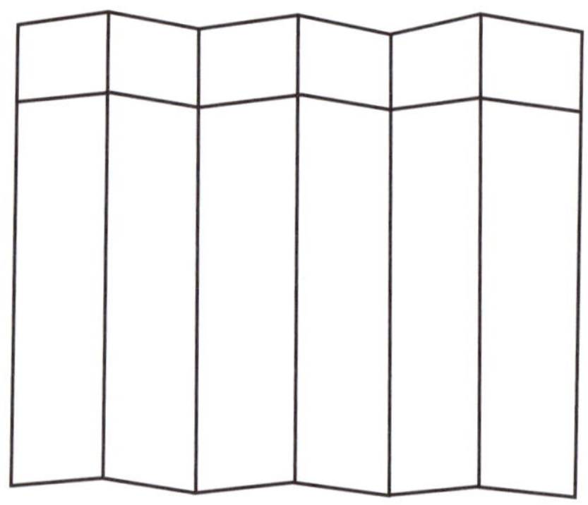

Web links:

https://ourworldindata.org/natural-disasters

https://www.nationalgeographic.com/environment/topic/natural-disasters-weather

Last accessed on 31 August 2021

1. The Indian Constitution

Warm up

Every word spoken in the Constituent Assembly, every debate and argument that went on among the members of the Assembly has been recorded in transcripts that run into 12 volumes. These books are known as *Constituent Assembly Debates* and help us understand the reason and logic behind whatever was included in the Constitution of India including how *Jana Gana Mana* became our national anthem. So, as we read about the Constitution of India, you can get information about the lengthiest constitution in the world by referring to these books.

After gaining freedom from British rule in 1947, the newly independent country needed a clearly defined set of laws and rules. The demand for a constitution was first made by the Indian National Congress in 1935. The unfair policies of the British and their **authoritarian** ways of working had created a **consensus** among the leaders and the people of India. They were certain that an independent India would be fair to all its people and that they would have a say in making the policies that would govern them.

In 1946, a Cabinet Mission from the United Kingdom was sent to India to plan the transfer of power from the British government to the Indian leaders. On December 9, 1946, the Constituent Assembly was formed. The Constitution of India was drafted by the Constituent Assembly.

The Constituent Assembly

The Constituent Assembly had around 300 members, who undertook the challenging task of writing the constitution for India in 1946. Dr B.R. Ambedkar was the chairman of the Drafting Committee. He is also known as the 'Father of the Indian Constitution'. The Constitution of India was adopted by the Constituent Assembly in 1949. It came into effect on January 26, 1950. The Constitution declared India a sovereign, socialist, secular and democratic republic and assured justice, equality and freedom to all Indian citizens.

Challenges Faced by the Constituent Assembly

1. The Congress won majority of seats in the elections for the Constituent Assembly. The Muslim League, which won a lower number of seats, started demanding a separate Constituent Assembly for the Muslims in India. During this time, communal riots broke out in different parts of the country, which resulted in the formation of two separate countries—India and Pakistan.
2. At the time of Independence, India had 565 princely states that were under the rulers and not the British. The status of these states was not clear and they were yet to be

authoritarian: enforcing strict obedience to authority at the expense of personal freedom; consensus: general or widespread agreement integrated into India. Some of the princely states were Patiala, Hyderabad, Mysore, Baroda and Kashmir.

3. India has diverse communities who speak different languages, follow different religions and have distinct cultures. The major challenge was to take care of the interests of diverse groups and maintain unity in diversity.
4. There were concerns for socioeconomic reforms and eradication of poverty as the condition of the people in India was dismal.

The Constitution of India

The Constitution of India originally had 395 articles, 22 parts and 8 schedules. Now the number of schedules is 12, after various amendments were made and added. It is the lengthiest constitution in the world and covers all aspects of governance and administration in detail. Over a hundred amendments have been made to the Indian Constitution as of 2019.

Importance of the Constitution

The constitution is an important document that contains a set of basic rules and laws that govern the country. The ideals that a country aspires to achieve are also laid out in the constitution to define the basic character of the country. The constitution also defines the nature of the country's political system. It was a crucial time for India when British rule ended and the country was truly independent of any external control. A decision was made about what kind of government India would have. The ideals of democracy and power to the people were upheld.

The constitution serves the very important purpose of safeguarding the interests of minorities. 'Rights for minorities should be absolute rights. They should not be subject to any consideration as to what another party may like to do to minorities within its jurisdiction', said B.R. Ambedkar in 1947. The minorities tend to be dominated by the majority, and situations can arise in a country when the interests and culture of the minority communities is threatened because of the majority, but the constitution safeguards the people.

The Preamble

The Preamble of India states that, 'We the people of India, having solemnly resolved to constitute India into a sovereign socialist secular democratic republic and to secure to all its citizens: justice, social, economic and political; liberty of thought, expression, belief, faith and worship; equality of status and of opportunity; and to promote among them all fraternity assuring the dignity of the individual and the unity and integrity of the Nation; In our constituent assembly this twenty-sixth day of November, 1949, do hereby adopt, enact and give to ourselves this constitution'.

FACT CHECK

The original constitution is kept in the library of the Parliament of India.

Features of the Indian Constitution

The salient features of the Constitution of India are:

Federalism: The makers of the Constitution understood that India is a vast and diverse country. It was not possible for a single government to govern the entire country. Therefore, India adopted a federal government with a central government at the centre and state governments to look after the states. Local governments were created to look after the needs of the people, and the Panchayati Raj was introduced to efficiently govern the villages of India. The Constitution contains three lists of subjects on which each level of the government can make laws. This is done to ensure that the powers and responsibilities of each level are clearly listed and that there are no clashes between them. The state governments derive their power from the constitution and not the central government.

Jawaharlal Nehru signing the Constitution of India

Parliamentary form of government: India is a representative democracy and the people exercise their power through representatives elected by them. These representatives are elected to various positions at different levels in the government. The people of India are guaranteed universal adult franchise through which they exercise the power to elect without discrimination on grounds of caste, religion, gender, region and language. There is a provision of bicameral legislature, which means that there would be two houses in the Parliament—the upper house or Rajya Sabha and the lower house or the Lok Sabha. As the names suggest, the Rajya Sabha represents the states and the Lok Sabha represents the people.

The Parliament House, New Delhi

Separation of powers: During the 18th century, the French philosopher, Montesquieu, propagated the idea of separating the powers of the three organs of the government. The Indian Constitution follows this idea propounded during the **French Revolution** in 1789. The three organs of the government—the legislature, the executive and the judiciary–have powers and responsibilities clearly differentiated from each other to ensure smooth functioning of the government. The legislature makes laws, the executive implements those laws and the judiciary enforces them. Thus, the three organs work effectively in tandem with each other.

Fundamental rights: Part three of the Indian Constitution contains the fundamental rights. These rights grant civil liberties to all the Indian citizens who were denied any rights during British rule. The fundamental rights are often referred to as the 'conscience' of the constitution.

The Constitution of India guarantees these fundamental rights—right to equality, right to freedom, right against exploitation, right to freedom of religion, cultural and educational rights, right to constitutional remedies and right to education. The Right of Children to Free and Compulsory Education Act, 2009, (RTE) provided by Department of School Education and Literacy, Ministry of Human Resource Development (MHRD) guarantees the right to education. A violation of any of these rights is punishable in any court of law.

French Revolution: a revolutionary movement in France that culminated in a dictatorship under Napoleon

Secularism: This means that there is no 'state religion' in India. Every individual is free to believe in and practise any religion he/she belongs to. The Constitution of India assures the Indian citizens that the state will not discriminate against any individual or a group on the basis of their religion.

Directive principles of state policy: The directive principles of state policy were included in the Indian Constitution to provide social and economic justice to the citizens of India. These principles aim at establishing a welfare state in India, where there will not be concentration of wealth in the hands of a few people. These principles are not enforceable by law.

What's in the picture?

Identify this person. Find out about the ideas contributed by him.

Fundamental duties: The fundamental duties were added to the Indian Constitution by the 42nd amendment, comprising a list of ten fundamental duties for all the citizens of India. Every citizen of India is expected to perform these duties.

A living constitution: The most significant feature of the Indian Constitution is that it is amendable. Keeping in mind the diverse nature of India, the makers of the Constitution made a provision to change certain parts of the Constitution to cater to the changing requirements of its citizens.

The first amendment to the Indian Constitution was made in 1951. Some important amendments of the Constitution are the 7th (reorganisation of states), 42nd (fundamental duties were added), 44th (right to property was removed as a fundamental right), 61st (18 years as the minimum age to vote) and 86th amendments (right to education added as fundamental right).

Fundamental Rights and Duties

Fundamental Rights

The basic fundamental rights guaranteed by the Indian Constitution are:

Right to equality: This right states that all persons are equal before law, and the laws apply equally to all the citizens of India. No one can be discriminated on the basis of religion, caste or sex. All public places, such as wells, playgrounds, hotels, hospitals, schools and shops are equally accessible to all people. The Constitution also prohibits the practice of untouchability.

Right to freedom: This right guarantees the following types of freedom.

1. Right to freedom of speech and expression;
2. Right to assemble peacefully and without arms;
3. Right to form associations or unions;
4. Right to move freely throughout the territory of India;
5. Right to reside and settle in any part of the territory of India;
6. Right to practise any profession or occupation, trade or business;
7. Right to education which entitles every child in the age group of 6 to 14, the right to free basic education, and
8. Right to information granting every citizen the right to know how the government works, what roles it plays and what its functions are.

Right against exploitation: This right prohibits human trafficking, forced labour and child labour.

Right to freedom of religion: The Constitution guarantees to all its citizens the freedom to practise, propagate and profess the religion of their choice.

Cultural and educational rights: According to this right, all minority communities, whether religious or linguistic, can set up their own educational institutions to preserve and propagate their culture.

Right to constitutional remedies: This right makes all other fundamental rights justiciable, as it allows the citizens to move the court of law if they feel any of their fundamental rights have been violated by any individual or state.

Case Study

Right to Education

The Constitution (86th amendment) Act, 2002, inserted Article 21-A in the Constitution of India to provide free and compulsory education for all children in the age group of six to fourteen years as a fundamental right in such a manner as the state may, by law, determine. The Right of Children to Free and Compulsory Education (RTE) Act, 2009, which represents the consequential legislation envisaged under Article 21-A, means that every child has a right to full-time elementary education of satisfactory and equitable quality in a formal school, which satisfies certain essential norms and standards.

Article 21-A and the RTE Act came into effect on 1st April 2010. The title of the RTE Act incorporates the words 'free and compulsory'. 'Free education' means that no child, other than a child who has been admitted by his or her parents to a school, which is not supported by the appropriate government, shall be liable to pay any kind of fee or charges or expenses that may prevent him or her from pursuing and completing elementary education. 'Compulsory education' casts an obligation on the appropriate Government and local authorities to provide and ensure admission, attendance and completion of elementary education by all children in the 6–14-year age group. With this, India has moved forward to a rights-based framework that casts a legal obligation on the central and state governments to implement this fundamental child right as enshrined in the Article 21A of the Constitution in accordance with the provisions of the RTE Act.

Q. How will the central government ensure that all states implement the provisions of RTE?

Fundamental Duties

Article 51A, Part IVA of the Indian Constitution, provides a list of fundamental duties of the citizens. It says it shall be the duty of every citizen of India:

1. to abide by the Constitution and respect its ideals and institutions;
2. to cherish and follow the noble ideals, which inspired our national struggle for freedom;
3. to uphold and protect the sovereignty, unity and integrity of India;
4. to defend the country and render national service when called upon to do so;

5. to promote harmony and the spirit of common brotherhood amongst all the people of India transcending religious, linguistic and regional diversities, to renounce practices derogatory to the dignity of women;
6. to value and preserve the rich heritage of our composite culture;
7. to protect and improve the natural environment including forests, lakes, rivers and wildlife and to have compassion for living creatures;
8. to develop the scientific temper, humanism and the spirit of inquiry and reform;
9. to safeguard public property and to **abjure** violence;
10. to strive towards excellence in all spheres of individual and collective activity so that the nation constantly rises to higher levels of endeavour and achievement.
11. to provide education to their children between the age of six and fourteen years. This duty was added to the original list by the 86th Amendment Act passed in 2002.

Green Earth

To protect and improve the natural environment, a fundamental duty, which is given in the Constitution, should be performed by all citizens.

Apply it!

Article 21A and article 45 are both related to education of students.

Article 21A is guaranteed as fundamental right, but Article 45 is a directive principle of state policy.

4 QUALITY EDUCATION

- Article 21 provides that the state shall provide free and compulsary education to children between 6–14 years of age.
- On the other hand Article 45 provides that the state shall endeavour to provide early childhood education and care for all children upto 6 years of age.
- A person of 6–14 years of age can move a court under 21A if he or she is not provided free and compulsory education.
- The case is not so with the article 45. No court can be moved against state for providing early childhood care and education to children upto six years of age.

Q. Why can people not go to court for non-compliance of provisions of Article 45?

World Connect

The Preamble of the Constitution of the United Stats of America states that: 'We the people of the United States, in Order to form a more perfect Union, establish justice, insure domestic tranquility, provide for the common defence, promote the general welfare, and secure the blessings of liberty to ourselves and our posterity, do ordain and establish this Constitution for the United States of America'.

Skill Builder

21ST CENTURY SKILLS

Life skills: Which neighbouring country of India has had to rewrite its Constitution? Why did they have to do it?

Information literacy: Collect news articles and pictures about the status of people in Myanmar and Nepal and the safeguards given in the constitution of these two countries. Do a comparative study between the constitutions of these countries and the Constitution of India. Present it in the form of a news collage or a PowerPoint presentation.

abjure: to solemnly renounce a belief, cause or claim

Wind up

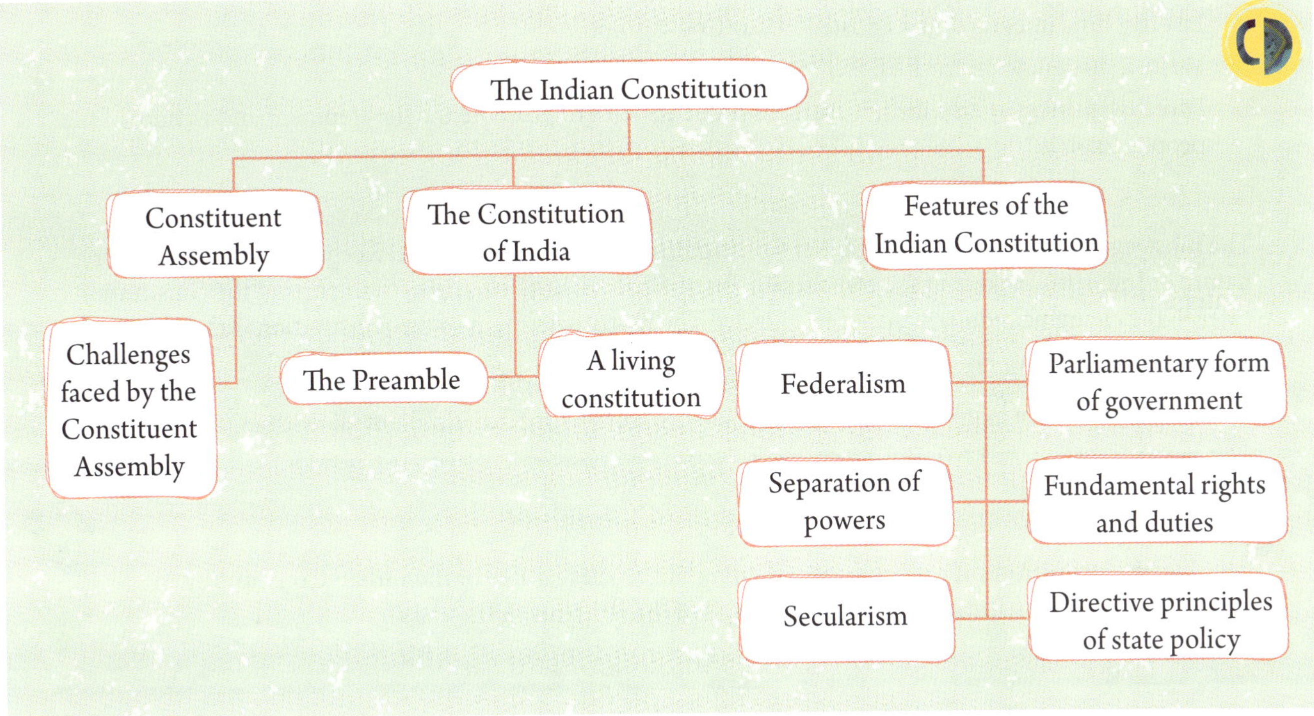

Exercises

A. Choose the correct answers.

1. A violation in any of the fundamental rights is
   a. acceptable by the courts
   b. punishable in any court of law
   c. tolerable by the justice system
   d. none of these
2. The Constituent Assembly had
   a. 200 members
   b. 300 members
   c. 600 members
   d. 250 members
3. This paved the way for the Constituent Assembly to start with the task of writing the constitution.
   a. Cabinet Mission
   b. Council Mission
   c. Cabinet Commission
   d. Union Mission
4. The absence of state religion is called
   a. socialism
   b. secularism
   c. federalism
   d. liberty

B. Write T for true and F for false.

1. The right to education prohibits trafficking of human beings. ☐
2. The right to freedom of religion makes all other rights justiciable. ☐
3. The right to freedom states that all citizens are equal before law. ☐
4. The right to constitutional remedies ensures that all minority communities can set up their own educational institutions. ☐

C. Answer these questions in brief.

1. What is a constitution and why is it important?
2. What is universal adult franchise?
3. What do you understand by separation of powers?

D. Answer these questions in detail.

1. List five fundamental duties enlisted in our Constitution.
2. Write a short note on the RTE Act.
3. Directive principles help the government frame policies to promote the development and welfare of the people. Explain.

E. Read the passage and answer the questions.

The most significant feature of the Indian Constitution is that it is amendable. Keeping in mind the diverse nature of India, the makers of the constitution made a provision to change certain parts of the constitution to cater to the changing requirements of its citizens. The first amendment to the constitution was made in 1951.

1. Why are amendments important?
2. What would have happened if the Indian Constitution was rigid and did not allow changes?

Think Big — Art integration

Design a constitution for your class, keeping the broad features of the Indian Constitution in mind. Your constitution should be fair to all of the students in the class.

Learning Tools

After reading the chapter, use major headings of the section to create an outline of the chapter.

Features of the Indian Constitution	Fundamental rights	Fundamental duties
....	....	....
....	....	....
....	....	....
....	....	....
....	....	....
....	....	....
....	....	....
....	....	....
....	....	....
....	....	....

Web links:

https://www.india.gov.in/my-government/constitution-india

Last accessed on 31 August 2021

2. Understanding Secularism

Warm up

Do you know that the term 'secular' was not always a part of the Preamble of the Indian Constitution? It was added to the Constitution in the 42nd Amendment.

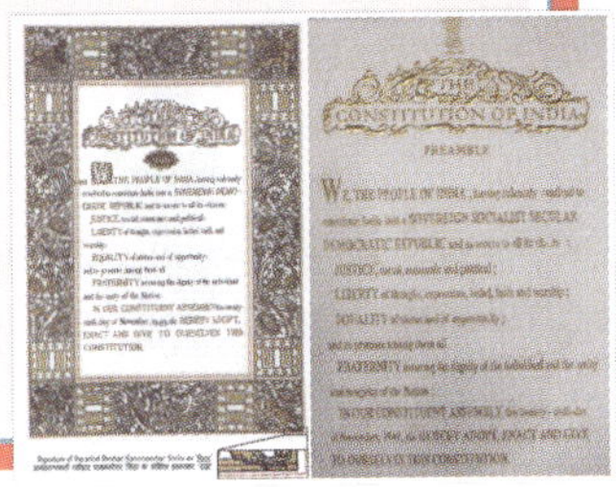

Secularism is one of the most significant ideals of the Preamble. According to the Constitution of India, the state will not be affected by religion. India does not have an official state religion. The government of a secular country treats the people from all the religions equally. It does not discriminate on the basis of religion. In other words, it does not **endorse** any religion. The festivals and important days of all religious communities are given equal recognition.

Why Secularism?

India is a secular nation

Have you ever wondered why India chose secularism? If the partition of the country took place on the basis of religion, why did India not proclaim itself to be a non-secular nation? Many countries in the world have an official state religion. The rules of these countries are completely different from the countries that do not have a state religion. Such a country is governed by religious heads and is called a theocracy. India preferred secularism over embracing one religion as the state religion because of its belief in the basic principle of equality. India is home to many religions and each has contributed in shaping the composite culture of India.

secularism: a system of social organization and education where religion is not allowed to play a part in civil affairs; endorse: declare one's public approval or support of

Religion, State and Politics

In a democracy, it is very important that religion and state power are separated. In today's world, every country has a population that follows different religions. People migrate from the country of their origin to other places in the world for better opportunities in life. Some religions are practised widely and some are followed by a smaller number of people. The basic **tenets** of democracy—liberty and equality–ensure that discrimination on the basis of religion is eradicated, irrespective of the number of people following it.

Interpretation of Religion

A modern democratic polity offers the freedom to practise a religion of your choice. An individual cannot be forced to practise the religion he or she is born into if he or she wishes to follow another religion. Sometimes people adopt or follow the ideals of many religions. In secular India, citizens enjoy the freedom to follow any religion of their choice.

In ancient times, the caste system was prevalent in the Indian society. The caste system was the hierarchical division of society based on one's birth. The system was followed rigidly and included the inhuman practice of untouchability. New religions, such as Buddhism and Jainism, used equality as their underlying principle.

Apply it!

More often than not, differences in religions have sparked violence and hostility amongst people. Make a peace dove using felt and give this symbol of peace to an Indian brother or sister who follows a different religion from you.

You will need, red felt, grey felt, scissors, cotton wool and red thread.

1. Make two cut outs of a heart, insert cotton wool in between the two and stitch them up together.
2. Make a cut out of a grey or white dove.
3. Use fabric glue to keep the dove in place. Then sew it on to the heart.

Your felt dove is ready!

Secularism in India

According to the Constitution of India, a secular state must ensure that:

- there is no inter-religious community domination;
- there is no intra-religious community domination;
- there is no state religion; and
- the religious freedom of individuals is guaranteed.

Some of the practices that explain the secular nation of the Indian state are:

1. Displaying national symbols and not religious symbols in the government and other important public buildings.
2. Avoiding restriction of the morning prayers to any one religion in all the government schools.
3. Celebrating all the religions with fervour and enthusiasm in all the public offices.

tenets: a principle or belief, especially one of the main principles of a religion or philosophy

Although the state upholds the principle of non-interference in religious affairs, it does make some exemptions. Some laws in India are sensitive to the needs of a particular religious community, and concessions are made in such cases.

The state sometimes purposely intervenes in religion to prevent the discrimination of a certain group of people by another group.

The Uniform Civil Code ensures that issues such as marriage, divorce and inheritance of property are treated fairly and according to the rules of a particular religion. The Indian Constitution distinguishes them from the other civil laws.

FACT CHECK

Many religious laws such as the Hindu Marriage Act, 1955, Muslim Personal Law, Christian Personal Law and the Special Marriage Act have been incorporated into the Indian Constitution under the Uniform Civil Code.

Difference between Western Secularism and Indian Secularism

In western countries, secularism means a complete breach between state and religion. The United States Constitution was amended to ensure that the legislature did not intervene in matters of religion. Read the amendment given below:

What's in the picture?

Which religions are represented by the symbols given here?

Why do you think religions need to have symbols?

Article [I] (Amendment 1—Freedom of expression and religion)

'Congress shall make no law respecting an establishment of religion, or prohibiting the free exercise thereof; or abridging the freedom of speech, or of the press; or the right of the people peaceably to assemble, and to petition the Government for a redress of grievances'.

In the United States of America, under no circumstance can the state interfere in religion or religion interfere in state affairs. The separation is to be strictly respected.

In India, the interpretation is different. To ensure equality of all citizens and religious communities, if the state has to intervene by making laws and allowing or banning certain practices, it would do so. For instance, the state can intervene in the Hindu caste system and abolish the practice of untouchability.

The Indian laws ensure that neutrality does not come at the cost of discrimination. If it does not intervene, then the constitutional principle of equality will be at stake. This is a yardstick by which we can say whether the intervention of state is to uphold human rights and to protect the Constitution or not.

Green Earth

Most religions preach living in harmony with nature and the environment.

Case Study

The Constitution and a Law by the Government

Article 1

'France shall be an indivisible, secular, democratic and social republic. It shall ensure the equality of all citizens before the law, without distinction of origin, race or religion. It shall respect all beliefs'.

In July 2014, France proposed a ban on Muslim women wearing the full-face veil called the niqab. This ban was upheld by the European Court of Human Rights. A case was filed by a 24-year-old French woman, who stated that under this ban, her freedom of religion and expression was being violated. However, French law dictates that no one can wear clothing that conceals the face in public places and if caught doing so, the person would be fined. A population of about five million Muslims reside in France.

1. What does the Constitution of France say about religion?
2. According to you, is the ban justified? Discuss and give reasons.

World Connect

John F. Kennedy was one of America's most influential presidents of the 20th century. On the topic of separation of Church from the state in 1960, he said 'I believe in an America where the separation of church and state is absolute where no Catholic prelate would tell the President (should he be Catholic) how to act, and no Protestant minister would tell his parishioners for whom to vote—where no church or church school is granted any public funds or political preference—and where no man is denied public office merely because his religion differs from the President who might appoint him or the people who might elect him'.

Skill Builder

21ST CENTURY SKILLS

Critical thinking skills: Have you read about persecution and incidents of violence based on religion from around the world? Take any one such incident and see what could have been done differently to turn the situation around.

Life skills: Make at least two rules to make your class secular. Find out if you have classmates from different religions in your class.

Collaboration: Ask your classmates and teachers about the festivals they celebrate, and list them in your notebook. This would help you understand the diversity that surrounds us.

Wind up

- Secularism
  - Why secularism?
    - Religion, state and politics
  - Secularism in India
    - Uniform Civil Code
    - Difference between western and Indian secularism

Exercises

A. Choose the correct answers.

1. Secularism means the absence of a
   a. state religion b. religion c. religious law d. religious head

2. India is a
   a. theocratic country b. secular country c. dictatorial country d. autocratic country

3. A theocratic nation follows this type of religion.
   a. Personal b. State c. Minority d. Majority

4. In India, there is intercommunity
   a. tolerance b. domination c. subjugation d. discrimination

B. Correct these statements.

1. In India, people are not allowed to change their religions.
2. In most countries, only one religion is found.
3. Minorities always tend to dominate.
4. Buddhism and Jainism propagated the caste system.
5. In the US, the state often interferes in religion.

C. Define:

1. Secularism
2. Theocracy
3. Uniform Civil Code

D. Answer these questions in brief.

1. How did secularism become a part of the Indian Constitution?
2. When does the Indian state interfere in the religious affairs of its citizens?
3. Secularism is the need of the world today. Give reasons for your answer.
4. What are the tenets of democracy?

E. Answer these questions in detail.

1. How is secularism in the US different from that in India?
2. List three practices that the Indian state follows to declare itself a secular state.
3. How did the caste system affect the secular perspective of the Indian people?

F. Read the passage and answer the questions.

In a democracy, it is very important that religion and state power are separated. History is a witness that politics of religion brings harm and divide the society. In today's world, every country has a population, which follows different religions. People migrate from the country of their origin to other places in the world for better opportunities in life. Some religions are practised widely and some are followed by only a small number of people.

a. Can you recall an incident from history, in which religion was the cause of the conflict?
b. Why is it important to separate religion and state power?

Think Big — Social emotional learning

Create a collage of photographs of all the students in your class and paste them on a chart. On that chart, join two photos of people who share similar beliefs using a red pen. Along the line, write how they are similar, for example, both are Hindu. Join two photos of people who share different beliefs and faiths using a green pen. Speak to these two people, find out two similarities between the two and write them along the green line.

Now, write a note on what you understand about secularism after doing this activity.

Learning Tools

Based on what you have studied in the chapter, write your own notes on the following.

Why secularism?

Religion, state and politics

Interpretation of religion

Secularism in India

Difference between western secularism and Indian secularism

Web links:

https://www.cvs.edu.in/upload/Secularism-in-India.pdf

Last accessed on 31 August 2021

3. The Indian Parliament

Warm up

The Parliament of India is the supreme law-making body of the country. This beautiful and imposing building was designed by Sir Edwin Lutyens and Sir Herbert Baker. The stately red sandstone structure includes many characteristic features of Mughal architecture and draws from the rich elements of Indian architectural style. The Central Vista Project is underway to renovate the building and modernise it to accommodate the demands of the changing times.

Our country has a long history of monarchy and people were under the rule of different dynasties and rulers in the ancient and medieval times. Under British rule, the status of the people of India was neither that of subjects nor of citizens. Today, we have the power to elect our representatives who form the government and rule on our behalf. In this, people have the power and they exercise this power through elected representatives.

Under the British, only some people were allowed to vote and universal adult franchise was granted to the people of India only after Independence. The absence of rights and freedoms under British rule had made it clear to the people that they did not want a similar administration in independent India. The national movement, thus, played a key role in preparing the people for their future role as citizens. After gaining Independence, the Constitution granted a representative democratic set-up in India.

Why Election and not Selection?

Elections involve the choice of a large majority of people and accommodate different communities that make up the population of our country. It is in the larger interest of the society. Selection involves the opinions of only a few people and can go against the wishes of a large number of people and favours only a few.

A government formed by the consent and approval of people is more likely to enjoy their support. People show their approval through electing representatives. These representatives also work well as they know that they carry the aspirations, faith and confidence people have shown in them.

Parliament

The Indian Parliament is also known as the *Sansad*. It is the legislative body of the country. The Union Legislature or Parliament makes laws for the whole country and is a symbol of India's democracy. It is a powerful institution as the people of this country elect their representatives who then exercise power on their behalf.

There are three sessions of the Parliament. They are the Budget Session, which takes place from February to May, the Monsoon Session, which takes place from July to September, and the Winter Session, which takes place from November to December.

The Formation of the Parliament

The Parliament consists of the President and the two Houses, the Lok Sabha or the House of the People and the Rajya Sabha or the House of States. The Lok Sabha is formed through general elections for which the country is divided into constituencies. The democratic principle of universal adult franchise consisting of the right to vote is guaranteed to all the citizens of India of 18 years or above in age. It empowers all adult citizens irrespective of education, income, gender, social status, caste or ethnicity.

Lok Sabha: The Lok Sabha consists of 545 Members. Of these, 543 members are elected, and * two Anglo Indians, who are elected from all over the country, are nominated by the President. Our country is divided into 543 constituencies and from each, one member is elected. The elected members are called MPs or members of parliament.

The Lok Sabha is the lower house of the Parliament but is more powerful than the Rajya Sabha. This is because the people directly elect the MPs who represent the people. Two members are nominated because the Anglo-Indian community is in a very small minority and might not get representation if left to the election like other communities. The Lok Sabha is elected for a fixed term of five years and gets dissolved at the end of that period. After this, general elections are held again. The Lok Sabha is presided over by the Speaker. The Speaker conducts the proceedings of the House in an orderly manner.

After the election results are tabulated, if a political party has to form the government, it should have secured at least half the number of seats or more. In political terms, this is called the magic number of 272. If a political party is not able to secure these many seats, then it can form an alliance with other political parties to attain the required number. If a party secures more than 272 seats, it can form a clear majority government. If they get into an alliance with other parties to form the government, then it is a coalition. The political parties that win some seats form the opposition. The largest among them is the opposition party.

An all-party meeting

Rajya Sabha: The Rajya Sabha is the upper house of the Parliament and represents the states of India in the Parliament. It has 250 members, of which 238 are elected and 12 are nominated by the President. These can be well-known people from any walk of life, who have made a significant contribution to their field of work. The Rajya Sabha is a permanent house and does not get dissolved after a fixed term. The members of the Rajya Sabha are elected by the MLAs or the members of the state legislative assemblies. One-third of the members of the Rajya Sabha retire after every second year. Each Rajya Sabha MP has a six-year term. The Vice-President of India is the chairperson of the Rajya Sabha by virtue of his/her post.

* Article 334, clause (b) of the Indian Constitution, provided for the nomination of two members of the Anglo-Indian community in order to ensure their representation in the House of the People and Legislative Assemblies of States. With the Constitution (104th Amendment) Act, January 2020, the implementation of this clause ceases.

Functioning of the Parliament

The Parliament begins with an address of the President. Article 87(1) of the Constitution states, 'At the commencement of the first session after each general election to the House of Representatives, the President shall address both houses of Parliament assembled together and inform them of the causes of the summons'.

Apply it!

Divide the class into two groups–one being the Lok Sabha and the other the Rajya Sabha. Divide classroom duties between the two. Do you think one can survive without the other? How would the country be affected if only one house, the Lok Sabha, made up the Parliament?

Question hour: The Parliament in session begins with a Question Hour in which the members of the opposition and other members can ask questions to the ministers and prime minister. The ministers have to answer these questions, and thus, they become accountable to the Parliament. The opposition keeps the ministers alert and answerable to the people about their policies. Law-making is also a very important role of the legislature.

RAJYA SABHA QUESTIONS & ANSWERS

Starred Questions: These are questions to which answers are desired to be given orally on the floor of the House during the Question Hour. These are distinguished in the printed lists by asterisks. 15 such questions are listed each day.

Unstarred Questions: These are questions to which written answers are given by ministers, which are deemed to have been laid on the Table of the House at the end of the Question Hour. Up to 160 such questions are listed each day in a separate list.

Short Notice Questions: Such questions can be asked orally in the House after the Question Hour or as the first item in the agenda where there is no Question Hour at a notice shorter than that prescribed for starred and unstarred questions. These must relate to a subject-matter considered by the Chairman to be of urgent public importance.

Parliament Forms the Government

The Parliament is the legislature and forms the executive. The legislature makes laws and the executive implements those laws. People commonly use the term, executive, interchangeably with the term, government. As per the results of the general elections, the party that has won more than half of the number of seats forms the government. The prime minister is the leader of the ruling party in the Lok Sabha. From the other MPs in the Lok Sabha, he/she selects a team of ministers who head different ministries like defence, external affairs and finance. Thus, it is their responsibility to implement the laws made by the Parliament through their ministries and the departments, which come under it.

Green Earth

The Environment Protection Act 1986 was enacted by the Parliament to protect the environment, where 'environment' included land, water, air, human beings and nature in all its diversity.

Election Commission of India

The Election Commission of India is responsible for conducting elections in the country. It plays a key role in forming our Parliament. The Chief Election Commissioner (CEC) is the head of the Commission.

The Election Commission of India conducts the election in all the constituencies across the country in a phased manner.

Before independence, India had a long history of people being treated unequally. The Constitution declared everyone as equal and advocated equal privileges and freedom for all. There were many communities like Dalits, that had to face discrimination and humiliation on the basis of their caste. Women were always relegated to the background and not considered capable of a public life or a career. To make the so-called backward communities at par with the rest of the society, the Constitution reserves some seats in the Parliament for the Scheduled Castes, Scheduled Tribes and OBCs or Other Backward Castes. These communities, it was feared, would lose out and not get represented in the Parliament in open elections. The Parliament is a very important institution of India and is a reflection of the Indian society as it has representatives from all sections of the society. Every community, whether majority or minority, should be able to voice the opinions freely and be heard.

Over the years, people of all communities have been able to win seats from different constituencies, thereby breaking the barriers between the rich and poor, educated and illiterate and so on. This diversity of representation in the Parliament is a unique feature of our country.

Case Study

The Election Commission organizes a 'Matdata Mahotsav' event to involve voters and citizens from all walks of life specifically women, youth, defence personnel, non-resident Indians, persons with disabilities and those from marginalised sections for enhanced sense of inclusion, greater awareness about the electoral process and strengthening SVEEP (Systematic Voters' Education & Electoral Participation) programme.

The voters' fest hosts national exhibition to showcase various dimensions of election management, which are, electoral roll, IT and technology, security, mobilisation of personnel and resources, voters' education, election material, expenditure monitoring and many more. A walk through the complete electoral process from registration to voting is given for voters to comprehend their duty and right of universal adult franchise better.

1. Why does the Election Commission organize activities like 'Matdata Mahotsav'?
2. What does 'Matdata Mahotsav' mean?

World Connect

Women are participating more in governance of the countries. The regional average of women in both houses in the world parliaments as per inter-parliamentary union in January 2019 was:

Nordic countries: 44%

Americas: 30.8%

Europe 28: 1%

Sub-Saharan Africa: 24.1%

Asia: 19.7%

Middle East and North Africa: 16.8%

Pacific: 19.5%

Skill Builder

21ST CENTURY SKILLS

Life skills: If you were elected to the Lok Sabha, list out two current issues that would be your priority.

Critical thinking skills: List five questions based on actual issues with your group members, which you will ask the ministers in the Lok Sabha during the Question Hour. Each member of the group must contribute at least one question.

Information literacy: When did the first Lok Sabha convene?

Wind up

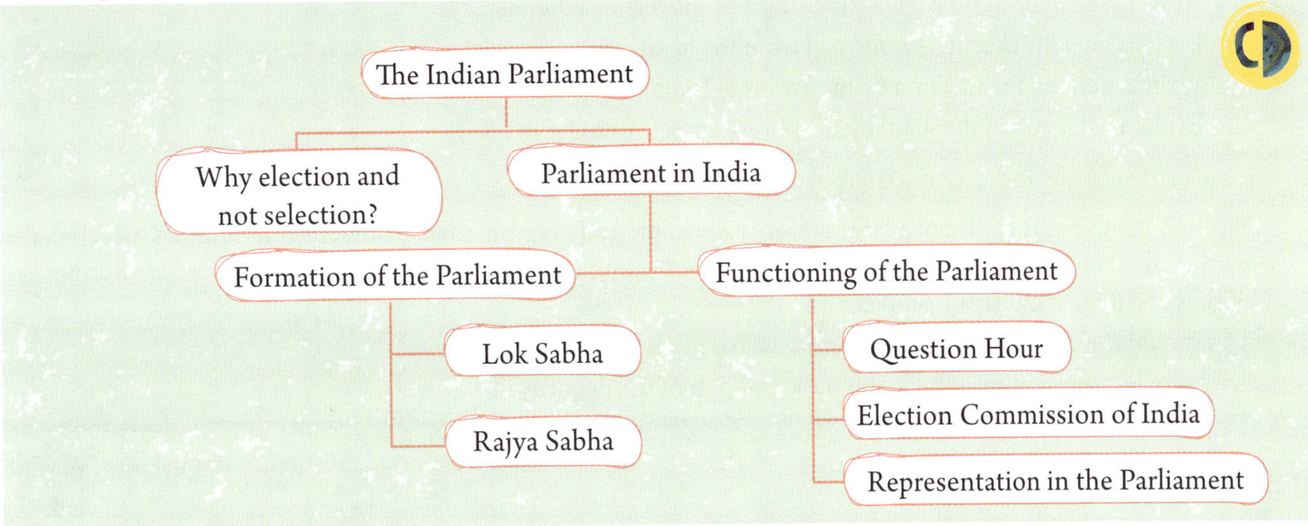

Exercises

A. Choose the correct answers.

1. The Lok Sabha is presided over by the
   a. Prime Minister b. Speaker c. President d. Chairman
2. Some seats in the Parliament are reserved for
   a. Scheduled Tribes b. majority communities c. Brahmins d. all of the above
3. After the general elections, the first session of both houses is addressed by the
   a. Prime Minister b. President c. Speaker d. Chairman
4. Questions which are related to matters of public importance are called
   a. unstarred b. short notice c. starred d. important

B. Explain the following terms.

1. Citizens
2. Coalition
3. Clear majority
4. *Sansad*
5. Starred questions

C. Correct the following statements:

1. The prime minister is the head of the Election Commission.
2. The Rajya Sabha is the lower house of the Parliament.

3. If a political party wins a clear majority, it can form a coalition government.
4. Under the British, everyone had the right to vote.

D. Answer these questions in brief.

1. What is a coalition?
2. What are general elections?
3. What is the role of the Election Commission in the formation of the Parliament?
4. What is the Question Hour?

E. Answer these questions in detail.

1. How do the opposition parties play a significant role in a democracy?
2. Explain how the executive is formed from the legislature.
3. Write a note on the Election Commission of India.
4. Explain what you understand by the phrase, 'magic number of 272'.

F. Read the passage and answer the questions.

Election involves the choice of a large majority of people and accommodates different communities, which make up the population of the country. Selection involves the opinions of only a few people and can go against the wishes of a large majority of people.

1. Should the government of the country be based on selection? Give reasons.
2. Why is it important to think about the opinion of the majority?

Think Big — English fun

Imagine that you have just become a member of the Lok Sabha. Write your first speech outlining your vision and hope. Remember to thank those who helped you, acknowledge people who have inspired you and speak about the needs of the electorate.

Learning Tools

Fold your chart along the dotted lines and list what you have learnt in the chapter under each head.

The Indian Parliament			
Why election and not selection	Parliament – formation and functioning	Parliament forms the government	Election Commission

Web links:

https://www.india.gov.in/my-government/indian-parliament

Last accessed on 31 August 2021

4. Laws

Warm up

Hammurabi's Code of Law is one of the most ancient and extensive codes of law from the 18th BCE. This code of the King of Babylon covers civil and criminal subjects, marriage, slavery, laws related to trade and family, details about penalties and punishments for each crime. The code promoted the punitive principle of 'an eye for an eye and a tooth for a tooth'. Discuss in the class if that an ethical principle of punishment or not.

The Constitution of India guarantees to all its citizens equality before law. This means that all citizens are considered equal before the law of the land. There will be no discrimination on any basis. Laws apply to all citizens and in the same manner. This is called the rule of law. The monarch has the supreme power over the kingdom in a monarchy. However, in the rule of law, the law is supreme and is considered more important than the people in power. The president, prime minister, ministers are not exempted from these laws despite their position. Everyone would be bound by the same laws.

Influence of History

During British rule, Indians suffered because of the lack of fair laws. By the early 20th century, leaders in India began protesting against the **arbitrary** laws of the British. The Indian society was caste-ridden before India gained freedom. The British made attempts to introduce social reforms but the Indian society was not ready to accept them and their efforts were considered as interference in the social and religious fabric of India eventually leading to the Revolt of 1857.

Therefore, there were two major problems for Indians—discrimination by the British and being treated unequally by the other affluent people of India. The makers of the Constitution understood these problems and sought to ensure that in an independent India, people did not have to face unequal treatment by others and the same written set of rules and laws were binding on the people as well as the authorities.

Arbitrary British Laws

The British government in India made many repressive laws. The Sedition Act passed by the British legislature in 1870 empowered the British to imprison anyone without a free trial. Anyone who criticized or exhibited disaffection for the British government in India was punished.

arbitrary: based on random choice or personal whim, rather than any reason or system

The Rowlatt Act, 1919 empowered the British to imprison Indians on mere suspicion. Punishments could be given without any trial by a court of law. Both Sedition Act and the Rowlatt Act were widely protested by Indian nationalists and the people. In one such protest against the Rowlatt Act on April 13, 1919, General Dyer opened fire on people who had gathered in Jallianwala Bagh in Amritsar. This massacre of men, women and children was widely protested in India and was even criticized by the British government.

Many lawyers fought for the cause of freedom during British rule. C.R. Das, Saifuddin Kitchlew, Dr Rajendra Prasad and Sardar Patel were a few lawyers who represented the people of India and the cause of nationalism. Various injustices of the British were highlighted by them during the court trials. Laws were now expected to be fair and just to all as against the earlier laws that were simply imposed on the people and were devoid of justice and equality.

Making a New Law

Laws originate from new situations and needs that may arise in society from time to time. A new law can be proposed by a group or single member of the parliament. A proposal for a new law is called a bill. The transformation of a bill to law generally takes a long time. The laws are made after proper discussion and deliberation. The decision is made on the basis of a majority.

There are two categories of bills—ordinary bills and money bills.

- Ordinary bills are those that can be introduced in either of the houses of Parliament.
- Money bills can be introduced only in the Lok Sabha. These are related to finances of the country and include imposition of new taxes, increase in the existing ones or abolition of any tax.
- A bill has to go through three readings and voting in each house of the Parliament.
- Once passed from the house where they were introduced, they are sent to the other house.
- The same procedure of three readings and voting is repeated and then they are sent for the approval of the President.
- The President may or may not send it back to the Parliament with suggested amendments twice. If suggestions are not accommodated then the President has to sign the bill the third time and it is passed.
- A bill thus becomes a law.

Role of the People

Sometimes it is not the members of Parliament (MPs) but the people who seek new laws to be made by Parliament. People raise issues and attract the attention of the Parliament through various ways. Democracy is successful only when the delicate balance of demand from the people and response from the government is maintained.

Green Earth

Laws such as the Environment Protection Act 1986 have been implemented to protect the environment from pollution and improve the quality of the environment.

India is a developing country and is making progress by leaps and bounds in all fields. Its pace of development has slowed down because of charges of corruption against various authorities and officials. Let us read the journey of the Jan Lokpal Bill to understand how the demand of the people for a corruption-free India became a movement. Thousands of people from across the country joined this anti-graft movement to end corruption.

Case Study

Lokpal Bill

The Lokpal bill was first introduced in the Parliament in 1968. It has a long history and underwent many twists and turns on its journey. The bill sought to establish a strong anti-corruption institution called the Jan Lokpal or the ombudsman. This authority was to be free of government control and supervised by the Election Commission of India and the cabinet secretary. The demand for this was raised by the people led by Anna Hazare, a social activist and leader, in 2011. A mass movement known as 'India Against Corruption' was launched.

According to the survey conducted by STAR News (now ABP News) and Nielsen, a market research company, 87 per cent of the 8,900 respondents of the survey supported the Jan Lokpal bill. The survey was conducted in 28 cities across the country. Almost a million people joined the *Times of India* online anti-graft campaign, in one of the biggest ever voting exercises held online. The Lokpal bill was finally passed by both the houses of Parliament in 2013. The 'I am Anna' caps became very popular with the people. Hundreds of people could be seen wearing these caps with pride in support of the movement.

- What is the role of a leader in this movement?
- How do we know that people supported the anti-graft movement?
- Do you think that wearing clothes with slogans or symbols are also a way of showing support for a cause?

Controversial Laws

Just as people play a key role in influencing the Parliament to make new laws, they also have the power to get **controversial** laws amended. Repressive laws are the laws that, in some way, interfere with the fundamental rights of the citizens. If the law is not in accordance to the Constitution, then the judiciary has the power to scrape it.

Section 66A of the Information Technology Act, 2000 was enacted in 2008 by the Parliament to protect the victims from cybercrimes. It brought those people who were allegedly causing annoyance, inconvenience, danger, obstruction, insult, injury, criminal intimidation, enmity, hatred or ill will using the Internet under the scanner of the law. While the law sought to protect people against Internet-related abuse, a petition was filed against it. Civil society groups argued that Section 66A violated the right to the freedom of speech and expression.

FACT CHECK

The Right to Information Act, 2005, is an act to provide information to the citizens under the control of public authorities to promote transparency and accountability in the working process of every public office.

In 2012, two young women were arrested under the Information Technology Act, 2000, for posting comments on the Internet against the government-sponsored shutdown of Mumbai following the death of a renowned political leader in Maharashtra. This caused widespread protests from people in all parts of the country. Following the protests, the Supreme Court of India repealed Section 66A of the Information Technology Act. Justice R.F. Nariman said, 'Section 66A is unconstitutional and we have no hesitation in striking it down'.

However, as responsible people, we must remember that while we enjoy the rights guaranteed in the Constitution, an effort must also be made to sincerely perform the duties of a citizen. A democracy can

controversial: giving rise or likely to give rise to public disagreement function only when people take a keen interest in the functioning of the institutions of the country. Electing representatives is not the end but the beginning of the responsibility for a citizen. A close observation of the work done by their elected representatives helps the citizens vote for the right candidate in the elections. People can participate in the government by being aware and raising their voice against any unjust laws or actions of the government. Supporting the government in its people-friendly initiatives is also the responsibility of the citizens.

Apply it!

The UN Women had launched a campaign called 'HeForShe' to end the worldwide problem of domestic violence and abuse of women. This initiative was started to sensitize men all over the world about the importance of gender equality. What is the significance of naming the campaign as 'HeForShe'?

World Connect

In South Africa, a policy of racial segregation known as 'apartheid' was followed. It was started by the white minority government formed by the National Party, which ruled over South Africa after World War II. The so-called blacks or the native people were discriminated against by the white minority government. Rules were not equal, and people suffered humiliation and unequal treatment in education, healthcare facilities and other public services. Gradually, people started protesting against the system. Along with internal disturbance, international pressure started building up on the government in support of the people's movement. The international community placed sanctions over the government. In wake of these developments, elections were conducted in South Africa for the first time and were won by the African National Congress under Nelson Mandela in 1994.

Skill Builder

21st Century Skills

Life skills: An almanac or a school diary contains all the rules of the school. Why do you think the rules of the school are written there? Think of what would happen if the school uniform, summer and winter timings other rules were not mentioned there.

Critical thinking skills: In India, the laws related to the protection of rivers are either too old or not strictly enforced. Form at least two laws within your group for the protection and cleanliness of rivers.

Communication skills: A democracy can function only when people take a keen interest in the functioning of the institutions of the country. Discuss this topic in the class.

Wind up

- Laws
  - Influence of history
    - Arbitrary British laws
      - Sedition Act, 1870
      - Rowlatt Act, 1919
  - Making a new law
    - Role of the people
      - Jan Lokpal bill
    - Controversial laws
      - Information Technology Act, 2020

Exercises

A. Choose the correct answers.

1. Money bills can only be introduced in the
   a. Lok Sabha b. Rajya Sabha c. Supreme Court d. high court
2. The Jan Lokpal bill was finally passed by
   a. one house b. both Houses of the Parliament
   c. Supreme Court d. Lok Sabha
3. The Right to Information Act was passed in
   a. 2005 b. 2006 c. 2002 d. 2010
4. Section 66A was repealed by the Supreme Court because
   a. it was too long b. it violated freedom of speech and expression
   c. it was redundant d. it violated the right to equality
5. Anna Hazare campaigned for
   a. Lokpal bill b. Domestic Violence bill
   c. Money bill d. Special Marriage bill

B. Correct these statements.

1. Ordinary bills can only be introduced in the Rajya Sabha.
2. The Right to Education makes information available to the people.
3. The Rowlatt Act came into force in 1920.
4. People do not have any role to play in making laws.
5. During British rule, laws were fair and just.

C. Arrange the sentences in the correct order.

1. The bill is sent to the other House. ☐
2. The President signs the bill. ☐
3. The bill is introduced. ☐
4. Voting of the bill takes place. ☐
5. The bill goes through three readings. ☐
6. The procedure is repeated. ☐

D. Answer these questions in brief.

1. What are money bills?
2. Differentiate between money bills and ordinary bills.
3. How did the British influence the process of law-making?
4. Name two arbitrary British laws.

E. Answer these questions in detail.

1. In what ways were the laws made by the British arbitrary?
2. Name two prominent lawyers of the British period. What were their contributions to the freedom struggle?
3. Why was Section 66A of the Information Technology Act repealed by the Court?
4. Explain the steps followed towards making a new law.

F. Read the passage and answer the questions.

Sometimes it is not the Members of Parliament but the people who seek new laws to be made by the Parliament. People raise issues and attract the attention of the Parliament through various ways. Democracy is successful only when the delicate balance of demand from the people and response from the government is maintained.

1. Why is it important for a democratic government to respond to the people?
2. Can you find out about one law that got made because of the demands raised by the people?

Think Big

Subject integration

Laws are required not only for the proper functioning of society but in mathematics, science and economics too. Name one law for each subject, and explain why it is important.

Learning Tools

Fill up the boxes with what you have learnt in the chapter.

Ordinary bills

....
....
....
....
....
....
....

Money bills

....
....
....
....
....
....
....

Controversial laws

....
....
....
....
....
....
....

Role of the people

....
....
....
....
....
....
....

Web links:

http://164.100.47.194/Loksabha/Legislation/Legislation.aspx

Last accessed on 31 August 2021

5. Judiciary in India

Warm up

This is the symbol of the Apex Court of India. It consists of the Ashoka Chakra and the National Emblem. Discuss with your classmates about the motto written in Sanskrit under the logo.

The main responsibility of the judiciary is to settle disputes between groups and individuals or groups and the government. All disputes are settled according to the rule of law. The judiciary protects the rule of law. It also safeguards the rights of individuals.

Structure of the Judiciary

India has a single integrated judicial system. The structure of the Indian judiciary is pyramidal, with the Supreme Court at the top, high courts below them and the district and the subordinate courts at the lowest level.

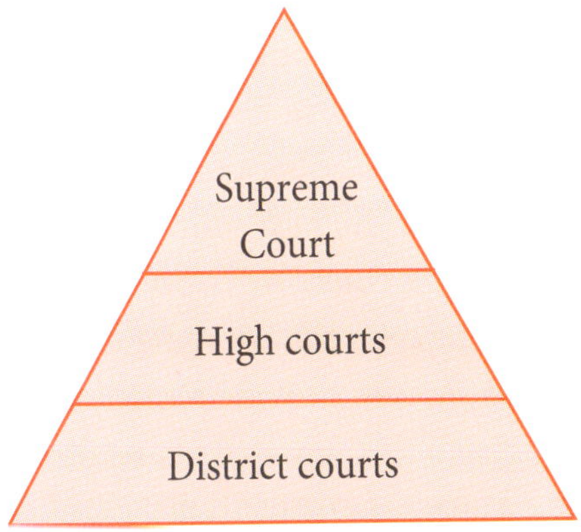

Judiciary in India

The judiciary resolves disputes, reviews laws and enforces the fundamental rights. It is responsible for resolving any disputes that may arise between two citizens, between a citizen and government, between two state governments or between the central and state governments. Courts are the final **arbitrators** on matters related to laws and their interpretation.

Integrated System of Judiciary

In India, there is a hierarchy of courts. The Supreme Court, high courts of the states and the subordinate courts are connected or integrated to each other. It works in two ways. If a person is not satisfied with the judgement of the lower court, the person can appeal to the higher court. A fresh appeal can be made in a higher court if they feel that justice has not been done. This provision of the judiciary is called appellate jurisdiction, a way to ensure full justice to a person. For example, in Manu Sharma vs. State (NCT of Delhi), (2010) 6 SCC 1 case, the lower court had acquitted the accused due to lack of evidence but the high court pronounced him guilty of murder. Under appellate jurisdiction, the Supreme Court upheld the decision of the high court, saying that it has analysed all the evidence and arrived at the correct conclusion. The verdict on the Jessica Lal case was one of the landmark judgments of the Supreme Court establishing the integrated judicial system in India.

arbitrator: someone who is chosen to settle a dispute

Appointment and Removal of Judges

The judges of the Supreme Court and the high courts are appointed by the President of India after consulting the Chief Justice of India (CJI). The Chief Justice of India recommends the names of four senior-most judges to the President.

The Chief Justice of India is the highest judicial position in India. He or she is appointed by the President of India. Usually, the senior-most judge of the Supreme Court is appointed as the Chief Justice.

A judge of the Supreme Court or the high courts can be removed only on the grounds of proven misbehaviour or incapacity. The removal of a judge must receive a majority support in both the Houses of the Parliament.

What's in the picture?

Identify this building, and say where it is located. What kinds of duties does it perform?

Jurisdiction of the Courts

You know that India has courts at the union level, state level and local level.

The Supreme Court: The Supreme Court of India has four kinds of jurisdictions—original, appellate, advisory and writ. Under the original jurisdiction, the Supreme Court hears the cases between two state governments or between a state and the central government. Appellate jurisdiction means that the Supreme Court is the highest court of appeal and any person can appeal to the Supreme Court against the decisions of the high court. Advisory jurisdiction means that the President of India can refer any matter of public importance to the Supreme Court. Under the writ jurisdiction, the Supreme Court can issue special orders called writs to provide remedy to the citizens whose fundamental rights have been violated. Such people can approach the Supreme Court directly.

- **Habeas Corpus:** It protects the people against unlawful detention and imprisonment.
- **Prohibition:** The Supreme Court and the high courts can prohibit the lower courts or magistrates from passing a judgement that exceeds their jurisdiction.
- **Certiorari:** A higher court can issue this writ to a lower court to transfer a case that has been pending because it is not in the jurisdiction of the lower court.
- **Quo Warranto:** This writ prevents public offices being taken over by someone who is not occupying it in a legal or lawful manner.
- **Mandamus:** This is issued to lower courts, public offices or officials, corporations or tribunals to instruct them to perform a public or statutory duty.

High Court

High courts deal with cases that come under the jurisdiction of the state. They can hear appeals from the lower courts. They also supervise and control the functioning of the courts below them. They can issue writs for restoring fundamental rights. All the union territories are attached to the high court of a neighbouring state.

District Courts

District courts deal with cases arising in the district. They also decide cases involving serious criminal offenses. The district courts appeal on decisions given by the lower courts.

FACT CHECK

The Supreme Court of India was inaugurated on 28 January, 1950.

Tribunals

As the number of cases reaching the courts increased manifold, many tribunals or special courts were established. These dealt with cases related to a particular sector. Although the tribunals do not have extensive powers to punish the offenders, they take considerable load off the regular courts. The National Green Tribunal (NGT) was set up in 2010 for speedy disposal of cases related to environment protection and conservation of natural resources. Securities and Exchange Board of India (SEBI) and Telecom Regulatory Authority of India (TRAI) are some well-known examples.

Litigation in India

Civil and Criminal law

The judiciary in India deals broadly with two kinds of cases—civil and criminal. A civil case can be filed for causing an injury, harm or violation of fundamental rights of an individual. Most civil cases pertain to issues such as divorce, employee-employer conflicts, buyer-builder conflicts, sale and purchase of goods or property, rental agreements, etc. The main objective is to get compensation for the affected party. Either of the people involved in a civil dispute should approach the court and file a petition.

A criminal offence is a 'crime against society'. Theft, harassment and demand for dowry are some examples of criminal offences. If a crime has taken place, the First Information Report (FIR) is lodged with the police. The police then investigate the crime. A case is then filed by the police in a court of law. Punishment for the person who has committed the crime is the primary objective of criminal law.

Judicial Review

If any law is made by the legislature, which is not in accordance with the Indian Constitution, the judiciary is empowered to review it. The judiciary can suggest changes to the law or repeal them. The court has the final authority to interpret the Indian Constitution.

Article 32 of the Constitution empowers the Supreme Court and Article 226 of the Constitution empowers the high courts to enforce the fundamental rights. If citizens feel that their fundamental rights are being violated by any person or government, they can appeal to the Supreme Court and high courts. The court issues orders or writs to protect these rights.

Public Interest Litigation

Courts in the country do not discriminate among the people on any basis and justice is available to all. However, many people avoid court cases as the court procedures are very complicated. It is extremely difficult for a layman to get paperwork done, approach a lawyer and bear the expense of the case. Sometimes the people who are suffering inhuman or exploitative conditions at work are too poor and incapable of demanding justice. They continue to suffer in silence as the people who are exploiting them are powerful and influential.

To solve these problems, a provision of Public Interest Litigation (PIL) was introduced by the Supreme Court in the 1980s. PIL has helped many people get justice as it has simplified the legal process considerably. Bonded labourers, slum dwellers and hundreds of poor people have benefitted from it. It is an inexpensive way to approach the court. A **nominal** court fee of Rs. 50 is charged for it.

nominal: a very small cost or charge

A PIL can be filed by an individual or organization on behalf of the people who are suffering or whose rights are being violated. A PIL can be filed in the high court or Supreme Court. A letter, postcard or telegram is also considered as valid PIL, and this saves valuable time and effort. A PIL helps the person filing it to take up causes of public welfare and environmental concerns.

Case Study

Rural Litigation and Entitlement Kendra vs. State of UP, on 12th March 1985

A PIL was filed against illegal mining in the Mussoorie–Dehradun belt, which was causing harm to the environment and disturbing the ecological balance of the area. The judgement in the case established the right to wholesome environment as an integral part of right to life and personal liberty guaranteed under Article 21 of the Indian Constitution.

Article 21 of the Constitution states that, 'No person shall be deprived of his life or personal liberty except according to procedure established by law'. According to the courts, the right to life includes the right to a living environment congenial to human existence.

The Supreme Court held that the right to environment is a fundamental right of every citizen of India and is included in the 'right to life' guaranteed under Article 21 of the constitution. The court further provides that the right to get pollution-free water and air is a fundamental right under Article 21. Following this decision, the right to a pollution-free environment was incorporated under the head of right to life and all the law courts within the Indian territory were bound to follow the same. This laid down the foundation of environmental litigation in India.

Q. How far have the states in India been able to implement these rights for their people?

Independence of the Judiciary

To ensure justice is delivered in a fair and unbiased way, the judiciary must stay independent of the influence or control of any other organ of the government. The separation of powers between the legislature, executive and judiciary is an important provision of the Indian Constitution that helps in achieving this.

The Constitution of India has ensured the independence of the judiciary through numerous measures. Some of these measures are:

1. The legislature is not involved in the process of appointment of judges. This ensures that party politics does not influence the appointments.
2. The judiciary is financially independent of the executive or the legislature. The salaries and the allowances do not need the approval of the legislature.
3. The judiciary has the power to penalize anyone who is found guilty of contempt of court. Being disrespectful or disobedient towards a court of law amounts to contempt of court.
4. The judges have a fixed tenure. Only in exceptional cases are the judges removed.

Issues in Judiciary

To fight a legal battle is very time consuming and it takes several years to settle it. The procedure and the paperwork involved are also very complicated for a common man. It requires a person to take time off from work and other engagements to appear before the court for a hearing. 'Justice delayed is justice denied' is a phrase used to describe the delays in resolving cases by the courts. The cost of employing a lawyer to present the case is also an issue in the judiciary for people who have limited financial means. The long road to justice needs to be shortened by removing avoidable delays.

The judiciary in India is often considered slow-paced, and cases take years to close. At the same time, the system of justice in India is also known to be thorough. It is time consuming, but the courts realize the importance of being sure that the guilty have been brought to justice with the help of clear and unambiguous evidence. Therefore, people have faith in the judicial system of our country and the competence of our judges.

Green Earth

With the growing use of Internet facilities and technology, efforts should be made to make judicial processes 'paper free'.

World Connect

The International Court of Justice is often called the 'World Court'. It was established by the United Nations in 1945 to resolve international disputes. It has its headquarters at Hague. It settles legal disputes between countries and takes decisions on legal matters submitted to it by the General Assembly. The Court has played an important role in the resolution of conflicts between countries.

Skill Builder

21ST CENTURY SKILLS

Life skills: Collect evidence to show that Judiciary is the protector of Indian Constitution.

Collaboration: In groups of four, prepare a PowerPoint presentation on the jurisdiction of the Supreme Court of India. Write an example of a case under each jurisdiction.

Information literacy: Prepare a list of the union territories of India and find out under which court's jurisdiction they fall under.

Wind up

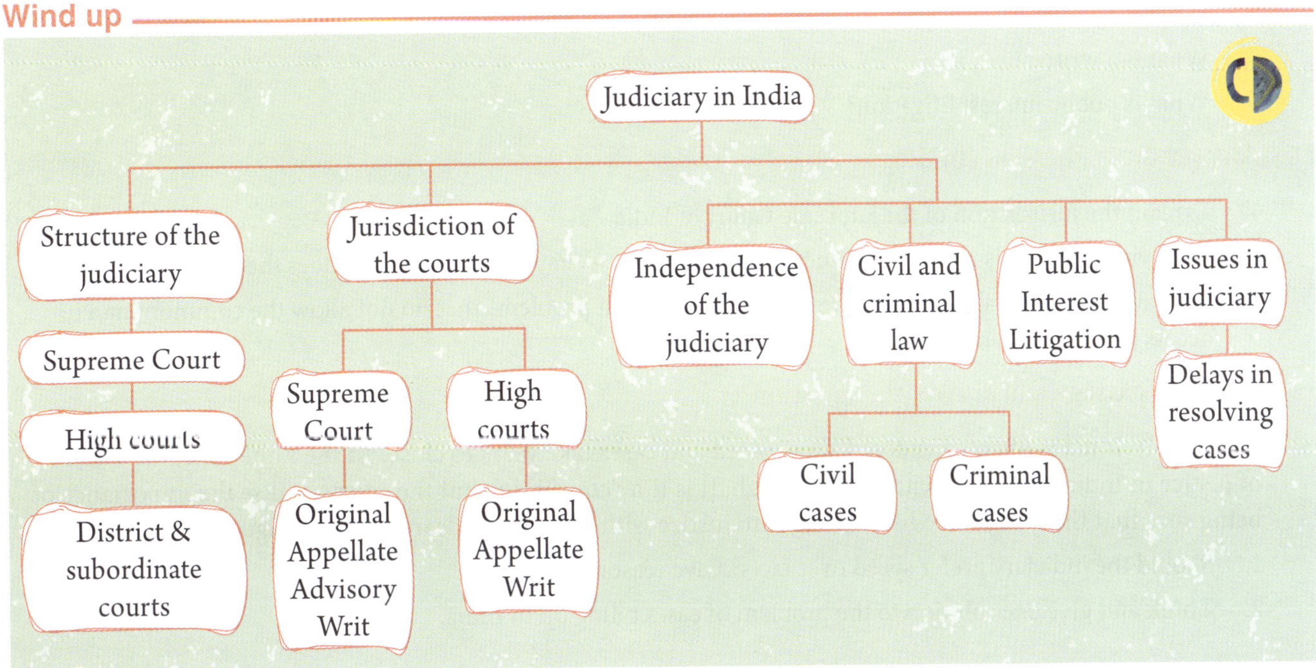

Exercises

A. Choose the correct answers.

1. The highest court in the state is the
   a. supreme court
   b. high court
   c. district court
   d. subordinate court
2. This writ protects the people against unlawful detention and imprisonment.
   a. Mandamus
   b. Habeas Corpus
   c. Quo Warranto
   d. Certiorari
3. This person presides over the Supreme Court.
   a. Chief Justice of India
   b. President of India
   c. Prime Minister of India
   d. Senior-most judge of a high court
4. This person is appointed by the President of India.
   a. Chief Justice of India
   b. Lawyer of a district court
   c. Lawyer of a subordinate court
   d. Judge of a high court
5. The structure of the Indian judiciary is pyramidal with this court at the top.
   a. High Court
   b. District Court
   c. Supreme Court
   d. Subordinate Courts

B. Correct these statements.

1. The judiciary in India is often considered to be fast-paced.
2. An FIR is lodged in civil cases.
3. Punishment for the offender is the main objective of civil law.
4. If a person is not satisfied with the judgement of the lower court, then he/she has to just accept it as final.

C. Answer these questions in brief.

1. What do you understand by 'independence of judiciary'?
2. How are the judges of the Supreme Court appointed?
3. What is an FIR?
4. What is a writ?
5. What is public interest litigation?

D. Answer these questions in detail.

1. Explain the jurisdiction of the Supreme Court of India.
2. Resolving disputes is a common function of the courts. What kinds of disputes does the judiciary resolve?
3. The law applies equally to all. However there are certain problems that do not allow the common man to access the courts. What are they?

E. Read the passage and answer the questions.

Judiciary in India is often considered slow-paced and cases take years to close. At the same time, the system of justice in India is also known to be thorough. It is time consuming but the courts realise the importance of being sure that the guilty have been brought to justice with the help of clear and unambiguous evidence.

1. Should the judiciary prefer speed over facts? Give reasons.
2. Think and give one solution to the problem of cases piling up in India.

Think Big

English Fun

Read the book *To Kill a Mockingbird*, and access the judicial system that existed during that period in America. Write a report on it.

Learning Tools

Complete the following chart and create a study guide for yourself on the chapter learnt.

Structure of the judiciary

....

....

....

....

Integrated system of judiciary

....

....

....

....

Jurisdiction of the courts

....

....

....

....

Litigation in India

....

....

....

Independence of the judiciary

....

....

....

....

Issues in the judiciary

....

....

....

....

Web links:

https://legalaffairs.gov.in/sites/default/files/chapter%207.pdf

https://main.sci.gov.in/constitution

Last accessed on 31 August 2021

6. Criminal Justice System

Warm up

In 1986, an 80-year-old woman sold her house to a newly married couple. The couple wanted to renovate the house before moving in, so they hired contractors. During the construction process, the builders found a box with jewellery worth rupees 5 lakh. When this discovery came to light, the old lady claimed that she had lost the box and, therefore, the money belonged to her. The couple who had bought the house claimed that the money was theirs as it was found on their land. The builder claimed the money belonged to him as he had found it. No existing law covered this dispute, so the judge hearing the case was required to make a decision that would create a new law. What decision would you have taken?

Conflicts between people or groups often arise in communities. If these conflicts cannot be resolved, we depend on the criminal justice system. Courts resolve cases of conflicts that occur in communities, maintain social order, **mitigate** crime and impose penalties on those who violate laws. According to the Constitution of India, every person who has violated a law has to be given a fair trial. Therefore, those accused of crimes are given protection against abuse through investigation and prosecution processes. Penalties are imposed depending on the proportion of the crime committed and are **reformative** in nature, giving an offender a second chance. It is the court's responsibility to see that justice is ensured to offenders and victims.

Criminal Justice System in India

The government is charged with certain duties and responsibilities that include enforcing law, arbitrating crime and correcting criminal conduct. To perform these duties, it relies on the criminal justice system. There are four agencies of the government that carry out these responsibilities. These are the police, the public prosecutor, the defence lawyer and the judge. While society plays an important role in determining the behaviour of people in a community, only the criminal justice system has the power to control crime and punish the criminals.

Broadly, the main objectives of the criminal justice system are:

- to prevent the occurrence of crime
- to punish the **transgressors** and the criminals
- to rehabilitate the transgressors and the criminals
- to compensate the victims as far as possible
- to maintain law and order in the society
- to deter the offenders from committing any criminal act in the future
- to enforce laws, arbitrate crimes and correct criminal conduct

Let us learn more about the practices of each agency of the criminal justice system.

mitigate: to make something less harmful; reformative: the action or process of improving something or someone; transgressor: a person who goes beyond the limit of what is legally acceptable

Role of the Police

The police force was instituted to maintain law and order within a state. Any crime or unlawful act is a threat to the law-and-order situation; therefore it is an important responsibility of the police to investigate every crime. They need to establish if a crime has actually taken place. If a matter is brought to the notice of the police by the people, the statement of the witnesses should be recorded by the police. If the police is certain of the evidence against an accused, they file a chargesheet in the court. This points to the offences of the accused. It is not the duty of the police, however, to decide whether a person is guilty or innocent.

If the police detains or arrests someone on the basis of evidence, the arrested person also has rights under Article 22 of the Constitution. Article 22 states that:

- No person who is arrested shall be detained in custody without being informed of the grounds of such an arrest.
- The arrested person shall have the right to consult and be defended by a legal practitioner of his choice.
- Each person arrested and detained in custody shall be produced before the nearest magistrate within a period of 24 hours.
- The arrested person cannot be detained in custody beyond the said period without the authority of a magistrate.
- An arrested person should be allowed to inform a friend or relative about the arrest and where he or she is being held.
- The arresting officer must inform the arrested person when she/he is brought to the police station of this right and is required to make an entry in the diary as to who was informed.

Judicial activism refers to the acts of the court in excess of and beyond the power of judicial review. It has taken place in India especially in the case of Article 22.

Case Study

Judicial activism 2015

Sheela Barse, a journalist and activist for prisoners' rights, wrote to the Supreme Court saying that of the 15 women prisoners interviewed by her in Bombay Central Jail, five admitted that they had been assaulted in police lock-up. Given the seriousness of the allegations, the College of Social Work, Bombay, was asked to visit the Bombay Central Jail to find out whether the allegations were true. The college submitted a detailed report, which, in addition to admitting that harassment and abuse against women were taking place, pointed out that the arrangements for providing legal assistance to prisoners were inadequate.

Police officers

The Court expressed serious concern about the plight of the prisoners who were unable to afford legal counsel to defend themselves. They said that not having access to a lawyer was the main cause of individual rights against harassment and torture not being enforced. It directed that:

1. Female suspects must be kept in separate lock-ups under the supervision of female constables.
2. Interrogation of females must be carried out in the presence of female police officers.
3. The magistrate before whom an arrested person is produced shall inquire from the arrested person whether she/he has any complaints against torture and maltreatment in police custody. The magistrate shall also inform such person of her/his right to be medically examined.

Q. How far do you think this directive of the apex court is followed by the police force in India?

Filing FIR

It is the responsibility of the police to file a First Information Report (FIR) in case of a cognizable offence such as murder, theft or kidnapping in which a police officer can make arrests without an arrest warrant. In case of a non-cognizable offence such as defamation, assault, cheating or forgery a police officer cannot arrest without a warrant and a NCR or non-cognizable report has to be filed.

An FIR or First Information Report is a document that officially registers that your complaint has been received and understood. It mentions the date, time, basic facts and details about the offence. The names of the accused and witnesses can be written in the complaint. FIR also records the details about the complainant. In case of the denial to lodge an FIR by any police officer, a complainant can either send a written report directly to a senior officer of the concerned police station or go to the high court or to a magistrate.

To lodge an FIR, visit the nearest police station preferably close to the crime scene and inform the police either orally or in writing. In case a verbal complaint is made, it is the duty of the authority recording the FIR to convert it into writing. First Information Report should be signed by the person giving the complaint. It is the duty of the police authorities to register the FIR in a record book. The police officer has to provide the complainant with a free copy of FIR. Once the FIR is lodged investigation begins, statements of the witnesses are recorded and the matter is referred to the court.

Guidelines for Investigation

It does not come under the **purview** of the police to declare a person guilty or innocent. Furthermore, the police force is required to follow guidelines specified by the court for the detention and interrogation of the arrested persons. The police cannot pass a judgement on its own. For investigation, it cannot torture or force a person to confess to having committed a crime. The confession of a crime in front of police or during investigation does not hold in the court because it could have been made under guilt when the accused was emotional about the crime having taken place or it could also be under pressure or done deliberately to mislead.

D.K. Basu, the Executive Chairman of Legal Aid Services, West Bengal laid down certain guidelines for the investigating officers. These are known as **D.K. Basu guidelines**. These include: actions of the state should be right, just and fair; torture for extracting any kind of confession would neither be right, just nor fair. Police personnel carrying out arrests and interrogation must bear accurate, visible and clear identification/name tags with their designations.

FACT CHECK

The National Legal Services Authority (NALSA) was established under the Legal Services Authorities Act, 1987, to provide free legal services to the weaker sections of the society and to organize Lok Adalats for amicable settlement of disputes.

A memo of arrest stating the time and place of arrest must be prepared by the police officer carrying out an arrest. It should be attested by at least one witness who is either a family member of the arrested person or a respectable person from the locality where the arrest is made. The memo should also be counter-signed by the arrested person. The arrested person may be allowed to meet her/his lawyer during interrogation but not throughout the interrogation. All bodily injuries on the arrested person should be recorded in the inspection memo, which should be signed by both the arrested person and the police officer making the arrest. A copy of the memo should be provided to the arrested person.

Role of Public Prosecutor

Public prosecution is an important component in the public justice system. The public prosecutor is appointed by the state and conducts prosecution on behalf of the state. He is an officer of the court and is required to present a truthful picture before the court. Even though he appears on behalf of the state,

purview: within the limits of an organization

it is equally his duty to see that the accused does not suffer in an unfair and **unethical** manner. He has to be truthful and impartial so that even the accused persons receive justice. The public prosecutor plays a dominant role in the withdrawal of a case from prosecution. He should withdraw from prosecution in rare cases; otherwise, the confidence of the public in the efficacy of the administration of justice will be shaken.

Role of Defence Lawyer

The defence lawyer represents the case on behalf of the defendant. To decide impartially, the judge and the jury must be able to hear the arguments of both sides. The defence lawyer presents all evidence to counter the prosecutor's arguments and challenges the facts presented by the prosecutor. A defence lawyer can be hired by a person or a company to defend them against the state in a criminal trial. If the court feels that a person is too poor to defend himself or herself in a case, then a defence lawyer can be provided by the court. The court gives equal hearing to all involved in the case and pronounces someone as guilty only when there is sufficient evidence against the person.

Green Earth

The Law Commission of India has proposed the establishment of 'Green Courts' to specifically look into matters related to the environment. The Supreme Court has raised the 'Right to Healthy Environment' as a Fundamental Human Right under Article 21.

Role of Judge

Judges play a crucial role in the justice system in India. They assess the evidence presented before them and impartially hear both sides of the case. They do not let their emotions affect the judgement. They pronounce the judgement at the end of the trial. In case a person is proven guilty, they decide the punishment as per the law and ensure that it is appropriate to the degree of the offence committed. In case a person is not proven guilty, the judge is instrumental in publicly restoring the social respect of the person and declaring him/her free of the charges.

Fair Trial

A trial conducted with all the elements of procedure is considered fair. The Hon'ble Supreme Court in the case of Zahira Habibullah Sheikh & Anr vs. State of Gujarat has held that 'the principle of fair trial now informs and energizes many areas of the law. It is reflected in numerous rules and practices... a fair trial obviously would mean a trial before an impartial judge, a fair prosecutor and atmosphere of judicial calm'.

Fair trial means a trial in which bias or prejudice for or against the accused, the witnesses or the cause, which is being tried, is eliminated. The courts have gradually expanded the meaning of fair trial to include various aspects of criminal procedure. For instance, the Supreme Court sometimes transfers cases from one state to another when it has been reasonably anticipated

District court

What's in the picture?

MAHATMA ARRESTE

MONTAGU EXPLAINS.

WHY MONTAGU RESIGNED.

ON CHARGE OF SEDITION.

HIS APPEAL TO THE PEOPLE

KEEP PERFECT PEACE

From what you have learnt about the criminal justice system in India, list the many ways in which the arrest of Gandhi was wrong and how it violated the freedoms and rights that the people of today's India have.

unethical: not morally acceptable

that the accused will not be given a fair trial or the court process may be interfered with. The 'right to silence' instructs that courts or tribunals should not be invited or encouraged to conclude that a suspect or an accused is guilty merely because he has refused to respond to questions put to him by the police or by the court.

Apply it!

The following table shows the statistics of crimes against women in India from 2017 to 2019.

Crime	2017	2018	2019
Rape	32559	33356	32033
Dowry Deaths	7466	7167	7115
Cruelty by husband or relatives	104551	103272	125298

Source: National Crime Records Bureau

- Which crime against women is rampant?
- Do you think the crimes have increased over the years? Why/Why not?
- How can women be protected against these?

World Connect

Scotland Yard is the Headquarters of the London Metropolitan Police. The force was created in 1829 by an Act passed by the British Parliament. The city of London was developing and becoming more populated in a rapid manner. It was the new centre of industrialization, and workers came from far and near in search of work in the newly established industries. The growing population led to law and order problems, and the old system of watchmen and guards were unable to deal with the situation. The Metropolitan Police was created to replace the old system. Crime Investigation Department (CID) was set up in 1878. As the force grew, it moved into a new office called the New Scotland Yard situated on the bank of river Thames. It is a highly competitive and professional force, and its services are sought for investigation of crimes across the United Kingdom.

Skill Builder

Critical thinking skills: Why do you think the criminal justice system of the country is sometimes inaccessible to the poor and underprivileged people?

Life skills: It is festival time and people are buying sweets for distributing to their family and friends and celebrate the festival. Reports of adulteration in sweets appear in the newspaper. Do you think it is a criminal offence to play with the health of so many innocent buyers? What would you do as a responsible citizen?

Information literacy: Find out about the POCSO Act and discuss why it is considered a draconian law.

Wind up

Criminal justice system in India

- Role of the police
  - Filing FIR for cognizable offence
  - Filing NCR for non cognizable offence
- Role of public prosecutor
  - Conducts prosecution on behalf of the state
- Role of defence lawyer
  - Represents the case on behalf of the defendant
- Role of judge
  - Fair trial

Exercises

A. Choose the correct answers.

1. Actions of the state should be
   a. biased and unfair
   b. right, just and fair
   c. lenient and merciful
   d. prejudiced and discriminatory
2. It is their responsibility to file the first information report.
   a. Judge
   b. Prosecutor
   c. Defence lawyer
   d. Police
3. Judges are expected to hear both sides of the case
   a. partially
   b. impartially
   c. both a and b
   d. none of these
4. The public prosecutor is an officer of the
   a. court
   b. executive
   c. parliament
   d. none of these

B. Establish the correct sequence of criminal proceedings.

1. The police records the statement of the witnesses. ☐
2. The judge pronounces the judgement. ☐
3. An FIR is lodged by the police. ☐
4. Witnesses are questioned. ☐
5. The accused is nabbed by the people. ☐
6. In a 'Hit and Run' case, a person is killed. ☐
7. The accused is produced before a magistrate. ☐

C. Correct the following statements.

1. The police force is allowed to torture people during an investigation.
2. The judge can quickly decide upon a case based on his/her feelings.
3. The police can detain anyone they want for interrogation.
4. A fair trial is when the punishment is harsh.
5. A public prosecutor represents the defendant in a case.

D. Answer these questions in brief.

1. What are the objectives of the criminal justice system?
2. How does the public prosecutor ensure justice?
3. What is the importance of witnesses in a case?
4. What is the role of a defence lawyer in a criminal case?

E. Answer these questions in detail.

1. List two differences between a cognizable and non cognizable offense.
2. Which provisions of Article 22 safeguard the rights of an arrested person?
3. According to the guidelines given by the Supreme Court, when can a trial be fair?
4. List the guidelines for investigation as specified by the court.

F. Read the passage and answer the questions.

The police force was instituted to ensure law and order within a state. Any crime or unlawful act is a threat to the law and order situation; therefore, it is an important responsibility of the police to investigate every crime. They need to establish if a crime has actually taken place. If a matter is brought to the notice of the police by the people, then the statement of the witnesses should be recorded by the police.

1. Find at least two points about the role of the police, from the above passage.
2. Apart from the points in the passage, list out some points about how the police helps the people.

Think Big

Integrate with maths

Conduct research on any one cognizable offence and the rate at which it increased or decreased over a period of three years. Present your findings in a graph.

Learning Tools

Fill up the boxes and create a study guide for yourself on the chapter studied.

Criminal Justice System in India Objectives:

....

....

....

....

....

....

....

....

....

Role of the police: ....

....

....

Filing FIR: ....

....

....

Guidelines for Investigation: ....

....

....

Role of public prosecutor: ....

....

....

Role of defence lawyer: ....

....

....

Role of judge: ....

....

....

Fair trial: ....

....

....

Web links:

https://bjs.ojp.gov/content/pub/pdf/wfbcjsin.pdf

Last accessed on 31 August 2021

7. Marginalization

Warm up

Not being given food under the mid-day meal schemes until other children have eaten, having to face constant humiliation, being forced to clean toilets, being made to sit separately from the other children, an everyday struggle to brave the discrimination and still get some education these are just some of the difficulties of children belonging to marginalised communities in our country. Is the time not ripe for a change?

Green Earth

The tribes of India and the world continue to be a valued source of study for the historians about the early humans. This is because many of the tribes have not changed their lifestyle in any significant manner and they live much like the hunters and gatherers.

India is a country with many different communities. People here are different from each other in various ways like education, socio-economic status, urban-rural divide and others. Despite the differences, there are some common factors in the way they lead their lives. However, some communities, even in this day and age, live in isolation, mostly away from the hustle and bustle of inhabited areas. They live in the forests that provide them a natural shield from the outside world. These are the tribal people of India. They are called marginalized because they live a primitive lifestyle and do not have access to many privileges and even some basic necessities of life.

The tribals are not a **homogenous** group and differ from each other in their beliefs, practices and rituals significantly. Each tribe falls into different categories of development, depending on its lifestyles and contact with the more developed areas. The tribes like Jarawas and Onges in the Andamans lead a very primitive lifestyle, whereas tribes like the Santhals are educated and have better lifestyles. These tribes are called *adivasis*. The term *adi* originated from Sanskrit and means 'from the beginning' and *vasi* means 'inhabitants'. Adivasi, therefore, means 'original inhabitants'. India has one of the highest number of tribal populations in the world.

The Constitution of India refers to the tribals as the Scheduled Tribes. The Constituent Assembly had declared India to be a country where all its people would be treated as equals. It identified groups of people who needed support in independent India for development and progress and called them the Scheduled Castes and Scheduled Tribes. People refer

homogenous: of the same kind

to the Scheduled Castes and Scheduled Tribes together, but the terms have different meanings. The Constitution referred to the lowest caste of the caste system of the pre-Independence times as Scheduled Castes. Scheduled Tribes could belong to non-Hindu societies and did not come under the purview of the caste system.

Historical Background

During British rule, measures such as permanent settlement and forest laws were enacted, which led to the reorganization of land holdings in the villages. Gradually, as new social structures emerged, the adivasis or the forest tribes were pushed to the lowest place in the social hierarchy. Then, forests that were home to the tribals were declared reserved and protected for use by the British, and the tribes were displaced. In independent India, to preserve the forests and wildlife, the government declared many forests as sanctuaries and national parks. This was a far-reaching measure to conserve the environment, but it shrank the areas available to the tribals.

Current Population

There is a significant tribal population in many states of India like Madhya Pradesh, West Bengal, Odisha, Rajasthan, Gujarat, Chhattisgarh and the north-eastern states. Karnataka, Tamil Nadu, Kerala, Andhra Pradesh and Telangana in the south also have a number of tribes. According to the census held in 2011, 8.6 per cent of India's total population are adivasis. The following table shows the percentage of tribals in the total population of the states.

Some states in India have a sizeable tribal population.

Chhattisgarh: 38%	Jharkhand: 26%
Odisha: 22%	Madhya Pradesh: 20%
Gujarat: 15%	Rajasthan: 12%
Maharashtra: 9%	Bihar: 0.9%

Mining and Plantations

Tea Plantations

Europeans and workers on a tea plantation

Tea plantations were set up in Assam by the British to promote the triangular trade between India, China and England. Requirement of cheap labour was huge in the large plantations, which covered a major part of Assam. The British forcibly recruited tribals of the Chota Nagpur region and adjoining areas into the Assam plantations. This forced migration of tribal people from the nearby areas to Assam was very harsh on the tribals, and hundreds of people died during their journey or perished due to disease and hardships. The labour had to enter into contracts with the planters that bound them to the plantations. They were not allowed to leave the plantation, meet their families or even fellow workers. When they tried to flee, they were killed by the British officials. The wages paid to them were extremely low, and they did not have any personal freedom.

Story of Mining

Tribals provide a major share of workforce in the mining sector of India. This has also led to the exploitation of the tribals. Chhattisgarh, one of the richest states in terms of mineral wealth, is mostly tribal dominated and heavily forested especially in areas like Bastar, Surguja, Korba and Dantewada. New mining projects are coming up in these districts, which are among the most backward districts of the state. Many extremist groups called Naxalites became active in the region as they resisted mining. The Maoists also known as Naxals are inspired by the political ideology of late Mao Zedong (Mao Tse Tung) who was a leader in China. They are active in the 'Red Corridor' from Andhra Pradesh to West Bengal including Bihar, Jharkhand and Chhattisgarh. The Chhattisgarh government has pitted the Adivasi population against the Naxals under the *Salwa Judum*, meaning 'peace march' or purification hunt' in Gondi language. This has divided the adivasis who were resisting industrial activity including mining. This conflict has led to the displacement of about 80,000 people in the state.

Stone Quarries of Maharshtra and Rajasthan

Women working in a stone quarry

Maharashtra is a state with many stone quarries, and Rajasthan is a major supplier of marble and sandstone to companies in India and abroad. Most workers in both the states are from the Scheduled Tribes. The issue of displacement of communities and inappropriate compensation is rampant here. The tribals agree to work in these quarries where working conditions are really inhuman as they want to supplement the family income. Women and children form a substantial part of the workforce, and child labour is widespread. Working in a **quarry** poses health hazards as workers constantly inhale harmful and injurious dust. Diseases like silicosis are common, which affect the workers, and is responsible for their early deaths. Women are said to take up the jobs in place of their husbands and run the risk of the disease to save their family members.

Development and Adivasis

As the rail and road network was built in India connecting remote areas of the country, it was seen as a sign of development and progress for the people. However, from the perspective of the Adivasis it proved to be not so beneficial. They were forced to provide labour for laying the tracks, and though this provided employment, it was not a natural way of life for them. They preferred to live in the forest and practice cultivation and collect honey, wax and other products for their use. The construction of the railways during the British period was a blessing in disguise for India. Tribals again were at a loss because large quantities of timber was required as sleepers for laying the railway tracks. The increased demand for timber led the British to the forests. In the process, the worst affected were the displaced forest communities and their use of forest resources was strictly regulated by laws. This created hardships for the people as they paid the price for the development.

quarry: a deep pit, from which stone or other materials are dug out

The newly constructed roads, railways and bridges connected the far remote areas in the country and helped the British traders immensely. They were able to take raw materials from the interiors and trade in them or use them for processing in the upcoming factories. However, this also brought the outside world closer to the forest tribes who were living in the shelter of the thick forests. No protection was given to them and their lands were invaded by the 'outsiders'.

Case Study

The Niyamgiri Hills are located in the Kalahandi and Rayagad districts of Odisha. In the thick forests of Niyamgiri, a tribe of indigenous people called Dongria Kodh live. A London-based mining company, Vedanta Resources, sought permission to set up bauxite mines in the region. This would have required the tribals to be displaced in the name of development. They would have had to leave the lands on which they had been living for generations and which they deeply loved and worshipped. Like all other tribes, Dongria Kodhs are experts in local forest, vegetation, plant and wildlife of the forest, grow various crops and depend on other resources for their survival. As news about the proposal of the mining company spread, local activists and organizations and international organizations like Amnesty International took up the cause of the tribals. In 2013, the Supreme Court in its first of a kind judgement said that the Dongria people must be consulted before any decision on the matter was taken. The Dongria people had meetings and unanimously voted down the building of mines in the area. The Supreme Court upheld the Right of the Dongria people to take decision in matters that would affect them. This is considered the landmark judgement of the Court to protect the true spirit of human rights and democracy.

A Dongria woman in a traditional attire

Q. How have the living conditions changed for the Dongria tribals after 2013?

Other Marginalized Communities of India

Who are the minorities? Adivasis are not the only marginalized community in India. According to Union Government of India, six religious communities—Muslims, Christians, Sikhs, Buddhists, Zoroastrians (Parsis) and Jains—are also considered the minority communities. The Constitution of India regards those communities as minorities who are fewer in numbers and have notably less population on the basis of their religion and language. The National Commission for Minorities (NCM) was set up by the Union Government of India in 1992 to protect the existence of minorities across India. The Commission looks after issues related to the minority communities of India under the National Commission for Minorities Act, 1992.

Apply it! E

In your village, town or city, who do you think are the marginalized groups? Give reasons why you think so.

The following table gives the percentage of the minority communities and the respective literacy rates compared to the total population.

Minority	Percentage in Population	Percentage of Literacy (as per Census 2011)
Muslims	12.4	57
Christians	2.3	74
Sikhs	1.9	67
Buddhists	0.8	71
Jains	0.4	86

Source: Census of India 2011

If you closely observe the table given above, you would notice that the literacy among the Muslims is the lowest. The Government appointed a committee under the chairmanship of Justice Rajinder Sachar to prepare a report on the social, educational and economic conditions of the Muslims in India. According to the Sachar Committee Report, one-fourth of Muslim children in the age group of 6–14 years have either never attended school or have dropped out of school. Only 50 per cent of Muslims who complete middle school are likely to complete secondary education compared to the 62 per cent at national level. The report has also drawn attention to the low levels of educational attainment among Muslim women in rural areas in both technical fields and higher education.

Constitutional Provisions

The Constitution provides many safeguards to protect the minorities in India. Article 46 of the Constitution states that, 'The State shall promote, with special care, the education and economic interests of the weaker sections of the people, and in particular, of the Scheduled Castes and Scheduled Tribes and shall protect them from social injustice and all forms of social exploitation'.

Article 30(1) provides that 'All minorities, whether based on religion or language, shall have the right to establish and administer educational institutions of their choice'.

Significance of the Tribal Culture

The tribals are known to be adept at forest conservation, contrary to the popular belief that they destroy the forests. They worship trees, mountains, rivers, the Earth and other natural elements. Sacred groves have been a traditional method of the tribes to protect the forests. Small patches of land are dedicated to local deities, and the tribals preserve and protect this patch of land with devotion. Thus, it becomes an excellent way of protecting the biodiversity of the area. Kerala has the highest number of sacred groves, followed by Maharashtra where there are around 1600 of them. Forest communities adopted the most scientific methods of cultivation. Although they have no education, their traditions show a deep understanding of nature conservation and judicious use of resources. Thus, they continue to play a key role in preserving the natural wealth.

According to the former head of the tribal language department of Ranchi University Giridhari Ram Ganjhu, 'Tribals are undoubtedly the first iron smelters who knew how to produce rust-free products. One will be amazed to see that the century-old trishul in Tanginath in Gumla has still not gathered rust. So, it is important to help these tribals pass on their knowledge to generations to come'.

Some Tribes in India

Bihar	Oraons, Munda
Odisha	Santhals Kondhs, Koyas, Gadabas, Juangs
Madhya Pradesh	Gonds, Bhils, Baigas
Andaman and Nicobar	Jarawas, Onges, Sentinelese
North eastern states	Naga, Garo, Khasi, Maram, Tripuri, Reang, Monpas, Bamons
Jharkhand	Kharia
Chhattisgarh	Korba, Abhuj Maria, Muria, Dhurvaa

What's in the picture?

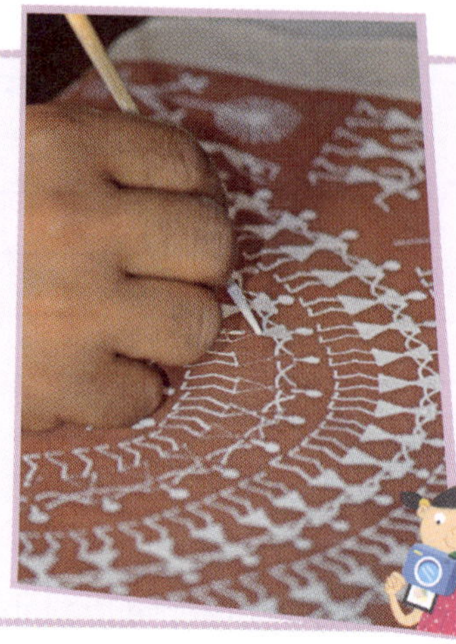

The Warli paintings are an exuberant example of tribal arts of India. These are made by the tribals of Maharashtra and the artists usually belong to the Warli and Malkhar Koli tribes.

What do you think this painting depicts?

World Connect

One of the oldest and most reclusive tribes living in the dense rainforest of Amazon is Mashco-Piro. In the recent past, there have been a few instances when the tribesmen clashed with the people who smuggle timber from the forest, drug traffickers and poachers who invade the privacy of the tribes in the process of conducting their illegal trades. The tribals have understood that they need weapons to fight these people, which can be sourced by attacking the remote villages and tourist camps on the fringes of the forest. Anthropologists feel that this contact can prove dangerous for the tribals as they can be killed in the violent encounters and get infected easily as they do not have the required immunity to fight the modern-day diseases.

Skill Builder

21st CENTURY SKILLS

Critical thinking skill: A lot is being done to bring the marginalized communities at par with the general population. Suggest three ways in which we as citizens can make a difference to the issue of marginalization.

Information literacy: Select any one state of India where tribes are still found. Make a presentation on the lives of the tribals of that state. Remember to include information about their dance, music, rituals, paintings, etc.

Wind up

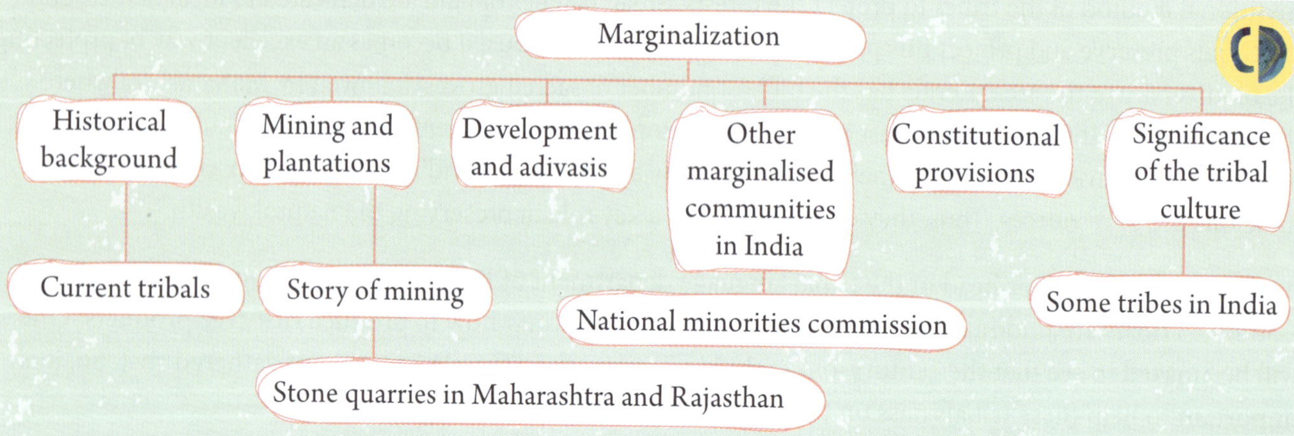

Exercises

A. Choose the correct answers.

1. Non-Hindu societies that did not come under the purview of the caste system
   a. Scheduled Castes b. Scheduled Tribes c. Naxals d. None of these
2. A traditional method of the tribes to protect forests
   a. Farming b. Composting c. Sacred groves d. None of these
3. The term 'adivasi' means
   a. backward b. original inhabitants c. tribe d. forest dweller
4. The minorities have been identified on the basis of their
   a. religion and language b. religion and festivals c. language d. region where they live

B. Correct these statements.

1. Among the minorities, Jains have the lowest literacy rate.
2. Sachar committee gave its report on the Muslim minorities.
3. Historians study the behaviour and lifestyle of the tribes to understand the foreigners better.
4. Tribals are found only in India.
5. Railway construction developed the tribals.

C. Unscramble the names of these states.

1. AHSODI
2. SMTRHHAAAAR
3. AAMYHD HRPESAD
4. DAAKRHHJN
5. RAHIB

D. Answer these questions in brief.

1. Who are the Scheduled Tribes?
2. What is the difference between Scheduled Castes and Scheduled Tribes?
3. Name some communities that are marginalized in India.
4. What is the role of National Commission for Minorities?
5. Why were the tea plantations set up by the British not beneficial for the tribal people?

E. Answer these questions in detail.

1. What do you understand by the term 'marginalized'?
2. Adivasis had to pay a heavy price for the development of the rest of the society. Explain.
3. In what ways is the tribal culture significant for the people?
4. List the issues faced by quarry workers.

F. Read the passage and answer the questions.

The tribals are not a homogenous group and differ from each other in their beliefs, practices and rituals significantly. Each tribe falls into different categories of development depending on its lifestyle and contact with the more developed areas.

1. Do you think greater contact with the outside world will benefit the tribes? Give reason for your answer.
2. Why do you think the tribal communities shy away from contact with the developed world?

Think Big

Design thinking

Find out about different tribes around the world and on a chart, paste their photos, the regions where they are from and list their unique characteristics.

Learning Tools

Create a two-tab book and use it for comparing and contrasting between different tribals and non-tribals and determining cause and effect, finding similarities and differences and more.

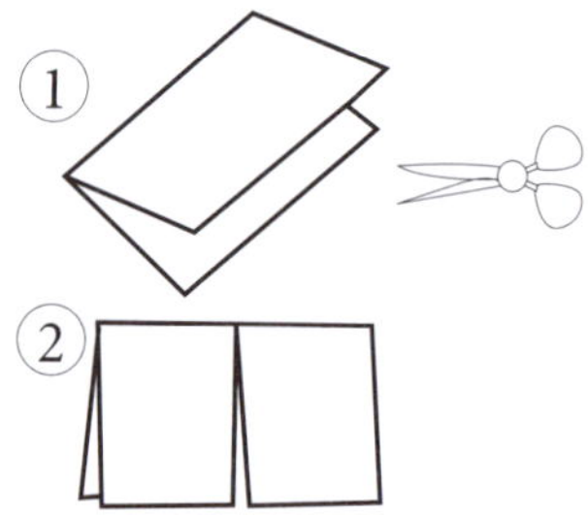

Web links:

https://www.lawctopus.com/academike/problems-marginalized-groups-india/

Last accessed on 31 August 2021

8. Challenging Marginalization

Warm up

Gaidinliu was born in 1915 in the Rongmei tribe of Manipur. As a young girl of 13 years, she joined a movement against the British and soon became a source of influence and inspiration for hundreds of Naga people who were fighting oppression by the British. Seeing the impact of her will and determination, the British arrested her and sentenced her to life imprisonment when she was just 16-years old. Jawaharlal Nehru met her in the prison and gave her the title of 'Rani'. She became famous as Rani Gaidinliu. She was freed in 1947, and the Government of India awarded her the Padma Bhushan in recognition of her contribution.

The Constitution and Marginalization

There are many marginalized groups in the Indian society. These groups have based their struggle for equality and dignity on the Constitution of India. The makers of the Constitution were aware of the complexities of Indian society and included provisions in the Constitution, which would best integrate different communities into the fabric of the new nation.

On 25 November 1949, Dr B.R. Ambedkar issued a grave warning in the Constituent Assembly: 'On January 26 1950, we will have equality in politics and inequality in social and economic life. We must remove this **contradiction** at the earliest moment, or else those who suffer from inequality will blow up the structure of political democracy, which this Assembly has so laboriously built up'. To guard against such an explosion of discontent, the Preamble of the Constitution clearly spells out the objectives of securing 'to all its citizens JUSTICE, social, economic and political' as well as 'EQUALITY of status and of opportunity'.

FACT CHECK

The Indian film industry has always tried to portray the positive and negative issues of the society. In 1936, a much talked about movie was made, which was based on the evil of untouchability. The film was *Achchut Kanya*. Franz Osten was a German filmmaker who directed the movie. It highlighted the evil practice of untouchability in India back then.

The Preamble stands as a testimony to the resolve of the makers of the Constitution to have justice and equality for all citizens. Apart from the Preamble, there are several other provisions in the Constitution that promote the cause of equality. The fundamental rights are universally applicable to all the citizens of India without any discrimination. There are also directive principles of state policy in the Constitution, which are meant to serve as guidelines to the government for policy making.

contradiction: a combination of statements, ideas, or features which are opposed to one another

Apart from Scheduled Castes and Scheduled Tribes, other minorities like Muslims, Parsis, Jains and Buddhists enjoy the protection and the safeguards granted to them for preserving and promoting their culture. The right to equality provides strength to the cause of equal treatment to all, and the cultural and educational rights empower them to practice and popularize their culture and set up institutions to propagate it.

What's in the picture?

The rights of which marginalized group are being fought for in the picture? Do people have a right to protest this way?

The directive principles of state policy in the Constitution also state that 'the state shall, in particular, strive to minimize the inequalities in income, and endeavour to eliminate inequalities in status, facilities and opportunities, not only amongst individuals but also amongst groups of people residing in different areas or engaged in different vocations'.

Harijans demonstrating outside the Boat Club in New Delhi, c. 14 September, 1981

In the pre-Independence era when caste discrimination was **rampant** and practised openly, a group of people were subjected to extreme humiliation and violation of dignity in the form of untouchability. The untouchables were considered so impure that their mere touch or shadow could make a person impure. Several social restrictions were placed on them and they were harassed and denied access to all facilities, which the other members of the society enjoyed. According to Dr B.R. Ambedkar, untouchables form an entirely new class, that is, the fifth *varna*, apart from the existing four varnas. Thus, untouchables are not even recognized under the caste system of Hindus. Their exclusion from the mainstream society was based on the belief that they are impure and harmful and that it was necessary to ostracize them for the overall benefit of the society.

Article 15(4) of the Constitution empowers the state to make any special provision for the advancement of any socially and educationally backward classes of citizens or for the Scheduled Castes and the Scheduled Tribes.

Article 17 of the Indian Constitution is a legislation that abolishes the practice of untouchability in any form. According to the provision of Article 17, 'enforcement of any disability arising out of untouchability' is a punishable offence in accordance with the law.

rampant: something flourishing or spreading unchecked

Apply it!

On 8 July, 1939, Vaidyanatha Iyer entered the temple with a group of Dalits and offered prayers. C. Rajagopalachari was the Chief Minister of Tamil Nadu and he supported the temple entry. He introduced a bill on the issue in September 1939 in the Legislative Assembly. This Bill was passed by the Assembly and it became a law in 1939.

Despite this, many Dalits are denied entry into temples and access to public places till today. More than 160 million people in India are still considered 'untouchables'.

Which shrine in south India were women allowed to enter in 2018? Why were people protesting against it?

Laws and Marginalization

Jats protesting for demand of quota

People of Scheduled Castes and Scheduled Tribes still live in poor conditions even after so many years of independence. The scenario is particularly **dismal** in the remote areas. They lead an isolated life. In villages, they are not allowed to enter temples; most of them do not even have basic dwellings. These socially deprived people do not have any drinking water or sanitation facilities. Literacy is still a distant dream for these people, and until and unless, they are educated, they would not be able to get jobs. There is an increasing recognition among policy makers that rising **militancy** in tribal areas is not merely a 'law and order' problem. The actual causes lie in the social, economic and political marginalization that tribal groups have experienced over the years.

Reservations were introduced in government jobs and educational institutions for the Scheduled Castes, Scheduled Tribes and Other Backward Castes as a means to provide more opportunities to these groups. As of 2016, 7.5 per cent of government jobs are reserved for the Scheduled Tribes, 15 per cent for the Scheduled Castes and 27 per cent for the Other Backward Castes. In the Lok Sabha, out of the 543 seats, 47 seats are reserved for the Scheduled Tribes and 84 for the Scheduled Castes.

Many relaxations are available to the SC and ST candidates for direct appointment to government jobs like relaxation of five years in the upper age limit, exemption from paying exam fees, relaxation in qualifications and experience required, and they can be interviewed separately if required. A Special Recruitment Drive was launched by the central government to encourage employment among the reserved categories. Many communities in India like the Patidars in Gujarat, Gujjars in Rajasthan and Kapus in Andhra

FACT CHECK

Gandhiji called the untouchables Harijans, the children of God. He undertook a famous march or *Padayatra* in support of the issue of dalit dignity in Odisha. Gandhiji recalled his mother telling him, 'you must not touch this boy, he is an untouchable'. 'Why not? I questioned back, and from that day my revolt began.'

dismal: of very low quality, sad; militancy: the use of confrontational or violent methods in support of a political or social cause

Pradesh are demanding reservations. The communities claim the status so that they can benefit from the schemes introduced by the central and the state governments. These protests often get violent and life and property are damaged.

The Scheduled Castes and Scheduled Tribes (Prevention of Atrocities) Act, 1989

The Scheduled Castes and Scheduled Tribes (Prevention of Atrocities) Act, 1989, was introduced because people from the Scheduled Castes and Scheduled Tribes were being subject to inhuman and derogatory practices by people of other communities. Violent attacks on Dalits and instances of Dalit homes and villages being set on fire were on the rise and this act prevents tribals from land encroachment. The act provided:

- to prevent the commission of offences and atrocities against the members of the Scheduled Castes and the Scheduled Tribes
- special courts for the trial of such offences
- the relief and rehabilitation of the victims of such offences

Some Schemes by the government for Scheduled Tribes:

- Vocational Training Centres in tribal areas empower the youth to earn their livelihood and make them independent.
- Efforts are being made to enrol 100% girls in schools so that the literacy rate among them increases.
- Scholarships programmes for Scheduled Tribes students
- Upgradation of merit of Scheduled Tribes students
- Meritorious students can avail financial aid for pursuing higher studies abroad.

Case Study

Article 23

Article 23 of the Constitution provides: Prohibition of traffic in human beings and forced labour. Any violation of this provision shall be an offence punishable in accordance with the law. This provision of the Constitution was openly being violated.

A letter was addressed to the Supreme Court of India by an organization called Bandhua Mukti Morcha, an organization dedicated to the cause of release of bonded labour, complaining about the prevalence of bonded labour in the quarries of the Faridabad District in the state of Haryana. The Supreme Court entertained a matter concerning release of bonded labour and treated the letter as a writ petition under Article 32 of the Constitution. The Court ordered an in-depth inquiry into the issue of the working conditions prevailing in the various quarries within the Faridabad district with particular reference to violation of provisions of the Bonded Labour System (Abolition) Act of 1976 and Inter-State Migrant Workmen (Regulation of Employment & Conditions of Service) Act.

The report submitted that the alleged stone quarries were full of dust and it was difficult for anyone to breathe. Some workers were not allowed to leave the stone quarries and were undergoing forced labour. There was no provision of pure water, or proper shelters, medical facilities or schooling for children. Some labourers were suffering from chronic diseases and no compensation was being paid to those who were injured in accidents on duty. Workers were paid nominal wages and often their family members were not permitted to take remunerative jobs elsewhere without the permission of the master. Quarries were located in a particular area away from habitation. On account of necessity for workmen in the area, people from different parts of the country were made to live there in harsh and inhuman conditions.

The Supreme Court ruled that to provide the basic facilities like water, shelter, medical facilities, education for children of the workers was completely the responsibility of the employers. It was observed that despite legislation against forced labour, it continued and stricter enforcement of laws were required.

Empathizing with the labourers, the court observed that for a loan taken at an exorbitant rate of interest, the debtor virtually sells himself to the creditor and gets bonded usually throughout his or her lifetime and renders service for the purpose of satisfying the debt. The creditor, anxious to exploit the situation, ensures that the debt is never satisfied and often on the traditional basis of pious obligation, the liability is inherited by the children of the original debtor. The system, thus, provides a built-in mechanism for continuation of the under-privileged section of the society by the privileged few living therein.

Q. Do you think the living conditions have improved now for the miners?

Prohibition of Employment as Manual Scavengers and their Rehabilitation Act, 2013

Manual Scavenging: Manual scavenging refers to the practice of manually cleaning, carrying, disposing or handling in any manner, human excreta from dry latrines and sewers. The practice of manual scavenging is linked to India's caste system where the so-called lower castes were expected to perform this job. Manual scavengers are amongst the poorest and most disadvantaged communities in India. There are health hazards related to this task. The Government encourages people to build only sanitary latrines so that the overall health of the society and its people can be improved. In 2013, the Prohibition of Employment as Manual Scavengers and their Rehabilitation Act, 2013, was introduced. As per this Act, a person engaging a manual scavenger is liable to get one year's imprisonment or a fine of INR 50,000 or both. An estimated 90 per cent of manual scavengers are Dalit women who face inequalities and discrimination based on their caste and gender and who are often exposed to violence and exploitation.

Right to Fair Compensation and Transparency in Land Acquisition, Rehabilitation and Resettlement Act, 2013

The Act states that if land has to be acquired for industrialization or development of essential infrastructure facilities, then the families affected due to their lands being taken, must be provided just and fair compensation. Adequate facilities should be provided to rehabilitate and resettle them so that even after acquisition, their socio-economic status develops and does not get impacted in a negative manner. This Act lends support to all those communities of tribals and Dalits whose lands were being forcibly acquired in the name of developmental activities. Baneshwar Fair is a unique tribal fair and one of the biggest in the country held annually in Dungarpur, Rajasthan. The Bhils from Dungarpur, Udaipur and Banswara constitute the major part of the gathering. Such fairs play an important role in encouraging the tribes to interact with the rest of the society, and in covert ways, it leads to their development as well.

Green Earth

Tribals from around the world are making significant contributions to forest conservation and preserving biodiversity and natural wealth. They use the trees, flowers and herbs for food and as medicines to heal.

The provisions of the Constitution and the schemes and laws by the government have brought marginal improvement to the lives of Dalits and Adivasis. An array of problems, however, continue to plague these communities. They still have to fight discrimination in society, and their rights are violated frequently. Dalit children are made to sit separately in schools, water sources are still not accessible to them, Dalits are subjected to violence and untouchability is practised, thus proving that only education and stricter enforcement of existing laws can bring about the desired changes.

World Connect

In Japan, a class of people who are considered untouchables are the Burakumin, who are at the lowest rung of the social order since the early 1600s when feudalism was practised. Feudalism was a system of hierarchy and privileges were given to the people on the basis of birth. A Burakumin faces segregation in the society and lives in extremely abysmal conditions. Although the Burakumin were freed and the class was abolished in 1871, they still continue to be discriminated against.

When Google Earth added an old medieval map of Tokyo to its online collection in 2006 in an attempt to connect to history and enrich resources, it faced opposition because the map points to the places where the Burakumin community lived and this was perceived as discriminatory.

Skill Builder

21ST CENTURY SKILLS

Critical-thinking skills: As a forest officer of your area, list out two ways in which you will protect the tribes living in the forest.

Life skills: Collect information on the illegal activities like poaching, which are widespread in the forests of India. Make a presentation on how it brings the tribals in conflict with such law breakers.

Information literacy: Collect information about the farmer's agitation of 2020–21 against the farm laws.

Wind up

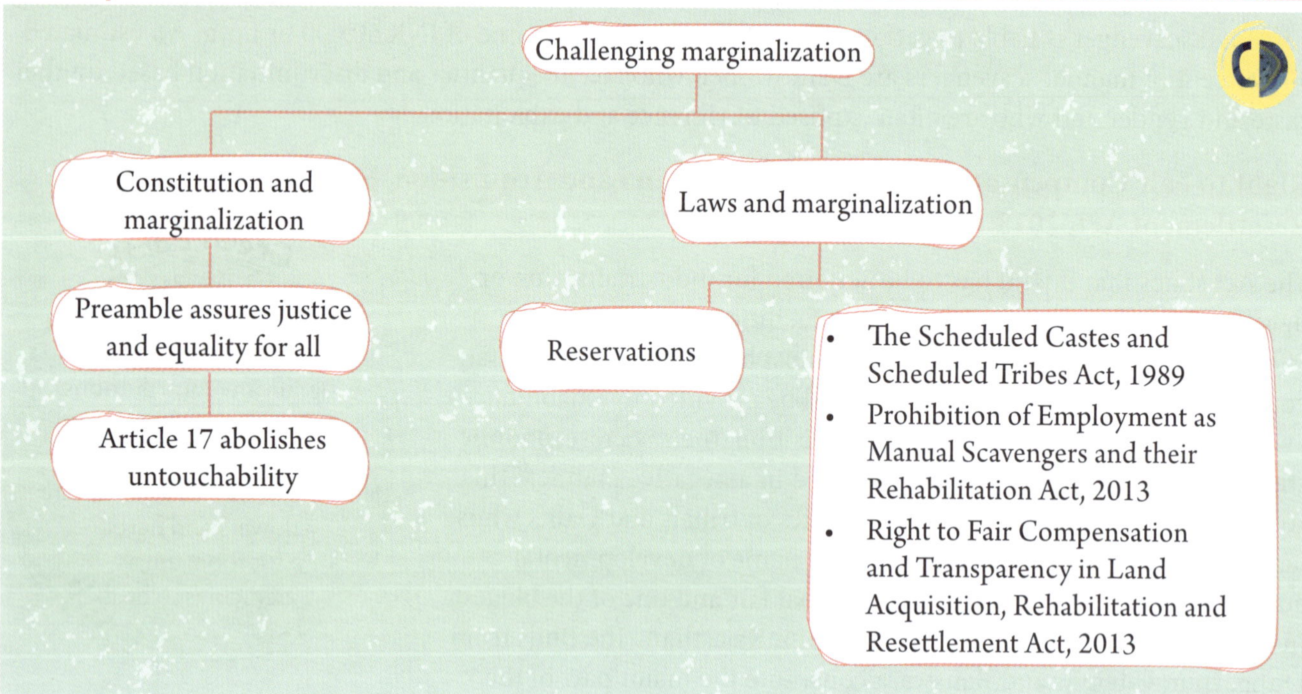

Exercises

A. Choose the correct answers.

1. Out of 543 seats, the number of seats that are reserved for the Scheduled Tribes in the Lok Sabha are
   a. 47 b. 84 c. 49 d. 79

2. Christianity is a

a. majority religion in India

b. minority religion in india

c. marginalized group

d. none of the above

3. Untouchability has been abolished by this article of the Indian Constitution.

a. 14 b. 17 c. 22 A d. 14 (5)

4. This means unequal or different treatment or harassment that causes harm.

a. Discrimination

b. Prejudice

c. Inequality

d. All of the above

5. Various benefits like these are given to the Scheduled Castes, the Scheduled Tribes and Other Backward Classes.

a. Scholarships b. Money c. Homes d. Rations

B. Fill in the blanks.

1. .... in Gujarat and .... in Rajasthan are communities that are demanding reservations.
2. Article .... of the Constitution empowers the State to make any special provision for the advancement of any socially and educationally backward classes of citizens or for the Scheduled Castes and the Scheduled Tribes.
3. .... refers to the practice of manually cleaning, carrying, disposing or handling in any manner, human excreta from dry latrines and sewers.
4. The .... has played a key role in protecting the rights of the tribals.
5. Working in a .... poses health hazards as workers constantly inhale harmful and injurious dust.

C. Correct the following statements.

1. Directive principles of state policy are enforced by law.
2. In our country, people following Hinduism are in a minority.
3. The Scheduled Castes and Scheduled Tribes Prevention of Atrocities Act was passed in 2016.
4. Untouchability is not practised now in India.

D. Answer these questions in brief.

1. What fear was expressed by Dr Ambedkar in the Constituent Assembly?
2. What do you understand by reservations?
3. Which organization filed a PIL against bonded labour?
4. List out some schemes introduced for the welfare of the Scheduled Castes and the Scheduled Tribes.

E. Answer these questions in detail.

1. What are the provisions of the Constitution, which protect the marginalized communities?
2. Name some communities which are demanding reservations now.
3. What would minorities gain by reservations?
4. Why was there a need to enable the Scheduled Castes and Scheduled Tribes Prevention of Atrocities Act?

F. Read the passage and answer the questions.

The Preamble stands as a testimony to the resolve of the makers of the Constitution to have justice and equality for all citizens. Apart from the preamble, there are several other provisions in the Constitution that promote equality. The Fundamental Rights are universally applicable to all citizens of India without any discrimination.

1. Justice and equality were made a part of Indian constitution based on inspiration from which country's constitution?
2. If equality was not an ideal listed in our constitution, how would it impact the people of India?

Think Big

Integrate with geography

Identify six tribal groups from around the world. On an outline map of the world, colour the regions where they are found. Note down the climatic zone where each tribe resides, and on a table, write about the lifestyle of these people.

Learning Tools

Make your own study guide by following these steps.

MAIN POINTS (*Note down the important headings and the main ideas*)

→ ....

→ ....

→ ....

→ ....

→ ....

→ ....

Keywords

- ....
- ....
- ....
- ....
- ....

Assess yourself (Use the questions at the end of the chapter to assess how much you have learnt and understood)

Web links:

https://www.savethechildren.in/child-protection/five-major-challenges-for-children-from-marginalised-indian-communities/
https://www.right-to-education.org/marginalised-groups

Last accessed on 31 August 2021

9. Development and Government

Warm up

The Government of India imposed various curbs and regulations on public movement, transportation, offices and schools to contain the spread of infections due to the coronavirus. State governments came up with their own guidelines to deal with the pandemic. The vaccination drive in India was pushed aggressively and in an organized manner to enable scores of people to get vaccinated and counter the pandemic. This highlights the crucial role played by the government in not just political affairs of the country but public administration as well.

Governance refers to the exercise of political and administrative authority at different levels to manage a country's affairs. It comprises institutions and representatives of the people, through which citizens and groups express their interests. A government also performs functions in accordance with the Constitution so that the citizens can enjoy their political rights. A government aims to provide all the basic amenities required to develop the society and ensure the welfare of people. Reforms in the existing systems are introduced from time to time by the government so that the economy of the country can be improved and poverty is eradicated.

FACT CHECK

Open defecation is one of the primary causes of diseases and infections in India. A UN initiative, 'Wherever The Need', addresses this issue by building eco-sanitation toilets for women.

Welfare of the People

Category	Rates from 1.4.2016 (Rs.)
Unskilled	368
Semi-skilled	407
Skilled	447

The government introduces schemes and makes laws for public welfare. The Minimum Wages Act was passed in 1948 to prevent the exploitation of workers and ensure a basic standard of living for them. Due to population, poverty and demand for labour in the industrial and construction sectors, workers were forced to work often without due **remuneration**. The government protected the interests of the workers with this Act. The minimum wages are revised from time to time for the advantage of workers.

Sanitation

The Central Rural Sanitation Programme, which was started in 1986, was one of India's first efforts to provide safe sanitation in rural areas. The concept of sanitation was expanded to include personal hygiene, home sanitation, safe water and proper garbage disposal. The overall health of the people in rural areas depends on multiple factors.

remuneration: pay, recompense

Nirmal Bharat Abhiyaan was launched with a vision to create awareness among the rural people about the importance of hygiene. The scheme aims to provide total sanitation coverage in the villages by 2022. People's participation is a key factor in making any campaign successful; therefore, the government has been making conscious efforts to involve the institutions of Panchayati Raj in the construction of toilets for each house and village schools. The rural sanitation scheme allocates funds for construction of toilets and money for improving awareness through advertisements, posters and campaigns on the need for toilets.

Prefabricated Public E-Toilets In Pune

School sanitation is highlighted as one of the important components under the Nirmal Bharat Abhiyan. The scheme focuses on toilet construction, combined with hygiene education, to promote early adoption of toilet usage in rural government schools. It stresses on the construction of separate toilets for boys and girls in co-educational schools to bring down the drop-out rate of girls from schools as they did not have toilet facilities in the school premises. In urban areas, a social service organization called Sulabh International had launched a sanitation movement. The organization has joined hands with the government to provide paid sanitation facilities, which are maintained well.

Swachh Bharat Mission, the 'Clean India' mission was launched on 2nd October 2014 to commemorate Mahatma Gandhi's birth anniversary. Millions of school and university students across India took a pledge to make India a clean country, at par with other countries. Clean up drives were organized in schools, offices and educational institutions to promote a culture of cleanliness.

What's in the picture?

How do clean roads and public places affect the way we live?

Healthcare

The urban areas in India have numerous private hospitals and clinics that provide quality health care. Big government hospitals not only provide good medical care and research facilities but also make medication available to the urban poor. Free medicines and medical care are available to the poor people in these hospitals.

The National Health Mission (NHM) is the umbrella programme of the government to provide health care. Two sub-missions of this programme were launched—the National Rural Health Mission and the National Urban Health Mission.

The mission aims to make quality health care affordable to the rural population, especially the marginalized communities. Under this mission the government launches various health schemes for eradication of diseases, preventing malnutrition among children and adults, immunization programmes and spreading awareness about seasonal diseases. The Pulse Polio Campaign has been a successful initiative under this scheme. It has eradicated polio by creating awareness about preventive medication.

Extensive campaigns are conducted by the government to promote and create awareness about the schemes. The schemes also involve public participation and are carried out by many volunteers and government health employees. The Central Government Health Scheme covers around 17 cities across India. This scheme provides health care facilities to all the government employees and their family members. Various schemes like Janani Suraksha Yojana spread awareness about nutrition and overall wellness of mothers-to-be.

The Pradhan Mantri Swasthya Suraksha Yojana, PMSSY, envisages the creation of tertiary healthcare capacity in medical education, research and clinical care in the underserved areas of the country. It aims at correcting regional imbalances in the availability of affordable/reliable tertiary healthcare services and augmenting facilities for quality medical education in the country.

Ayushman Bharat Yojana or Pradhan Mantri Jan Arogya Yojana or National Health Protection Scheme was launched in 2018 to provide health insurance for the poor. Government has made provision for medical fund for poor patients for diseases like cancer and disability.

Case Study

Public Distribution System

The public distribution system is an integral part of the government's responsibility. The main objective of the Department of Food and Public Distribution is to ensure food security for the country through effective procurement and distribution of grains. Food grains procured from different areas have to be stored properly; then, they have to be transported and delivered to the distributing agencies from where they can reach the people. The work is done on a simple principle that stocks are sourced from surplus regions and given to meet the requirements of deficit regions. For example, Punjab, Haryana and Madhya Pradesh have surplus produce of wheat. Compared to deficit areas like southern parts of India, where rice is the main crop. The food grains thus distributed are priced at low and affordable rates so that the poor in India can benefit.

Q. What are the main features of the Public Distribution system?

Water

To a large part of the country, clean drinking water is still a distant dream. Piped water supply is available to approximately 69 per cent of the population in urban areas across the country. Water supply is available for limited hours even in big cities. In rural areas, people have to rely on open wells, hand pumps and sometimes even village ponds for drinking water. Women still walk miles to arrange water for their families. Most natural water sources are contaminated by sewage and agricultural runoff. According to the World Bank, 21 per cent of communicable diseases in India are related to unsafe water.

Green Earth

The Government of India is making a notable effort in conserving the Wetlands of India under the National Wetland Conservation Programme.

Water for supply is generally taken from improved and not improved sources. Some improved sources are the piped water, bore wells and harvested rainwater. Water supplied by local vendors, open and unprotected wells and springs and tanker water are considered not improved sources. The government makes efforts to supply safe drinking water to households. The Ministry of Drinking Water and Sanitation releases funds under the National Rural Drinking Water Scheme to the state governments for increasing and improving the supply of drinking water in their respective states.

Education

The education system in India is often considered better than most other countries. It is a major factor in promoting the economic development of India. The subject of education is listed under the concurrent list in the Constitution. As a result, both the Central and the state governments can take initiatives to provide facilities of elementary and higher education.

The Constitution of India under Article 21-A guarantees the right to free and compulsory education to children from 6–14 years of age. The Right to Education Act came into force in 2010. Under this Act no child, other than a child who has been admitted by his or her parents to a school not supported by the government, shall be liable to pay any kind of fee or charges or expenses, which may prevent him or her from pursuing and completing elementary education. 'Compulsory education' makes it obligatory for the government and local authorities to provide and ensure admission, attendance and completion of elementary education by all children in the 6–14 age group. A programme called Sarva Shiksha Abhiyaan was launched to promote elementary education in India.

With a view to enhancing enrolment, retention and attendance and simultaneously improving nutritional levels among children in the primary classes, the National Programme of Nutritional Support to Primary Education (NP-NSPE) was launched as a Centrally Sponsored Scheme on 15th August 1995. In 2001, MDMS became a cooked Mid Day Meal Scheme under which every child in every government and government-aided primary school was to be served a prepared mid day meal with a minimum content of 300 calories of energy and 8–12 gram protein per day for a minimum of 200 days. Its funds and outreach to unaided schools has been increased periodically.

Rashtriya Madhyamik Shiksha Abhiyaan RMSA is a major scheme launched in March 2009, with the vision of making secondary education of good quality available, accessible and affordable to all young persons in the age group of 15–16 years. Integration of information and communication Technology in schools is considered a part of the RMSA. It enables the students to be more connected to the developments around the world, be more technology savvy and acquire more well-rounded personalities. Hostel facilities for girls, Inclusive Education for the Disabled at Secondary Stage and vocational education were also taken as sub-parts of the RMSA from 2013–14. The Mahila Samakhya Scheme realized the importance of education in women empowerment. Importance was stressed on encouraging more girls to enrol in schools, to bring down the dropout rate of girls from schools and thus, to empower them.

The Saakshar Bharat Scheme aimed at promoting adult literacy especially in the villages. The aim was not just to make the adult population literate but also to spread awareness about social issues and inequalities which exist in society.

Railways

The Indian Railways is the third largest network in the world, which covers almost 66,000 km. In the Rail Budget of 2016, the government proposed to **decongest** railways by building dedicated freight corridors to separate passenger and goods traffic. This would enable faster movement of both goods and passengers. The government has also adopted the Public Private Partnership model so that private

Railways, India

decongest: to ease crowding or clogging in an area

companies can invest in improving the railways. Tourism is a source of revenues for the railways; so, trains promoting tourist destinations and UNESCO World Heritage sites in India will also be started. The government has also taken steps to introduce luxury trains and high speed trains to improve the services of the Indian Railways.

The National Urban Transport Policy was made in 2006. The Policy proposed to improve transport networks in the urban areas. Under the mass rapid transit system, the government has introduced metro trains in some cities to ease traffic on the roads and enable people to commute within the city. Metro services are used by thousands of commuters within the cities to reach their destination.

Apply it!

Smart Cities

The government has introduced the scheme of making 100 smart cities in India. The total number of 100 smart cities has been distributed among the states and union territories on the basis of an equitable criteria with each state/union territory having at least one.

Uttar Pradesh leads the way with 13 smart cities, followed by 12 in Tamil Nadu and 10 in Maharashtra.

Under this scheme, the objective is to promote cities that provide infrastructure and give a decent quality of life to its citizens. It also aims at the application of 'smart' solutions to developmental issues. The focus is on giving an identity to the city based on its main economic activity, such as local cuisine, health, education, arts and craft, culture, sports goods, furniture, hosiery, textile, dairy, etc.

Conduct a research and list the advantages and disadvantages of smart cities.

Roads and Street Lighting

Roads are the lifelines of a country. An elaborate network of roads is crucial for the economic development of the country. Connecting rural areas to urban areas and increasing access to remote parts through roads boost the development of agriculture, industry, trade and markets. The government, therefore, makes efforts to ensure an ever-widening network of roads by building highways, expressways, elevated corridors, overbridges and underpasses to facilitate swift movement of traffic. With almost 33 lakh km of coverage, the road network in India is the second largest in the world. The Pradhan Mantri Gram Sadak Yojana was introduced by the Central government to increase rural connectivity and construct all-weather roads to develop the rural areas. It also aimed to upgrade the existing network of roads in the country.

The government provides not only the road network but also streetlights. In most cases, the municipalities and corporations look after street lighting. The Union Ministry of Urban Development has instructed all state governments to change the streetlights within their states to LED lighting. There are approximately 27.5 million streetlights in India. The energy, thus, saved would amount to 5,000 MW of electricity consumption over three years.

Sources of Finance

Large amounts of funds are required by the government to provide these facilities and carry out developmental work. The main source of funds for the government is the taxes that people pay. Just like there is a demarcation of powers and responsibilities of each level of government given in detail in the Constitution, there is a detailed allocation of the sources of finance for the different levels of government. Some of the taxes are property tax, income tax and goods and services tax (GST).

World Connect

The Intergovernmental Panel on Climate Change is an initiative of the United Nations. The Panel is formed to review and assess the scientific reports to understand and contain climate change. The membership is open to all the member countries of the United Nations. Currently, there are 195 members in the IPCC. The Governments meet to review the developments and take decisions about the work programme to be adopted in the future.

Skill Builder

21st CENTURY SKILLS

Life-skills: How would you tackle the issue of heavy traffic on the roads, if you were provided an opportunity?

Critical thinking skills: Do you think there should be a penalty for dirtying the roads?

Wind up

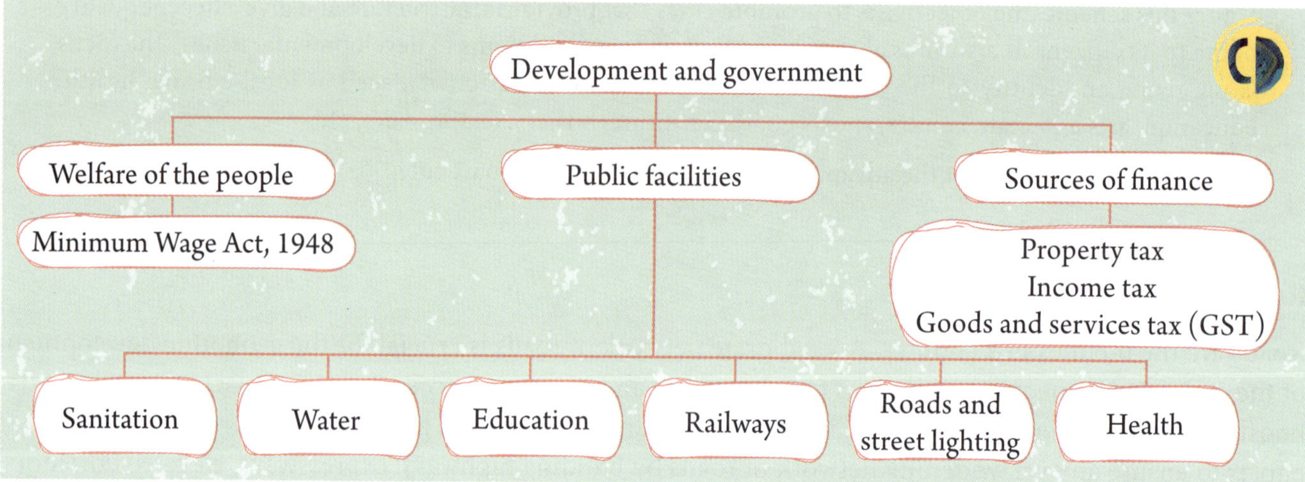

Exercises

A. Choose the correct answers.

1. The road network of India is the
   a. largest in the world   b. second largest in the world
   c. biggest in the world   d. shortest in the world
2. Sulabh International is a
   a. government organization   b. social service organization
   c. NGO   d. private entity
3. School sanitation is highlighted as one of the important components under the
   a. Sulabh International   b. Swachh Bharat Mission
   c. Nirmal Bharat Abhiyan   d. none of the above

4. Streetlights have to be provided by the
   a. residents
   b. government
   c. charities
   d. electricity companies
5. Through Public Distribution System, the government ensures that this reach the masses.
   a. clothes
   b. food grains
   c. books
   d. shoes

B. Write down the main purposes of these government schemes in the given table.

Rashtriya Madhyamik Shiksha Abhiyaan	
Mahila Samakhya scheme	
Saakshar Bharat	
Pradhan Mantri Gram Sadak Yojana	
Swachh Bharat Mission	

C. Correct the following statements.

1. The Food Corporation of India is responsible for providing mid-day meals.
2. A programme called Sarva Shiksha Abhiyaan was launched to promote secondary education in India.
3. Grants and loans are a source of funds for the central government.
4. Roads are required only in the urban areas.
5. The current wage for skilled labour is 100 rupees.

D. Answer these questions in brief.

1. What are the responsibilities of the government?
2. What is the Minimum Wages Act? Why is it important?
3. List out the main features of the Nirmal Bharat Abhiyaan.
4. How has the Pulse Polio campaign helped in countering the challenge of polio?

E. Answer these questions in detail.

1. What are the 'improved' and 'not improved' sources of water?
2. List the steps taken by the government to ensure a network of roads and street lighting.
3. Elaborate the schemes made by the government to promote health care in India.
4. What are the sources that finance these facilities provided by the government to imporve welfare of the people.

F. Read the passage and answer the questions:

The government provides not only road network but also streetlights. In most cases, the municipalities and the municipal corporations look after street lighting. The Union ministry of Urban development has instructed all the state governments to change the street lights within their states to LED lighting.

1. Why is LED lighting important?
2. List out some measures to make markings on highways and streets more user friendly.

Think Big

Integrate with geography

Procure a map of the area where your school is located. Separate the routes frequented by trucks and other commercial vehicles from the ones used mainly by people for commuting. Work out dedicated corridors for the two to decongest the roads.

Learning Tools

Create a usable timeline by using an Accordion Book Foldable. Insert the names of rural settlement patterns in one section and the types of urban settlements in another. Add characteristics of each group to help you remember the chapter.

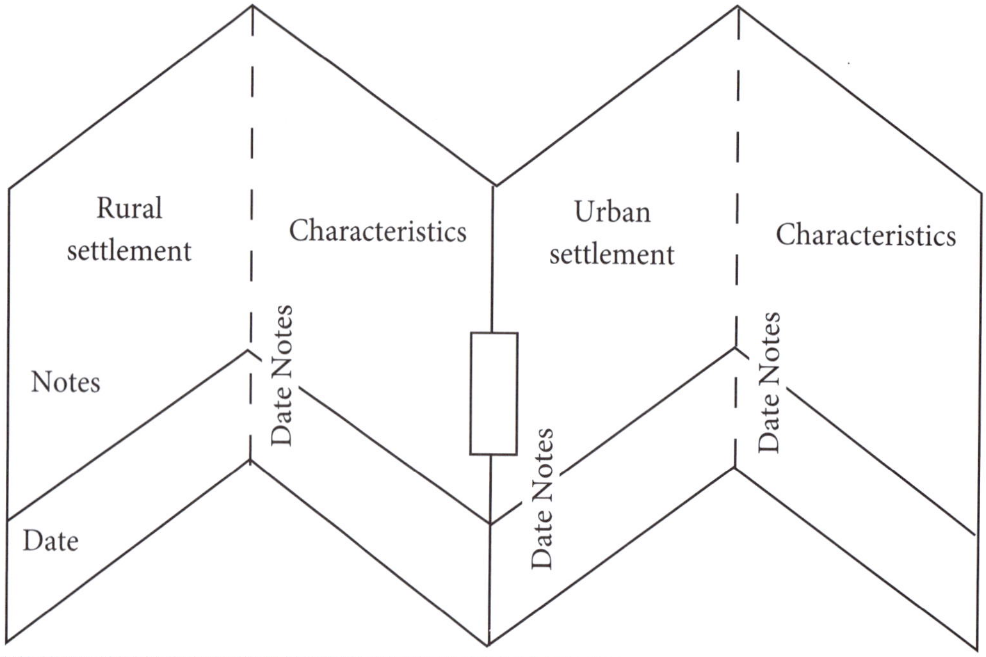

Web links:

https://nios.ac.in/media/documents/secsocscicour/english/lesson-17.pdf
https://www.britannica.com/place/India/Health-and-welfare

Last accessed on 31 August 2021

Being and staying happy is never an easy thing. So many things bring us down so sometimes, we need ideas to take us back on the road to happiness, life satisfaction and resilience. Here are a few things you can do.

#1 Appreciate the Good in Each Day

Make a list of things for which you're grateful and express your gratitude to people who have made a difference in your life.

#2 Stay Positive

Practice optimism and make it a habit. You can list your strengths focus on improving yourself for the better. Letting go of painful memories also help to making a happier you!

#3 Practice Acts of Kindness

Our happiness also depends on how happy the people we surround ourselves with are. Life becomes richer and more meaningful if you try to improve the lives of others.

#4 Nurture Relationships

Stay close to people you know and like. Listen to them, appreciate them, share with them and support them.

#5 Take Care of Your Body

If you have a strong and healthy body, you are happier. Eat healthy, exercise and show enthusiasm in all that you do to create a happier you!

#6 Commit to Your Goals

Choose goals that are personally rewarding, authentic, challenging and flexible. Believe in your ability to achieve those goals and reward yourself after a goal is met.

Where is your happy place?

A happy place is somewhere where you feel calm and are most relaxed. Write about your happy place in the spaces below.

ASSESSMENT 1

History

Max Marks: 80

A. Multiple choice questions

10 × 1 = 10

1. Who started the *Bengal Gazette* in India?
   a. James Mill
   b. James Augustus Hickey
   c. Joseph François Dupleix
   d. William Johns
2. Who was the first Governor General of India?
   a. Lord Cornwallis
   b. Lord Wellesley
   c. Warren Hastings
   d. Lord Mountbatten
3. The Battle of Buxar took place in the year
   a. 1764
   b. 1757
   c. 1784
   d. 1857
4. Who introduced the Ryotwari System?
   a. Holt Mackenzie
   b. Sir Thomas Munro
   c. Charles Cornwallis
   d. Zamindars
5. Gandhi started the Champaran Movement for these farmers.
   a. cotton
   b. wheat
   c. indigo
   d. none of these
6. The Garo tribals rose in revolt under the leadership of
   a. Togan Sangma
   b. U Kiang Nangbah
   c. Haripur
   d. Surchandra
7. The Industrial Revolution began in Britain in this century.
   a. 15th
   b. 17th
   c. 16th
   d. 18th
8. The first cotton textile mill was opened in
   a. Surat
   b. Bombay
   c. Ahmedabad
   d. Madras
9. Who started the Asiatic Society?
   a. Sir William Jones
   b. Warren Hastings
   c. William Bentinck
   d. Raja Ram Mohan Roy
10. When was the Right to Education Act passed?
   a. 2010
   b. 2015
   c. 2009
   d. 2019

B. Answer the following.

[2 × 4 = 8]

1. How did James Mill divide the history of India?
2. What do you mean by the policy of paramountcy?
3. Write short note on Alluri Seetha Ram Raju.
4. Why did the British want to educate the Indians? Write two reasons.

C. Answer these questions in brief.

[Attempt any 2] [3 × 2 = 6]

1. Explain three Sources that helped to Study the Colonial Period.
2. Write any three drawbacks of the Land Revenue Systems introduced by the British.
3. Distinguish between the ideas of orientalists and anglicisits.

D. Read the following passage and answer the questions.

[3]

The Indian Rebellion of 1857 was a major in India in 1857–58 against the rule of the British East India Company. It began in the form of a mutiny of sepoys of the Company›s army in Meerut soon erupting in many parts of India. The rebellion posed a considerable threat to British power in that region.This rebellion has been called many names throughout history. Some are the Sepoy Mutiny, the Indian Mutiny, the Great Rebellion, the Revolt of 1857, the Indian Insurrection, and the First War of Independence. After the first strains of the rebellion took place, the rebels declared 81-year-old Mughal ruler, Bahadur Shah Zafar, the Emperor of Hindustan. The East India Company's response came rapidly as well. With help from reinforcements, Kanpur was retaken by mid-July 1857, and Delhi by the end of September. However, it then took the remainder of 1857 and the better part of 1858 for the rebellion to be suppressed in Jhansi, Lucknow, and especially the Awadh countryside. The large princely states, Hyderabad, Mysore, Travancore, and Kashmir, as well as the smaller ones of Rajputana, did not join the rebellion.

1. In which year did the first war of Indian independence start?
2. Where did the rebellion of 1857 begin?

E. On the outline map of India locate and name the centers of the 1857 revolt. [3 × 1 = 3]

1. Kanpur
2. Lucknow
3. Jhansi

Geography

A. Multiple choice questions [1 × 10 = 10]

1. The climate found in the Mediterranean region
   a. hot and dry summers, cool and moist winters
   b. long winters and moderate to high annual precipitation mostly in the form of snow
   c. a cold winter season and warm and wet summers
   d. none of them
2. Air and sunlight are examples of
   a. ubiquitous resource
   b. non-renewable resources
   c. actual resources
   d. none of these
3. The horizon consists of the subsoil is
   a. C Horizon
   b. B Horizon
   c. D Horizon
   d. none of these
4. Two examples of conventional resources are
   a. solar energy and wind energy
   b. petroleum and natural gas
   c. bio-gas and tidal energy
   d. none of these
5. The leading coal producing countries are
   a. USA, Russia, China, Germany and France
   b. Iran, Iraq, Kuwait, Saudi Arabia
   c. Paraguay, Norway, Brazil
   d. All of them
6. Desert soil is found in
   a. western Rajasthan and parts of Gujarat
   b. Jammu and Kashmir, Uttar Pradesh and West Bengal
   c. north-west Deccan Plateau
   d. some parts of Tamil Nadu
7. The process in which the bare ground is covered with a layer of organic matter like straw or husk to retain soil moisture is known as
   a. terrace farming
   b. contour ploughing
   c. crop rotation
   d. mulching
8. The forest which is found in Southeast Asia and India is
   a. tropical deciduous forests
   b. Mediterranean forests
   c. coniferous forests
   d. grasslands
9. An initiative which is not taken for conservation of forests is
   a. protecting the forest reserves
   b. increasing the area under forest cover
   c. encouraging the practice of shifting agriculture
   d. protection of forest from forest fire
10. This mineral is found in large quantities, in South Africa and Australia
    a. gold
    b. diamond
    c. mica
    d. none of these

11. This is often referred to as 'black gold
    a. coal   b. petroleum   c. iron ore   d. none of these
12. Buildings, roads, machinery and vehicles are examples of
    a. human resources   b. human-made resources
    c. actual resources   d. none of these

B. Answer these questions.

1. Explain any four methods to conserve soil. [2]
2. What is the difference between Intensive Agriculture and Extensive Agriculture? Give three differences. [3]

C. Give reasons. [5]

1. We need to conserve the forest resource
2. Xerophytic plants are grown in deserts.
3. Tropical Rainforest appears to be green throughout the year.
4. Regur soils are also known as black cotton soil.
5. Natural gas is advantageous than coal and petroleum.

D. On an outline map of the world, mark and label [5]

1. a tropical desert
2. a region in the world which faces water scarcity
3. the temperate grasslands
4. an important petroleum producing country
5. an area of coniferous forest

E. Label the following. [5]

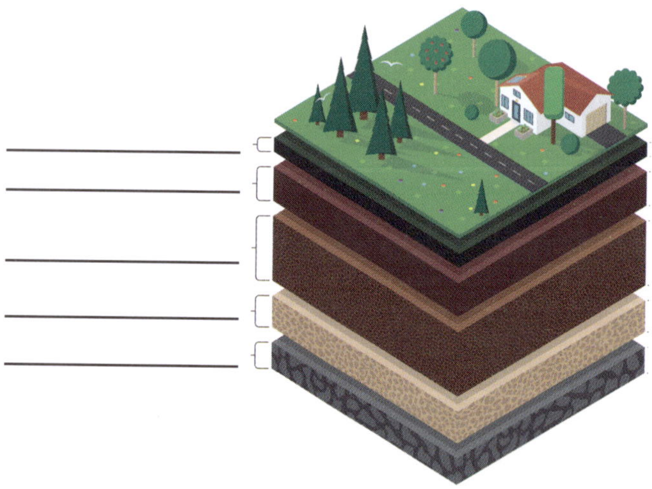

Social and Political Life

A. Multiple choice questions [1 × 8 = 8]

1. Which one of the following is not a challenge faced by the Constituent Assembly?
   a. Diversity   b. Unity
   c. Princely states   d. Economic condition
2. India opted for more than one level of government. This feature is
   a. federalism   b. secularism   c. democracy   d. sovereignty

3. Which of the following is a feature of Indian secularism?
   a. Inter-religious community domination
   b. Intra religious community domination
   c. Official religion
   d. No official religion
4. Countries which have an official religion are known as
   a. democracies b. theocracies c. secular countries d. republics
5. He or she presides over the Lok Sabha.
   a. President b. Prime Minister c. Chief Minister d. Speaker
6. Questions in Parliament which can be answered orally are called
   a. starred questions b. unstarred questions c. short notice questions d. important questions
7. These bills can only be introduced in the Lok Sabha
   a. extra ordinary bills b. money bills c. ordinary bills d. law bills
8. Controversial laws are looked into by the
   a. President b. Prime Minister c. Judiciary d. Executive

B. Answer these questions.

1. Explain the Parliamentary form of government in India. [2]
2. In what ways is Indian secularism different from that of the western countries? [2]
3. Why is the question hour important? Give two reasons to explain. [2]
4. How does a bill become a law? [3]

C. Passage Based [3]

A democracy can function only when people take a keen interest in the functioning of the institutions of the country. Electing representatives are not the end but the beginning of the responsibility for a citizen. A close observation of the work done by their elected representatives helps the citizens to vote for the right candidate in the elections.

1. Why is electing representatives not enough?
2. How can a good choice of candidates be made in the elections?
3. When can democracy be called successful?

ASSESSMENT 2

History

Max Marks: 80

A. Multiple choice questions

10 × 1 = 10

1. Who was a leading reformer of the Parsis?
   a. Dadabhai Naoroji b. Keshab Chandra Sen
   c. Raja Ram Mohan Roy d. Ishwar Chandra Vidyasagar .
2. The practice of having more than one wife is known as
   a. sati b. dowry c. polygamy d. widowhood
3. Narayana Guru was a social reformer from
   a. West Bengal b. Maharashtra c. Kerala d. Tamil Nadu
4. Who wrote the famous book Gulamgiri (slavery)?
   a. Jyotiba Phule b. Kandukuri Veeresalingam Pantulu
   c. Periyar d. Dr Ambedkar
5. Delhi is located on the banks of the this river.
   a. Ganga b. Yamuna c. Krishna d. none of these
6. A British Presidency
   a. Delhi b. Bombay c. Ahmadabad d. Nagpur
7. When was Rabindranath Tagore awarded the Nobel Prize for Gitanjali?
   a. 1913 b. 1920 c. 1915 d. 1925
8. Who was known as 'Frontier Gandhi'?
   a. Abdul Gaffar Khan b. Bhagat Singh c. Jawaharlal Nehru d. Gandhiji
9. Who was the president of Constituent Assembly?
   a. Subhash Chandra Bose b. Rabindranath Tagore c. Jawaharlal Nehru d. Dr Rajendra Prasad
10. When was the first nuclear explosion of India conducted in Pokhran ?
    a. 1975 b. 1980 c. 1974 d. 1990

B. Answer the following.

2 × 4 = 8

1. What do you mean by Bhoodan Movement?
2. What was the significance of the Prarthana Samaj?
3. How did the printing Press help the people to voice their feelings?
4. What was Gandhi-Irwin Pact?

C. Answer these questions in brief.

[Attempt any 2] 3 × 2 = 6

1. What are the three challenges faced by the newly independent India?
2. Write short note on Acharya Vinoba Bhave.
3. Briefly explain European Contribution to Indian Literature. any three]

D. Read the following passage and answer the questions.

3

The term *caste* derived from the Portuguese word *casta*, meaning 'race, lineage, breed' and, originally, 'pure or unmixed (stock or breed.. There is no exact translation in Indian languages, but *varna* and *jati* are the two most approximate terms. The four castes were the Brahmins (priestly people., the Kshatriyas (rulers, administrators and warriors., the Vaishyas (artisans, merchants, tradesmen and farmers., and Shudras (labouring classes. This categorization implicitly had a fifth element, being those people deemed to be entirely outside its scope, such as tribal people and the untouchables.

Jati, meaning *birth*, is mentioned much less often in ancient texts, where it is clearly distinguished from *varna*. There are four *varnas* but thousands of jatis. The jatis are complex social groups that lack universally applicable definition or characteristic, and have been more flexible and diverse than was previously often assumed.

1. What do you mean by the word caste?
2. Name the four varnas.
3. What do you understand by the word jati?

E. On an outline map of India locate the following places of the freedom movement. [3 × 1 = 3]

1. Lahore 2. Jallianwala Bagh 3. Chauri Chaura

Geography

A. Multiple choice questions [1 × 12 = 12]

1. Manufacturing of steel and cloth weaving are examples of
   a. primary activity b. secondary activity c. tertiary activity d. none of these
2. Mid-latitude temperate grasslands practice
   a. plantation agriculture b. extensive commercial agriculture
   c. intensive subsistence agriculture d. none of these
3. Banana, coffee, tea, cashew and rubber are crops grown in
   a. mixed farming b. dairy farming c. truck farming d. plantation agriculture
4. Jowar, bajra and ragi are examples of
   a. cash crops b. fibre crops c. millets d. beverage crops
5. Pottery, baskets, textiles and jewellery are examples of
   a. small-scale industries b. cottage industry c. large-scale industries d. none of these
6. Bhilai Steel Plant is an example of
   a. public sector industries b. mineral-based industries
   c. basic industries d. all of them
7. The people in the age group of 15–65 years are
   a. working population b. dependent population c. productive population d. none of these
8. West Bengal, Odisha, Andhra Pradesh and Tamil Nadu are very prone to
   a. floods b. cyclones c. earthquakes d. all of these
9. Gujarat, Chhattisgarh and central Maharashtra are examples of
   a. drought-prone areas of India b. flood prone areas of India
   c. Earthquake prone areas of India d. none of these
10. Regarded as the 'Manchester of Japan'
    a. Osaka b. Tokyo c. Nagasaki d. none of these
11. Sugar industry is an example of
    a. private sector industries b. agro-based industries
    c. consumer industries d. all of these
12. Brazil, India, Cuba, China, Thailand, Mexico and USA are major producers of
    a. sugarcane b. tea c. jute d. coffee

B. Answer these questions.

1. Name two causes for the occurrence of earthquakes? [1]

2. What type of soil is suitable for cotton cultivation? [2]
3. Give two differences between the geographical conditions for rice and wheat cultivation. [2]
4. What are the factors that helped Ahmedabad to become a textile centre? [3]

C. On a map of the world, mark and label the following: [5]

1. Location of an iron and steel industry in North America
2. A maize growing country of South America
3. An area of high population density in Europe
4. An earthquake-prone area of Asia
5. An area practicing Commercial Grain Farming

D. On a map of India, mark and label the following: [5]

1. TISCO
2. Manchester of India
3. Silicon Valley of India
4. A flood prone area
5. An area of Zone V of Earthquake

Social and Political Life

A. Multiple choice questions. [1 × 8 = 8]

1. This is the highest court in India
   a. Tribunal   b. High Court   c. Supreme Court   d. District court
2. Which one of the following is not a right of an arrested person?
   a. to be informed about the grounds of arrest   b. to be produced before a magistrate
   c. to return home   d. to inform a friend or a relative
3. Represents the state in a criminal case
   a. public prosecutor   b. defense lawyer   c. judge   d. police
4. Tea plantations under British rule were exploitative because
   a. employed cheap labour   b. workers not allowed to leave
   c. long working hours   d. all of the above
5. The region in states like Andhra Pradesh, Chhattisgarh, West Bengal and some others where Naxals are active areas is called
   a. White corridor   b. Red corridor   c. Blue corridor   d. Naxal corridor
6. Equality in the preamble of the Constitution refers to
   a. equality of status and opportunity   b. equality of wealth
   c. equality of education   d. equality of livelihood.
7. Reservations for scheduled tribes were introduced
   a as the government favoured them   b. as they were endangered
   c. to give them opportunities at par with the rest   d. to make them most important in society
8. This is a programme to promote elementary education in India
   a. Nirmal Bharat Abhiyaan   b. Janani Suraksha Yojana
   c. National Health Mission   d. Sarva Shiksha Abhiyaan

B. Answer these questions.

1. Give two reasons to show that an independent judiciary is very important in a democracy. [2]
2. Give any two points to show that tribal culture is an important and integral part of our culture. [2]
3. List out some schemes of the government for the welfare of the scheduled tribes. [2]
4. In what ways does the Minimum Wages Act help the workers? Give any two points. [3]

C. Passage Based [3]

A criminal offense is a 'crime against society'. Theft, harassment and demand for dowry are some examples of criminal offenses. If a crime has taken place, the First Information Report (FIR) is lodged with the police. The police then investigate the crime. A case is then filed by the police in a court of law. Punishment for the person who has committed the crime is the primary objective of criminal law.

1. Why are criminal offenses called crimes against society?
2. What is an FIR?
3. Why is it important to punish the law breakers?

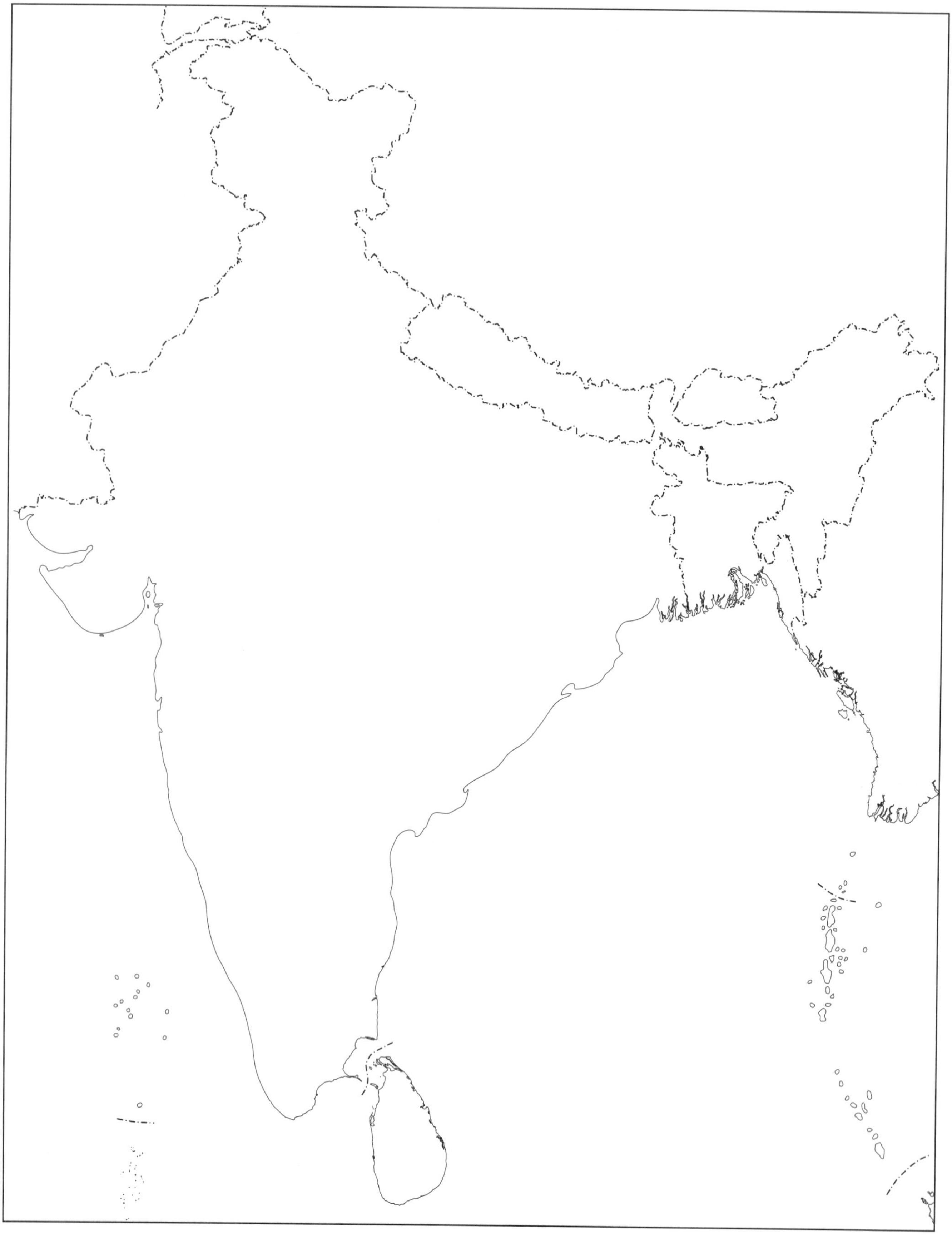

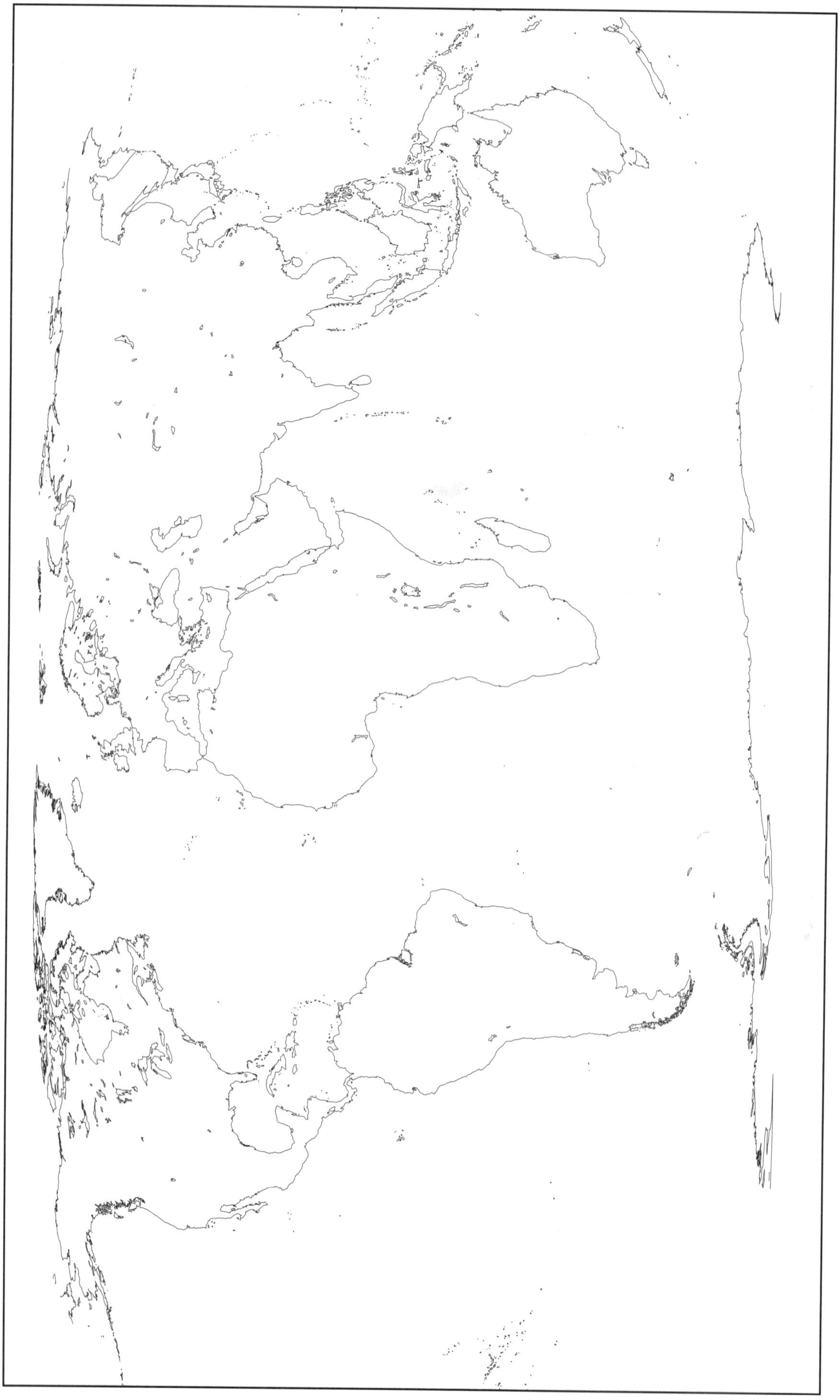